Academic Growth in Higher Education

Academic Growth in Higher Education

Questions and Answers

Edited by

Helena Pedrosa-de-Jesus and Mike Watts

BRILL
SENSE

LEIDEN | BOSTON

All chapters in this book have undergone peer review.

Library of Congress Cataloging-in-Publication Data

Names: Pedrosa de Jesus, Helena, editor. | Watts, Mike, editor.
Title: Academic growth in higher education : questions and answers / edited by Helena Pedrosa-de-Jesus, Mike Watts.
Description: Boston : Brill Sense, [2019] | Includes bibliographical references and index.
Identifiers: LCCN 2018046674 (print) | LCCN 2018051899 (ebook) | ISBN 9789004389342 (Ebook) | ISBN 9789004389328 (pbk. : alk. paper) | ISBN 9789004389335 (hardback : alk. paper)
Subjects: LCSH: Education, Higher--Aims and objectives--Europe. | Learning and scholarship--Europe. | Student-centered learning--Europe. | Inquiry-based learning--Europe. | Academic achievement--Europe.
Classification: LCC LA628 (ebook) | LCC LA628 .A34 2019 (print) | DDC 378.4--dc23
LC record available at https://lccn.loc.gov/2018046674

Typeface for the Latin, Greek, and Cyrillic scripts: "Brill". See and download: brill.com/brill-typeface.

ISBN 978-90-04-38932-8 (paperback)
ISBN 978-90-04-38933-5 (hardback)
ISBN 978-90-04-38934-2 (e-book)

Copyright 2019 by Koninklijke Brill NV, Leiden, The Netherlands.
Koninklijke Brill NV incorporates the imprints Brill, Brill Hes & De Graaf, Brill Nijhoff, Brill Rodopi, Brill Sense, Hotei Publishing, mentis Verlag, Verlag Ferdinand Schöningh and Wilhelm Fink Verlag.
All rights reserved. No part of this publication may be reproduced, translated, stored in a retrieval system, or transmitted in any form or by any means, electronic, mechanical, photocopying, recording or otherwise, without prior written permission from the publisher.
Authorization to photocopy items for internal or personal use is granted by Koninklijke Brill NV provided that the appropriate fees are paid directly to The Copyright Clearance Center, 222 Rosewood Drive, Suite 910, Danvers, MA 01923, USA. Fees are subject to change.

This book is printed on acid-free paper and produced in a sustainable manner.

CONTENTS

Acknowledgements   VII
List of Figures and Tables   VIII
Notes on Contributors   XI

1 Introduction
  Debates and Dilemmas   1
      Helena Pedrosa-de-Jesus, Júlio Pedrosa and Mike Watts

2 Developments and Challenges in Widening Participation in HE
  A Reflection from Portugal   12
      Júlio Pedrosa

3 Teaching, Learning and Research
  An Analysis of the Academic and Political Agenda   19
      Carlinda Leite

4 The Advent and Implications of SoTL
  Overview of the Initiation and Development of SoTL Internationally   31
      Vaneeta D'Andrea

5 A University Learning and Teaching Unit
  Work in Practice   43
      Fiona Denney

6 Challenging Physics Lectures through Questioning and Collaborative Work
  Research Developed in Portuguese Higher Education Institutions   59
      Nilza Costa

7 Using an Understanding of Cognitive Styles to Enhance Pedagogy   74
      Carol Evans

8 The Effects of Collaborative Learning on Students' Achievements and Skills According to Their Learning Styles within an E-Learning Environment
  Qatar University   88
      Aisha Fadl A. A. Al-Kaabi and Sarmin Hossain

9 Promoting University Students' Inquiry-Based Learning through
   Use of Questioning
   Review of Previous Research and Description of New Research in Japan   102
      Yoshinori Oyama and Emmanuel Manalo

10 Student-Centred Inquiry and the Awareness of One's Own
   Lack of Knowledge
   Building Unknowns about Objects   117
      José Otero and Cleci T. Werner da Rosa

11 Can 'Feed-Forward' Work?
   University Students' Perceptions of Their Preflective Practice   130
      Richard Malthouse and Jodi Roffey-Barentsen

12 Research, Design, Approaches and Methods   145
      Helena Pedrosa-de-Jesus, Mike Watts and Betina da Silva Lopes

13 Approaches to Student Inquiry-Led Learning   160
      Helena Pedrosa-de-Jesus, Aurora Coelho Moreira and Mike Watts

14 Academics' Conceptions about Teaching and Its Implication
   towards Pedagogical Innovation   171
      Betina da Silva Lopes

15 Models of Teachers' SoTL   186
      Helena Pedrosa-de-Jesus, Cecilia Guerra and Mike Watts

16 Assessment and Feedback   200
      Helena Pedrosa-de-Jesus, Aurora Coelho Moreira,
      Betina da Silva Lopes, Cecília Guerra and Mike Watts

17 Teacher Reflections   217
      Helena Pedrosa-de-Jesus and Mike Watts

18 Summary   229
      Helena Pedrosa-de-Jesus and Mike Watts

   Index   233

Acknowledgements

First, Mike is grateful for the institutional investment, collegiate cooperation and supportive camaraderie at the Department of Education, Brunel University London and, for which, sincere thanks. Then his hearty appreciation to Ruth, his darling wife and best friend, and his family Sian, Rhian, Oscar, Rosie, Lily, Joel, Conor, and Dylan.

Helena would like to sincerely thank the Department of Education and Psychology and the Research Centre on Didactics and Technology in the Education of Trainers University of Aveiro, Portugal, for all the institutional support and the hosting of the three main research projects that have inspired this book. She is especially thankful to her wonderful and supportive family, her husband Júlio, sons Miguel and Paulo, daughters-in-law Alda and Iola, grandsons Pedro, Luís, André and Miguel.

We are both indebted to Fundação para a Ciência e a Tecnologia (FCT), Portugal, for their financial support over the years: POCTI/CED/36473/2000; POCI/CED/59336/2004; PTDC/CPE-CED/117516/2010, as well as to our colleagues Adelaide Almeida, António Correia, Ângela Cunha, Fernando Gonçalves, José Teixeira-Dias, Sónia Mendo, and to all chemistry and biology students from the University of Aveiro, who were involved over the years.

Special thanks are also due to Dr. Hans van der Meij, from University of Twente, the Netherlands, a consultant in one of our projects.

Figures and Tables

Figures

6.1	Example of a conceptual question in a physics class (adapted from Oliveira et al., 2009, p. 99). 61
6.2	General description of the work developed by Oliveira (2011). 68
9.1	Correlations between total number of questions, cognitive cost of question generation, and lack of knowledge about question generation. 107
9.2	Correlations between total number of factual questions and easiness of question verbalization, and between total number of thought-provoking questions and cognitive cost of question generation. 108
9.3	Question matrix used during the training phase of study 2. 109
9.4	Changes of number of factual and thought-provoking questions across the phases of the study. 110
9.5	Total numbers of questions that students in the "control" and "experimental" classes generated. 112
11.1	Respondents and their programmes. 136
11.2	Respondents' areas of study. 137
11.3	Thinking ahead about a learning task. 137
11.4	Providing information early. 138
11.5	Clear thinking about tasks. 138
11.6	Being analytic. 139
11.7	Dependent on the nature of the task. 139
11.8	Used a range of sources. 139
11.9	The PReflective model. 140
12.1	Example of a semi-annual compilation of students' written question within a specific curricular unit and his personal selection of those he considered to be most relevant for his/her learning path. 154
14.1	The process of changing teaching conceptions – two different models. 172
14.2	Main differences between two broad teaching conceptions according to David and co-authors model. 172
14.3	David Kember and co-workers' "five-teaching-conceptions-two-orientations-to-teaching" model (based on Kember, 1997, p. 260). 173
14.4	Main teaching conceptions of university teachers' according to Prosser and Trigwell. Based on Prosser, Trigwell, and Taylor (1994, pp. 200–204). Original labels A, C, D, E and F for teaching conceptions was maintained, in order to facilitate cross interpretations of the reader between this particular chapter and the original studies. 173

14.5   Teaching approaches of academics (based on Trigwell, Prosser, & Taylor, 1994).   174
14.6   PTA identification through the ATI responses of two academics.   176
14.7   The question sheet strategy: Global description and an illustrative example.   176
15.1   The role of feedback and academic self-reflection on academic growth.   189
15.2   Maintenance/adaptation/innovation academic practice (MAI model).   190
15.3   The instructional coaching meetings.   190
15.4   Teaching strategies used by Teacher A (2012/2014).   191
15.5   Teaching strategies used by Teacher B (2012/2014).   192
15.6   Teaching strategies used by Teacher C (2012/2014).   193
15.7   Teaching strategies used by Teacher D (2012/2014).   194
16.1   Feedback strategies developed in the teaching context of 'Evolution' (2006/2014).   204
16.2   Translation of quality criteria of students' posts into a quantitative mark for assessment purpose.   206
16.3   Students' posts on the ODF over three months.   206
16.4   Categorization of the teachers' posts according to Garrison et al.'s (2001) model 'teaching presence'.   207
16.5   Example of one type of feedback posted by the teacher's to the students' on the OFD710.   207
16.6   Transcripts of an excerpt from the student debates highlighting examples of oral feedback given by the teacher.   209
16.7   Levels of student skills and competencies assessed during group discussion.   210
16.8   Example of the teacher's written feedback profile considering the critical analysis of one group of students.   211
16.9   Example of the teacher's written feedback profile considering the critical analysis of one group of students.   212

Tables

4.1.   Summary of number of presentations at UK international SoTL conferences 2001–2003 by overall topic, type of scholarship and country of origin.   35
5.1.   Interviewee data.   54
5.2.   Interview questions.   55
6.1.   Context and participants of the studies carried on in stage 1.   63
6.2.   Context and participants of the studies carried on in stage 2.   67

7.1.	Components of a personal learning styles pedagogy (Evans & Waring, 2014).	78
8.1.	The main results of the research.	96
9.1.	Examples of questions participants generated.	106
10.1.	Scheme for categorising unknowns about objects, and examples of the corresponding questions.	122
12.1.	Research around undergraduate science at the University of Aveiro (2000–2015).	146
12.2.	Questions coding throughout the 'Aveiro project'.	155
16.1.	Quality of co-constructive written formative feedback (Pedrosa-de-Jesus & Guerra, 2018).	203

Notes on Contributors

Aisha Fadl A. A. Al-Kaabi
is Assistant Professor of Education at Qatar University. She gained a BA in Arts and Education in 1992 through the Faculty of Education, Qatar University, and holds a Special Diploma in Education Qatar University from 1998. She received a Master's degree ICT and Education from the School of Education, Leeds University, UK in 2006, and achieved her PhD in Education at Brunel University in 2016. Aisha began work at Qatar University as a laboratory supervisor and became a Laboratory Training Supervisor, then became Teaching Assistant until October 2017. She now teaches a range of education modules in, for example, 'Research Methods' and 'Technology for Children' and runs numerous staff workshops on Blackboard at Qatar University.

Aurora Coelho Moreira
is currently a post-doctoral researcher in the field of science communication, being a member of the Centre for Functional Ecology of the University of Coimbra, Portugal. Her main professional interests focus on the promotion of public awareness and understanding of science, as well as scientific culture and scientific literacy, being involved in different projects for diverse types of public in these fields. Her recent work has been mostly developed at the Botanical Garden of the University of Coimbra and at the Exploratório, Ciência Viva Science Centre, as a member of the direction board since 2015. With a master degree in Communication and Education in Science and a PhD in Didactics of Science, both from the University of Aveiro, her main research interests have been mainly on questioning and inquiry-led learning, both in formal and non-formal settings.

Nilza Costa
is a full professor in Education in the Department of Education and Psychology (DEP), University of Aveiro (UA)/Portugal, being responsible in DEP for the area of Didactics and Educational Technology. She is a founding member of the Research Centre "Didactics and Technology in Teacher Education" (CIDTFF), allocated in DEP/UA, and external financed by the Portuguese Science and Technology Foundation (FCT), since its creation in 1994. She was the coordinator of CIDTFF, between 2012–2016, leading 80 researchers from UA and other Higher Education Institutions. She was, during five years, the Coordinator of the Integrated Centre of Teacher Education in UA. Her main research interests are: teacher education and staff development from secondary to higher education; science/physics education; and evaluation and assessment in education. In the last thirty years she has been responsible for

several research projects (at a national and international level), an author and/ or co-author of several publications and a supervisor of more than 20 PhD students (mainly from Portugal, but also from Brazil and Africa). She has been invited to give key lectures at many universities in Europe, Africa and Brazil.

Betina da Silva Lopes
is presently a post-doctoral researcher at the Research Centre "Didactics and Technology in Teacher Education", Department of Education and Psychology, University of Aveiro (Portugal). Her current work is focused on International Cooperation for Development in Science Education. She graduated as a biology and geology teacher in 2004 at the University of Coimbra (Portugal) and she has been also involved in research around education since 2007, developing topics such as: quality of teaching and learning in higher education, academic development, curricular internships and its relation to graduate employment. She is also active in science dissemination initiatives for the general public and currently she collaborates on the project SaltScience (http://sal.spq.pt/). She is a proud mother since 12/2013.

Vaneeta D'Andrea
has held academic posts in the USA and the UK for over forty years and had held professorships at City University (personal chair), the Open University and the University of the Arts London, where she is now Professor Emerita. She has been a policy advisor on secondments to the Higher Education Quality Council (UK) and for the Higher Education Funding Council for England (HEFCE). She has consulted universities, governments, and higher education NGOs on a range of higher education issues in Africa, Central Asia, Asia, Europe, the Gulf States, North and South America and Southeast Asia. Her recent publications include topics ranging from: branding in higher education, educational development, educational research methods, higher education policy, quality enhancement in higher education, excellence in teaching in higher education, the research-teaching nexus and scholarship of teaching and learning (SoTL). She has also received numerous fellowships, awards and honours for her work in higher education.

Fiona Denney
is professor and Director of the Brunel Educational Excellence Centre at Brunel University London. Fiona has worked in UK universities for 20 years – both as an academic and as a senior professional member of staff. In 2003, she left full-time lecturing to take up a post in Educational and Staff Development at Queen Mary, University of London (QMUL) where she established a programme of training for researchers, worked with colleagues on the

teaching qualification for new academic staff and helped develop and deliver a leadership programme for senior academic staff. In 2007, Fiona moved to King's College London's Graduate School where she had responsibility for the development of researchers, senior research staff and doctoral supervisors. At King's, Fiona built a team for researcher development and with colleagues, developed the first King's coaching service for researchers and academics. Her post at Brunel is an academic one, and she is enjoying the return to doing research on doctoral supervision and academic leadership.

Carol Evans

is chair in higher education at the University of Southampton, UK and co-director of the Centre for Higher Education at Southampton (CHES). She is a National Teaching Fellow and Principal Fellow of the Higher Education Academy (HEA), UK, and an Associate member of the HEA. Carol was President of the Education, Learning, Styles, Individual differences Network (ELSIN) (2009-2015). She is the UK Vice Chair for the International Federation of National Teaching Fellows (IFNTF). She is also the international officer for the Committee of the Association of National Teaching Fellows (CANTF). Carol is editor-in-chief of the new *Higher Education Pedagogies* journal and Associate Editor of the *British Journal of Educational Psychology*. She is a Visiting Professorial Fellow at the UCL Institute of Education, UK. She has worked in school and higher education contexts (education and medicine). She is passionate about enhancing learning and teaching through an understanding of individual differences in learning with a focus on cognitive styles and enhancing assessment feedback practice.

Cecilia Guerra

is Postdoctoral Research Fellow at the Research Centre "Didactics and Technology in Teacher Education", Department of Education and Psychology, University of Aveiro (Portugal). She holds a PhD in Multimedia in Education (2012), a Master's degree in Communication and Science Education (2007) and a Degree in Teaching of Biology and Geology (2002). She has participated in research projects and collaborated in the organization of scientific events. She was also a teacher assistant in the higher education context and an in-service teacher trainer. She has several publications in the areas of Science Education, Educational Technology and Academic Development. She holds a technical production, the Courseware Sere: "The human being and natural resources".

Sarmin Hossain

holds a BSc (Hons) Mathematical Science Degree from City University, London, UK; PGCE in Mathematics Secondary from the Institute of Education,

London, UK; MSc and a PhD in Information Systems from Brunel University London, UK. She began her academic career as a Research Associate in Mathematics Education in the Department of Education and Professional Studies, Kings College London. She joined Brunel in January 2011 as Lecturer in ICT in Education. That same year she became the PGCert ICT Secondary Course Coordinator, responsible for leading and managing the overall the ICT Course. Sarmin's academic background and work experiences in engineering education have enabled her to develop research interests in three of the STEM areas: Information Communications Technology (ICT), engineering and mathematics.

Carlinda Leite
is Full Professor at the Faculty of Psychology and Educational Sciences, University of Porto, Portugal. She is a member of CIIE Research Center Administration, where she is also a Senior Researcher. Her area of specialty is Educational Sciences, Curriculum Studies – that includes Curriculum Theory and Development, Conception and Evaluation of Projects, Curriculum Innovation, Learning Evaluation, Institutional Evaluation, Multiculturalism Education and Teacher Training. Since 2009, she has been a member of the Agency A3ES that evaluates and undertakes the accreditation, in Portugal, of the higher education courses. She has published various articles with peer review and book chapters.

Emmanuel Manalo
is a tenured professor at the Graduate School of Education of Kyoto University in Japan. He completed his PhD in psychology from Massey University in New Zealand. Emmanuel's research interest concerns the development of effective teaching and learning strategies, the educational uses of diagrams, the application of critical thinking to information evaluation, and variations in the cognitive cost involved in the use of different learning strategies. He has published over 100 refereed research articles and book chapters. Recently he guest edited a special issue of the journal *Thinking Skills and Creativity* on how failure can be beneficial for learning.

Richard Malthouse
is Lecturer in education at the University of East London. He has extensive experience in teaching and learning in a range of educational settings such as Further and Higher Education, the MoD, Police Service, various airlines and governmental agencies in the United Kingdom, United Arab Emirates and Romania. His research interests focus upon aspects of reflective practice, police culture and students' approaches to study. He has published widely

on the subject of Contemporary Education and is a Fellow of the Higher Education Academy. He teaches at all levels and contributes to programmes at undergraduate and masters level in Contemporary Education and Criminology.

José Otero

is Emeritus Professor in Science Education at the University of Alcalá (Madrid, Spain) and has been a Visiting Scholar in several U.S. Universities. His research interests have focused on text comprehension, metacognition, and, in particular, comprehension monitoring and question asking in science education. He has been responsible for several graduate and PhD programs in these areas, and has participated in consultancy and research projects involving universities of Europe, North, Central, and South America. He has served on the editorial board of science education journals and educational psychology journals such as *Metacognition and Learning* and *Journal of Educational Psychology*.

Yoshinori Oyama

is an associate professor in the Department of Education at Chiba University in Japan. He received his PhD in Education from the Graduate School of Education of the University of Tokyo. He is in charge of teacher education for students training to become teachers in elementary through to high schools. His main research areas include teachers' questioning skills training, and promoting pupils and students questioning skills for lifelong learning. Recently, he and co-author Manalo proposed "the Hemingway effect" in human motivation, which elucidates the conditions when failure to finish a task can be beneficial.

Helena Pedrosa-de-Jesus

has been Associate Professor with Habilitation for Full Professor, at the Department of Education and Psychology, University of Aveiro, Portugal, being responsible for the area of studies concerning Science Education, Supervision and Academic Development in Secondary and Higher Education. Before joining the University, Helena has been a school teacher for twenty years, where she was involved in teacher training as a supervisor of trainees. Her main research areas include Science Education and Questioning in teaching and learning in schools and University, with special emphasis on the role of questions to promote inquiry-based learning. In the last fifteen years Helena has been responsible for three major research projects financed by the Portuguese Science and Technology Foundation (FCT) to investigate the role of questioning for developing innovative teaching and learning approaches in Higher Education. Helena's research programs have always involved international collaboration, originating an extensive list of journal and conference papers, as well as book chapters.

Júlio Pedrosa

has been a full professor in the Chemistry Department of the University of Aveiro from 1988 until 2009. Being a founding member of the University and of CICECO – University of Aveiro Institute of Materials, he continues with his academic work in this Institute, focused in HE policies and governance, institutional and programme evaluation and accreditation, knowledge exchange between HE Institutions and external partners. Vice-Rector for seven years, elected Rector of the University from 1994 until 2001, was President of the Portuguese Council of Rectors (1998–2000), Minister of Education of Portugal (2001–2002) and elected President of the National Council for Education (2004–2009). Being involved in Institutional evaluation and accreditation of Universities in the period 2004–2013, Júlio has evaluated HEI in Denmark, Ireland, Italy, Latvia, Lithuania, Portugal, Spain and Turkey. He is currently a member of the Register Committee of EQAR, the European Quality Assurance Register, nominated by EUA, and coordinates a team established to develop a study about the Portuguese Higher Education System, its achievements, challenges and future developments, on demand of Gulbenkian Foundation, in Lisbon

Jodi Roffey-Barentsen

is Senior Lecturer in Education at the University of Brighton. She is responsible for, and involved with, a suite of degree programmes in education, including EdD and PhD programmes. She has extensive experience in teaching and learning in a range of educational settings, such as schools, Further and Higher Education institutions, and also large government organisations (MoD and Police Service). Her main research interest is in the field of Reflective Practice. Jodi works as a consultant for an international exam board, is peer reviewer of educational research (journals/conference papers), and is a Fellow of the HEA.

Mike Watts

is Professor of Education with research interests in the learning and teaching of science (STEM), in schools and beyond. Mike enjoys 'naturalistic' people-orientated research projects in both formal and informal educational settings and has conducted major studies of learning interactions in the UK and abroad. His recent work looks at how learners' own questions can be used as a basis for inquiry-led learning, the ways in which feelings and emotions shape learning, and ways in which classroom technologies can be used to enhance inquiry-based teaching. He was awarded (2003) a Higher Education Academy National Teaching Fellowship for excellence in teaching and (2004) was elected a Fellow of the Institute of Physics and Chartered Physicist. He has

NOTES ON CONTRIBUTORS   XVII

been external examiner for the National University of Ireland, consultant to the Teaching Council for Ireland, and to universities around the world. Mike has published widely in the field of science education through his reviews, books, journal articles and many conference papers. He teaches at all levels and contributes to programmes at undergraduate, post-graduate, masters and doctoral level within Brunel's Department of Education.

Cleci Teresinha Werner da Rosa
is a PhD in Scientific and Technological Education and words as a post-graduation counselor at the University of Passo Fundo, Brazil. She coordinates the research group called "Scientific and Technological Education" and researches on Science Education, specifically the themes related to the didactic science laboratory and metacognition. She has recently researched approaches of metacognition with the investigative approach and with scientific literacy.

CHAPTER 1

Introduction
Debates and Dilemmas

Helena Pedrosa-de-Jesus, Júlio Pedrosa and Mike Watts

Introduction

This is a book in three parts. In this introductory part we outline the scope of the book, its purposes and directions, along with a brief précis of the chapters to come. In Chapter 2 we have invited Júlio Pedrosa to outline some of the key changes taking place in higher education across Europe, and Vaneeta D'Andrea to sketch some of the key issues surrounding the scholarship of teaching and learning (SoTL). Like Júlio, we are watchful of the changes taking place and, like Vaneeta, we are keen advocates of SoTL and see such scholarship as a worthy goal of professional development and growth for teachers in higher education. This is not a new perspective but, as we discuss later, remains a worthwhile and achievable aspiration for teachers and lecturers of all disciplines at this tertiary level of education.

Each chapter in the second part details distinctive work undertaken within universities around the world. These are multilevel interventions within university departments that drive towards change. They are commonly place-based and are usually situated in bounded geographic settings that may be referred to as local communities. They range from Brazil to Spain, Qatar to Japan, although many are clustered around studies undertaken in Portugal and the UK. This is, in part, a consequence of a long-standing project based at the University of Aveiro in Portugal where, over a period of some fifteen years, research in teaching and learning at university level has generated a substantial body of contiguous work, including an array of masters dissertations, PhD theses, agency reports, project websites, journal articles and books – not to mention working papers, PowerPoint presentations, classroom materials and online tutorials. Just as important has been the organisation of three international seminars based on this work, in 2004, 2010 and 2015. These three day-long seminars have not only presented and discussed the output of the 'Aveiro Project' but have also drawn together a network and community of like-minded colleagues and friends. We have been hugely privileged to work with some outstanding people over the course of a decade or more: students at many different levels, teachers of various hue and stripe, colleagues from diverse disciplines and institutions, many of whom are contributors to this volume. Our intention is that these chapters in Part 2 provide a broad international context, raise some of the key questions and debates in our field of study.

In the third part, we present some of the main outcomes of the Aveiro Project. The work we have undertaken can be set into six broad inter-related themes: first, in aiming to be learner-centred throughout our work. Whether in terms of formal teaching, informal support, assessment and feedback, we have worked to increase the active participation of learners: it is often their voices that dominate the research papers we have published. Rather than diminish the role of the teacher, in many respects this makes their organisation and management of learning increasingly more important – if somewhat more difficult. Second, we have sought to explore leaner differences, looking to cater for individual and group differences where we find them. This differentiation has been, for example, in the ways that learners ask questions, tackle problems, undertake learning tasks quite generally, and how different teachers might – and have – responded to these. Third, we are earnest believers in inquiry-based learning, where natural inquisitiveness and questioning drives a search for answers and understanding. This aspect of our work has been active from the very start, and entails not just a cognitive approach to questioning, the content and delivery of a question, but also the affective, emotional dimensions that accompany the processes of question-asking.

Fourth, we covet criticality. A fairly constant thread through the major parts of the Aveiro Project has been the development of 'critical beings' within schooling, undergraduate and post-graduate university studies. While this may seem *de rigueur* for courses at tertiary levels, our sense is that there is much more to be done to enhance learner criticality. Our fifth thread has been an interest in the processes of research and its methodologies. Our primary instinct has been to use qualitative approaches to research although we have also used correlational statistics where such methods are apposite. For us, naturalistic qualitative research brings high context validity or, what some call, normative validity, in that we have enjoyed researching real-time learning and teaching, in situ, in ways in which other teachers and researchers will recognise quite easily. Finally, our sixth thread is an overwhelming concern for the development and academic growth of our teaching colleagues. Their capacity to innovate and reflect on practice has been at the heart of the work. At times we have used the analogy of an orchestral conductor with the task of orchestrating meaningful outcomes with a mixed-motivated, mixed-skilled group of musical (and sometimes non-musical) players. The analogy works only so far, of course, but gives some force to the complex work of the teacher.

While these six threads are exemplified in our chapters of the third part, we spend time here discussing their origins and expansion through the phases of the overall project.

Being Learner-Centred

The Bologna Declaration has had an important influence on teaching and learning in higher education. Portuguese higher education institutions, as are many institutions world-wide, are undergoing a series of educational reforms to promote more student-centred approaches to teaching and learning, a consequence of the so-called 'Bologna process'. This is presented as a 'window of opportunity to introduce pedagogic and curricular reforms' (Veiga & Amaral, 2009), from direct knowledge transmission to the development of knowledge-generation competencies by students. The Bologna Declaration was an intergovernmental initiative between a voluntary collection of signatory countries with the original goal of achieving a European Higher Education Area (EHEA) by the year 2010. The overall initiative has been an instrument of the European Community within the EC Treaty (articles 149 and 150, 2005) and its purpose, as stated in its formal priorities and 'action lines', was to create a broad framework for higher education to enable comparability within a flexible system and to promote the European Higher Education Area for the benefit of all of the countries involved. It has not been intended to create standardised or uniform higher education across the European Higher Education Area, but initiated a concerted movement to promote innovations to respond to the increasing diversification of publics and contexts in higher education observed worldwide. That said, there have been a number of policy threads that have assumed the status of a 'push for conformity', student-centred learning being one of these. Student-centred learning was not actually among the thematic areas that were tackled directly in the Bologna Declaration at its inception. However, many of the priority work plan themes discussed early on in the process tackled aspects that helped make learner-centred education more of a reality. This included flexibility tools such as ECTS, mobility, improved recognition, qualification frameworks and others. Also, parts of the ministerial conferences communiques reaffirmed the importance of the educational mission of universities. Student-centred learning was fully taken into the process during the Leuven/Louvain-la-Neuve ministerial conference, in 2009. This constituted an important reassertion of the teaching mission of higher education, which – while central to the creation of a coherent European Higher Education Area – had initially been often overlooked in the development of the 'Bologna process':

> We reassert the importance of the teaching mission of higher education institutions and the necessity for ongoing curricular reform geared toward the development of learning outcomes. Student-centred learning requires empowering individual learners, new approaches to teaching and learning, effective support and guidance structures and a curriculum focused more clearly on the learner in all three cycles. Curricular reform will thus be an ongoing process leading to high quality, flexible and more individually tailored education paths. Academics, in close cooperation with student and employer representatives, will continue to develop learning outcomes and international reference points for a growing number of subject areas. We ask the higher education institutions to pay particular attention to improving the teaching quality of their study programmes at all levels. This should be a priority in the further implementation of the European Standards and Guidelines for quality assurance. (Leuven/Louvain-la-Neuve communique)

Many of the initiatives we describe here have taken place at a 'local' level within departments, subject areas and individual classrooms, and may – or may not – have happened under the umbrella of an 'institutional mission' to change. There is an old adage that all educational innovation acts to make a teacher's life more difficult, and there is some truth here, in that empowering individual learners on 'high quality, flexible and individually tailored education paths' requires considerable investment of personal resource. This is an issue that reappears throughout the chapters to follow.

Differentiating Learning

Our approach to learner differentiation has been to explore students' responses to a variety of learning tasks. For example, even while we have used David Kolb's (1984) experiential learning theory of development, we have pushed and pulled at this model in order to meet our own purposes. In one instance we used Kolb's 'cone of experiential learning' where he differentiates between three broad developmental stages: acquisition, specialisation and integration. Our aim was to chart the mode and content of students' questions, and used these three descriptors to help manage our emerging data. Not only did this approach prove useful but gave quite unexpected and interesting outcomes (Moreira, 2012), so that student questions posted to an online discussion forum showed much higher levels of thinking and integration of ideas and possibilities than might otherwise have been expected. Other contributors in this volume discuss differentiation more fully so that, while Aisha Al Kaabi and Sarmin Hossain look further at Kolb's work, Carol Evans takes a more sweeping view of different styles and approaches.

Inquiry-Based Learning

It will have already become apparent that inquiry, questions and questioning have been a core aspect of our work. The importance we attach to the asking of questions lies in the ways in which the composition and delivery of questions has on thinking and understanding, on the learning that takes place in and around a question and on expressing the diversity in students' learning approaches. Our argument is that the questions asked by learners are indicative of their need for interaction with both teachers and other students within sessions, for understanding within the domains in which they are working and studying, and for some resolutions in their thinking. For example, the question 'What does this mean?' asks for a definition for a specific term. The question may have been formulated spontaneously or brewed over a period of time, may have been presented openly and orally within a classroom, individually in a quiet moment during a tutorial, written as comment to a lecturer, or as a personal comment during a period of reading. Whenever, or however, the point of utterance, the question signals puzzlement, curiosity, perplexity, doubt, challenge, wonder, incongruity – and more. All of these states of thinking are worthwhile and a necessary prelude to the construction of meaning. In some cases, asking even poorly formed and tentative questions can indicate an active, interrogative attitude that not only looks for appropriate information and opinion, hunts for conceptualisation and meaning in the subject matter, but also seeks some determination of the worth of what is read or heard.

In the development work that underpins this experience, teachers have adopted approaches to teaching that tune not only with their own and learners' questions, but also with the substance and nature of particular subject disciplines. There is strong evidence that if 'good' conditions are created (appropriate conditions conducive to the generation and asking of student questions) then students will ask and respond to a range of questions – specifically, learners will ask questions when they have high levels of self-confidence and self-esteem within the learning context, and when their questions are seen to be valued. It is this context of sprit of inquiry we look to develop and, in Part 2, the work of Jose Otero in Madrid, Yoshinori Oyama and Emmanuel Manalo in Japan, give life to this through their studies.

Being Critical

Critical thinking is seen as one of the very highest orders of cognitive abilities not just in Portugal, of course, but in universities across the world. It is recognised as a key competency in higher education, particularly for science and technology, in terms of an:

Attitude of critical appreciation and curiosity, an interest in ethical issues and respect for both safety and sustainability – in particular as regards scientific and technological progress. (Commission of European Communities, 2005, p. 15)

Allied to our work on questioning, our supposition throughout has been that, if we require pre-university, undergraduate and post-graduate students to be critical thinkers, then one vehicle for achieving this is to enable them not just to ask critical questions *per se*, but to be critical questioners in the round. This may seem like a fine distinction: Surely a person who asks a critical question is, per force, a critical questioner? For us, though, the issue is much more than simple semantics: we favour the second sense of 'critical being' as advocated by Barnett (1997). Like Barnett, we have argued against a form of critical thinking 'window dressing', where students are taught to 'go through the critical motions', what Barnet calls 'the critical thinking industry', by which he means a mechanistic 'study skills' approach. Rather, we are interested in developing students who are 'critical questioners', fostering the actions and processes of critical questioning with a degree of understanding and intensity that flavours all of their studies.

Our own approach has been to explore the context in which criticality can best operate; the disposition of the critic: his or her self- and other-awareness as they are being critical, and the composition and delivery of the criticism. One of our most recent studies has looked at the effects of students' own peer review and feedback on each other's work, the ways in which critical comment was generated, proffered and accepted (or not!). The general consensus among the 140 or so students involved in the exercise was very positive although, not surprising, some of the students critique might not have been delivered well, some not received well: there are certainly skills and competencies to be learned!

Methodology

Our research has a decidedly qualitative bent, generated on the whole through face-to-face interactions, classroom observations, individual interviews, discussion groups. Needless to say, we have also undertaken considerable documentary analysis, scrutinised test and examination results, followed on-line discussions in forums and communities, employed surveys and learning inventories, and many other approaches. Throughout, we have had a keen eye to rigour, significance and impact, not least because the funding bodies have demanded this of us. This impetus has pushed us to develop validation processes that have allowed us to feel confident that the ideas we have generated, the claims we have made, the outcomes we have published are as solid as we can make them. We have adopted quantitative methods where appropriate but, generally, our sense of significance lies not in formulaic tests, but in the broader value, worth, of the work we have been doing. The data we have cited throughout our many papers are illustrative rather than exhaustive; our purpose has often been to illuminate the phenomena – tacit and explicit – of learning and teaching, rather than detailed statistical analyses of learners' and teachers' overt behaviours. In this vein, we frequently offer exemplar quotes from interviews, field-note entries from the observational data, comments collected online to support our on-going arguments. As Crowe and Watts (2014) note, young people deploy a growing range of 'mashed' and innovative textual forms in a range of social contexts offline and online. The use of these terms acknowledges not just the tenor of student ways of life but also, for instance, the embeddedness of digital technologies, text and practices such as mobile phones, social networking sites and online forums in the discursive lives of young people in contemporary culture and acts to reinforce this placement.

Academic Development and Growth

The core of the book, of course, lies in supporting teachers' academic development and growth. The *Teaching and Learning International Survey* (OECD, 2009, p. 49) describes professional pedagogical training and development as those 'activities that develop an individual's skills, knowledge, expertise and other characteristics as a teacher'. In this vein, a report to the European Commission on 'Improving the Quality of Teaching and Learning in Europe's Higher Education Institutions' (European Commission, 2013, p. 13) states that: 'A good teacher, like a good graduate, is also an active learner, questioner and critical thinker'. The same report recommends that: 'All staff teaching in higher education institutions in 2020 should have received certified pedagogical training' (p. 64). We pay much more attention, of course, to this set of issues as the book progresses.

The Chapters of the Book

The chapters in Part 2 describe a range of studies from around the world. These case studies are designed as a viable way to test a variety of community level interventions. We appreciate that multi-level interventions introduced in one community are likely to 'look' different in other communities where policies, community alliances, agencies and population composition are different. Even if we could match at all levels chosen for the intervention, communities do not share the same dynamics; and complex systems change in different ways and at different rates. For this reason we prefer to avoid the trap of assuming that any two cases 'matched' on demographics, or other factors can be identical. Instead, we invite readers to make a 'comparative case analysis' that rests on the comparison of these interventions within their own institutions that are culturally and structurally congruent. This means that, while entering into these accounts, the reader will encounter some congruence: similarity of purpose and conceptual framework that guides the variety of activities and actions. There is always something to be learned by how others do things.

First we have four studies that look at issues teaching and learning across higher education, and within institutions quite broadly. Júlio Pedrosa begins by focusing primarily on the changes and challenges with the university and polytechnic system in Portugal and, given the given broader access to higher education in the country, pointing to the need for courageous innovation in teaching and learning. In Chapter 3, Carlinda Leite tests the policies and pressures not simply for teaching, student learning and academic research as individual professional tasks, but the viability of the composite sense of teaching-learning-research. None of this trinity, she argues, merits over-riding preference over the others and so the professional imperative in higher education is to find ways to manage all three as interwoven threads. In addition, the more this can involve the student, the better. Vaneeta D'Andrea follows this with an authoritative overview of the 'scholarship for teaching and learning' (SoTL) movement, its genesis, current state and prospects for the future. This is an important contribution, not just because we set one of the broad goals of our work to be academic growth in the direction of enhanced SoTL, but also because of the growing political pressures for 'teaching excellence' – not only in the UK but elsewhere in the world. Fiona Denney picks up this story with a strongly personal and professional route into managing and developing an educational development unit within a university in the UK, the tasks and challenges in working with academics to shape professional improvements.

In Chapter 6, Nilza Costa illustrates innovations in the teaching of an introductory physics course for engineering students through peer tutoring and collaboration. Carol Evans follows this in Chapter 7, and sets out a Personal Learning Styles Pedagogy (PLSP) as an example of an inclusive participatory cognitive styles pedagogy that acknowledges the multifaceted nature of cognitive style working at different levels of cognitive functioning and in relation to different style families. It is, she says, 'about promoting self-regulation in learning through an understanding of styles'. As such, it sits easily within our pursuit of learner centeredness. Aisha Al Kabbi and Sarmin Hossain then take the discussion a step further. In their work in Qatar, they explore the over-lapping complexity of working with students across two domains: their learning style as reported by David Kolb's Learning Styles Inventory, and their propensity to work individually or collaboratively in small groups. As foreshadowed in Carol's work, both the learning context and the learning task can be shown to be important in fostering good outcomes and achievement from students' work.

Chapters 9 and 10 present two studies that focus on students' questioning. Yoshi Oyama and Emmanuel Manalo describe three studies within their own university in Japan to discuss students' self-generation of questions for the purposes of better learning is an integral part of inquiry-based learning. They are worried about students' lack of spontaneity in using the questioning strategy for their own learning, and explore ways through which they can promote routes into inquiry-based learning. Jose Otero and Cleci Werner da Rosa follow this with a close examination of students' formulation of questions through what they know and don't know. This involves a discussion of the nature and primacy of 'unknowns' in students' learning and the implications of these for teaching and learning. The last chapter in this part deals with reflective feedback. In Chapter 11, Richard Malthouse and Jodi Roffey-Barentsen discuss students' propensity to pre-reflect, what they call PReflection, the type of thinking they engage in before embarking upon a new task. They report that, on the whole, students like to start the thinking process well in advance of a deadline, and the majority generally has clear ideas of what is expected of them. Richard and Jodi argue that this is an important aspect of students' academic direction.

The chapters in Part 3 describe the work of the Aveiro Project. These comprise reports of intervention studies undertaken over a fifteen-year period from 2000 to 2015 at the University of Aveiro, Portugal. We use Schensul's (2009) sense of interventions, as efforts to introduced planned change into – in this case – a tertiary education system. Consistent with Hawe et al.'s (2009) work, we think of interventions as systematically planned, conducted and evaluated education-based cultural products, intercepting the lives of people and institutions in the context of multiple events and processes that are intended to speed or produce change towards a desired outcome. In this case, we evaluate the interventions on the basis of their capacity to build change towards the desired goal of 'increasing SoTL'. The interventions we discuss in each chapter are visibly multilevel, they address change efforts at multiple institutional levels in the hope that effects at each level will forge synergistic links facilitating movement toward the overall desired change. In each chapter it is possible to identify *macro* (at the institution and policy level), *meso* (departmental and resource level) and *micro* (individuals, teachers, students, groups, classes, friends and online communities) – all interacting both directly and indirectly. Many recent articles and books in the areas of higher education refer to 'community based' research, that is to say, research conducted in community settings and usually together with various sectors of designated collectives. This raises immediate questions about the definition of communities. Communities may be as large as a year cohort of 150 students on a foundation course, student groups of 25 or 30 within elective modules or tutorials, working groups of six or so, or scattered respondents within an online chat forum.

In Chapter 12, members of the team discuss the over-arching approaches to research that we have adopted, the broad design and methods we have used over time. Our discussion and description of research in this part of the book is of a specific kind, driven by a particular ethos and sense of 'research probity'. The thrust is towards participative, naturalistic research where educational researchers work alongside their academic colleagues in collaborative endeavour. We then move to focus in Chapter 13 on university students' student-centred learning and, in particular, the nature of student questions. This chapter explores both those occurring naturally and the conditions required to 'hot-house' these within university lecture rooms. As outlined in Chapters 9 and 10 in Part 2 above, students' questioning is often recognized as a fundamental, higher level capacity, associated with the development of other core competences, such as critical thinking, problem-solving, and reflecting capabilities, attaining an important role in the context of science education. Chapter 14 considers university teachers' own conceptions of and reflections on teaching. Teachers shape their teaching through a series of perspectives of what it means to teach and learn at university level. This chapter explores two such broad perspectives and the implications these have for the practice of teaching within university programmes. We follow this with a discussion of the development and evolution of teacher activities, and their growth within different models of teaching and learning within the Aveiro project, in particular as they approach our goal of SoTL. The following chapter explores some of the outcomes of assessment and feedback on teachers' work and, of course, on students' learning. The overall discussion and comments on these issues derive from a series of studies that comprise the 'Aveiro Experience'.

Chapter 17 draws out some reflections from the lecture room. The collaborating university teachers at the heart of the project reflect on the processes and products of the project. Finally, in Chapter 18, we summarise the book with some concluding comments. Bringing this book together has been a powerful and very collaborative venture and we are enormously grateful the time and energy required by all of our contributions in the development of a wide-reaching and interesting text.

References

Barnett, R. (1997). *Higher education: A critical business.* Buckingham: Open University Press.

Commission of European Communities. (2005). *Proposal for a recommendation of the European parliament and of the council on key competences for lifelong learning.* Retrieved December 6, 2015, from http://ec.europa.eu/education/policies/2010/doc/keyrec_en.pdf

Crowe, N., & Watts, D. M. (2014). 'We're just like Gok, but in reverse': Ana girls – empowerment and resistance in digital communities. *International Journal of Adolescence and Youth, 21*(3), 379–390.

European Commission. (2013). *Report to the European commission on improving the quality of teaching and learning in Europe's higher education institutions.* Luxembourg: Publications Office of the European Union.

Hawe, P., Shiell, A., Riley, T., & Pattison, P. (2009). Theorising interventions as events in systems. *American Journal of Community Psychology, 43*(3–4), 267–276.

Kolb, D. A. (1984). *Experiential learning: Experience as a source of learning and development.* Englewood Cliffs, NJ: Prentice Hall.

Moreira, C. A. (2012). *O questionamento no alinhamento do ensino, aprendizagem e avaliação* (Unpublished PhD thesis). University of Aveiro, Aveiro.

Organisation for Economic Co-Operation snd Development. (2013). *Creating effective teaching and learning environments first results from TALIS.* Retrieved from http://www.Sourceoecd.Org/Education/9789264056053

Schensul, J. J. (2009). Community, culture and sustainability in multilevel dynamic systems intervention science. *American Journal of Community Psychology, 43*, 241–256.

Veiga, A., & Amaral, A. (2009). Survey on the implementation of the Bologna process in Portugal. *Higher Education, 57*, 57–69.

CHAPTER 2

Developments and Challenges in Widening Participation in HE

A Reflection from Portugal

Júlio Pedrosa

Introduction

The development and diversification of higher education offers in Portugal, in the last sixty years, has already been seen as a case study. In fact, looking at figures for the period before the political changes of 25th of April 1974, one can observe that in the decade between 1959–1960 (22481 students) and 1969–1970 (48,199 students, 43.5% being female), the student numbers in the four existing public universities more than doubled (Machete, 1968; UNESCO, 1975). This demand for higher education has continued to a peak in 2003, with 400,831 students attending a network of universities and polytechnic institutions, public and private, covering the whole of Portugal. These developments have opened access to students coming from a wide range of cultural, social and economic backgrounds, while there is ample evidence for the need to go further in this process (Almeida & Vieira, 2012; Callender & Sá, 2014; Engrácia & Baptista, 2018; Pedrosa, Teixeira, Moreira, & Santoalha, 2017; Williams, 2017).

In the same period, higher education systems have been through major developments around the world. This process has been seen (Trow, 1974) as a succession of three major phases: the 'elite phase', in which only around 15% of the age group which usually enters higher education institutions was acceding to HE institutions; the 'democratization period' where between 15–50% of that age group participates in HE, and a third development period designated as 'universal HE', with a participation of more than 50% of the age group. Such changes are associated with political, social and economic contexts that have configurations, stimuli and frameworks varying with countries, opening avenues for even more challenging HE developments (Bokor, 2012; Maskell & Robinson, 2002; Neave & Amaral, 2012; Santos & Bonito, 2015).

Surprisingly, the European Union panorama on widening access is seen as being not very encouraging (European Commission, 2014):

> There is therefore a long way to go before a convincing, evidence-based, European-wide picture of progress in widening access is possible to obtain ... Both bridging programs and recognition of prior learning are an access feature of about half of the European higher education systems. However, clear geographical patterns are visible, as they remain most prevalent in the north and the west of Europe. There are few examples of an alternative route accounting for more than 10% of entrants.

The developments in access to HE have had drivers which vary from country to country, but it is useful to have a view about the meaning of 'widening the access', and a recent contribution identifies target groups which, at least in the UK, are considered in the policies strategies and actions (Moore, Sanders, & Higham, 2013). These authors consider that,

> Widening participation students are not a homogeneous group. They may have a range of identities, diverse social characteristics and come from a variety of backgrounds ... the following key target groups were identified: People from lower socio-economic groups; Mature students; Part-time learners; Learners from ethnic minority groups; Vocational and work-based learners; Disabled learners; Care leavers.

One could say that, in Portugal (Santos Silva & Serrano, 2015), the trends in the widening of access to HE would not differ much from those mentioned by Moore, Sanders and Higham. However, recent studies (CNE, 2015; Figueiredo et al., 2017) support a view indicating the need to create opportunities of access to HE for mature students, vocational and work-based learners with special attention given to secondary school leavers from fragile economic, social and cultural contexts.

Diversification and Differentiation in HE Offers

Policies related to the design of higher education institutional systems have varied with time and from country to country (Bokor, 2012; Gurin, Dey, Hurtado, & Gurin, 2002). The trends and the drivers for these changes observed in the last fifty years would deserve attention and adequate investigation (Bailey, Jaggars, & Jenkins, 2015; Bahr, 2012; Ma & Baum, 2016). In any case, one could consider that the need to respond to changes in secondary education and the different entry profiles of candidates, together with needs of society requiring a variety of outcome capacities, knowledge, competences and experiences are among the main contextual factors.

In a recent work on the Portuguese higher education system, there is evidence that policies that have offered recognition of prior learning, and that have opened secondary education to adults over 23 years old, have had an increasing impact on entry to HE, mainly via the polytechnic network (Pedrosa et al., 2017). The same study adds evidence to what has already been referred to (CNE, 2015; Figueiredo et al., 2017), that there is a clear need for continuing, or even reinforcing, the openness of HE to professional secondary school graduates and to the 'under-qualified' adult population (Engrácia & Baptista, 2018). Indeed, the presence of students from lower socioeconomic backgrounds is still far from adequate standards (Williams, 2017). In addition, in Portugal, compulsory education was recently extend to 18 years old, with two main choices on the secondary schools – professional/vocational or sciences/humanities – with the increase in demand for secondary professional education, now close to 50% of the choices, having strong impact on HE access.

The issues of diversification of offers, the factors influencing the changes in demand and participation in HE, government policies with particular attention to access policies and systems, are present more and more in the HE agendas of countries that have given a high priority to widening participation in HE (EC/Eurydice, 2014). In recent work focused on HE in the USA and the UK, Dougherty and Callender (2017) have explored the similarities and dissimilarities of higher education policies in the two countries with an eye to what each country can learn from the other with regard to reducing social class and racial/ethnic differences in higher education access and success. These authors conclude by saying that

> progressive policies run up against the enduring class, racial/ethnic, gender, and other inequalities that fundamentally structure English and American society ... Perhaps the most important policy strand is the one that focuses on improving information and advice during primary and secondary school.

Also Chowdry, Crawford, Dearden, Goodman, and Vignoles (2013) refer to the inequality of access to university for socio-economically disadvantaged pupils remain a major policy issue and present evidence that pupils from lower SES backgrounds are much less likely to participate in HE then pupils from higher SES backgrounds. Policy makers who are interested in increasing participation among pupils from lower SES backgrounds need to intervene earlier to maximize their potential impact.

The analyses of widening access that put the emphasis on critical questions are also valid for Portugal and I would consider that all the issues mentioned above deserve full attention and investment of political and institutional stakeholders. However, I also believe that more recognition and investment should be added to the academic work required to develop, test and consolidate capacities and innovative approaches to designing curricula, research and pedagogic approaches.

This is intended to be a contribution to integrate the widening of higher education to distinct publics with the challenging demands that those developments pose to institutions and all the professionals dedicated to offering the public good that is Higher Education. The University of Aveiro is one of the first Portuguese institutions to have opted for have polytechnic and university schools inside the organization. This experience has shown that students entering into the polytechnic schools would benefit from having distinct pedagogic approaches. One of such schools (Águeda School of Science Technology and Management), which has also often been mentioned as a case study, has adopted and consolidated problem-based learning as the favoured teaching and learning approach (Alarcão, 2007; Oliveira, 2007). The recognition of the relevance of those developments is expressed by the involvement of José Manuel Oliveira, the leading figure of the PBL experience in Águeda since the start, in the promotion of similar pedagogic approaches in the University of Aveiro, Águeda Polytechnic School and in other seven Polytechnic schools in Portugal (Personal communication, 12th April 2018).

The Bologna Process or a Missed Opportunity for Change

The so-called Bologna Process has been understood (or misunderstood?) in different ways across Europe. Being involved, and having followed the preparation and approval of the Bologna Declaration as Rector of a university and President of the Portuguese Council of Rectors, I was very much in favour of a reorganization of degrees, their curricula and the offer of HE in such a way that students could be better prepared for entering in a fast changing world, open to the need of lifelong learning. In Portugal, the Bologna Declaration and its developments have deserved attention of academics, higher education institutions and other national entities such as the National Council for Education, CNE (CNE, 2009; Santos, Alarcão, Andrade, & Costa, 2008; Veiga, 2015). One of the main areas of diversity in the approaches to follow the Bologna Declaration was the adoption of a 3+2 (bachelor + master) scheme to engineering programmes or establish an integrated master (a five-years degree programme leading to a master degree diploma in engineering). This last option was at that time adopted by all universities in Portugal. The debate that is on-going in the country, associated with the analysis and discussion of the OECD evaluation draft report (CNE, 2018), shows that the issue of integrated masters or 3+2 options is again in the agenda.

A question might be raised, however: how can political decision makers, institutional leaders and academics enter in such a process without a previous investment in finding answers to the following questions:

- In this country, community, society, which parts of the public are to be seen as potential candidates for acceding to higher education?
- Having identified the potential candidates, in a widening the access to higher education process, what set of programmes, curricula, pedagogic contexts and approaches are required?
- How should the institutions organize themselves, select, educate and train staff to be involved in the teaching and education of such students once they enter the Institutions?

Our recent study (Pedrosa et al., 2017), in which it was possible to hear a wide spectrum of stakeholders voices, showed that these critical questions can find answers if adequate involvement of partners is promoted.

Final Points

This is a contribution in which there is evidence that the widening of the access to higher education has been a trend in many countries. It is believed that such process will be present in all countries that are far from having reached the desired levels of participation in HE.

There is also enough evidence for accepting that those processes lead to situations in which institutions and academics are asked to respond in a professional and successful way to distinct publics. Teachers are asked to face and educate students differing in motivation, capacities, levels of engagement in studying, learning abilities and life projects.

Apparently, the issue of widening the access, looking for the reasons behind this trend and for the types of diversity in candidates for those processes has been addressed in many studies and publications. However, some authors refer that there is not yet enough attention and work dedicated to the pedagogic issues associated with the opening of HE to new publics. Anyway, for European contexts there are some very recent inspiring contributions on teaching and learning approaches (European Commission, 2014; Baeten, Struyven, & Dochy, 2013; Henard & Roseveare, 2012). This book is a serious and relevant contribution to respond to such a gap and it offers evidence that the projects developed in the University of Aveiro, associated with what is published here opened a door which should continue open. Why not evolve from that basis to a structured framework for a questioning-based learning (QBL) approach to teaching and learning designed and tested to respond to a wide variety of students in a classroom?

References

Alarcão, I. (2007). Changing to project-based learning: The role of institutional leadership and faculty developments. In E. de Graaff & A. Kolmos (Eds.), *Management of change: Implementation of problem-based and project-based learning in engineering* (pp. 69-82). Rotterdam, The Netherlands: Sense Publishers.

Almeida, A. N., & Vieira, M. M. (2012). From university to diversity: The making of Portuguese higher education. In G. Neave & A. Amaral (Eds.), *Higher education in Portugal, 1974-2009: A nation generation* (pp. 137-159). Dordrecht: Springer.

Baeten, M., Struyven, K., & Dochy, F. (2013). Student-centred teaching methods: Can they optimise students' approaches to learning in professional higher education? *Studies in Educational Evaluation, 39*, 14-22.

Bahr, P. R. (2012). Student flow between community colleges: Investigating lateral transfer. *Research in Higher Education, 53*, 94-121.

Bailey, T., Jaggars, S., & Jenkins, D. (2015). *Redesigning America's community colleges: A clearer path to students success*. Cambridge, MA: Harvard University Press.

Bokor, J. (2012). *University of the future*. Melbourne: Ernst & Young.

Callender, C., & Sá, C. (2014). *Acesso ao Ensino Superior*. Lisboa: Fundação Francisco Manuel dos Santos.

Chowdry, H., Crawford, C., Dearden, L., Goodman, A., & Vignoles, A. (2013). Widening participation in higher education: Analysis using linked administrative data. *Journal of the Royal Statistical Society, 176*(2), 431-457.

CNE – Conselho Nacional de Educação. (2015). *Acesso ao Ensino Superior: Desafios para o Século XXI*. Lisboa: CNE – Conselho Nacional de Educação.

CNE – Conselho Nacional de Educação. (2018). *Seminário Ensino Superior em Portugal, uma estratégia para o futuro*. Lisboa: CNE – Conselho Nacional de Educação.

Engrácia, P., & Baptista, J. O. (2018). *Percursos no Ensino Superior: Situação após quatro anos dos alunos inscritos em licenciaturas de três anos*. Lisboa: Direção-Geral de Estatísticas da Educação e Ciência (DGEEC).

European Commission. (2014). *Report to the European commission on new modes of learning and teaching in higher education*. Luxembourg: Publications Office of the European Union.

European Commission/EACEA/Eurydice. (2014). *Modernisation of higher education in Europe: Access, retention and employability 2014* (Eurydice Report). Luxembourg: Publications Office of the European Union.

Figueiredo, H., Portela, M., Sá, C., Cerejeira, J., Almeida, A., & Lourenço, D. (2017). *Benefícios do Ensino Superior*. Lisboa: Fundação Francisco Manuel dos Santos.

Fry, H., Ketteridge, S., & Marshall, S. (2009). *A handbook for teaching and learning in higher education* (3th ed.). New York, NY: Routledge.

Guerreiro, J., Costa, A., Ferreira, A. L., Maia, C., Baptista, J. O., Queiroz, J., Teixeira, J. S., Silva, J. A., Alarcão, M., Barrias, P., & Teixeira, P. (2016). *Relatório sobre a avaliação do acesso ao ensino superior (diagnóstico e questões para debate)*. Lisboa: MCTES.

Gurin, P., Dey, E., Hurtado, S., & Gurin, G. (2002). Diversity and higher education: Theory and impact on educational outcomes. *Harvard Educational Review, 72*(3), 330–366.

Henard, F., & Roseveare, D. (2012). *Fostering quality teaching in higher education: Policies and practices*. Paris: OECD (IMHE).

Ma, J., & Baum, S. (2016). *Trends in community colleges: Enrolment, prices, student debt, and completion*. New York, NY: The College Board.

Maskell, D., & Robinson, I. (2002). *The new idea of a university*. Thorverton: Imprint Academic.

Moore, J., Sanders, J., & Higham, L. (2013). *Literature review of research into widening participation to higher education*. Bristol: HEFCE.

Oliveira, J. M. (2007). Project-based learning in engineering: The Águeda experience. In A. Kolmos & E. de Graaff (Eds.), *Management of change: Implementation of problem based and project based learning in engineering*. Rotterdam, The Netherlands: Sense Publishers.

Pedrosa, J., Teixeira, P. N., Moreira, M. J. G., & Santoalha, A. M. (2017). *Educação Superior em Portugal: Uma Nova Perspectiva*. Lisboa: Fundação Calouste Gulbenkian.

Santos, L., Alarcão, I., Andrade, A. I., & Costa, N. (2008, April 1–3). *Formação de professores e processo de Bolonha: o "caso" da Universidade de Aveiro*. Comunicação apresentada no 4° Encontro Internacional da Sociedade Brasileira de Educação Comparada, Porto Alegre (PUCRS). Retrieved from http://www.sbec.org.br/evt2008.php

Santos, R. S., & Bonito, J. (2015). *Pensar e Construir a Universidade no Século XXI*. Boa Vista: EDUFRR.

Santos Silva, A., & Serrano, A. (2015). A gestão do acesso ao ensino superior: Entre a massificação e a regulação. In M. L. Rodrigues & M. Heitor (Eds.), *40 Anos de Políticas de Ciência e de Ensino Superior* (pp. 647–660). Coimbra: Almedina.

Trow, M. (1974). Reflections on the transition from elite to mass to universal higher education. *Daedalus, 99*, 1–42.

UNESCO. (1975). *Para uma Política de Educação em Portugal*. Lisboa: Livros Horizonte.

Veiga, A. (2015). Análise do sistema de ensino superior após o processo de Bolonha. In M. L. Rodrigues & M. Heitor (Eds.), *40 Anos de Políticas de Ciência e de Ensino Superior* (pp. 591–606). Coimbra: Almedina.

Williams, J. (2017). *Addressing the completion challenge in Portuguese higher education: Summary report*. Cambridge, MA: M-RCBG Associate Working Papers.

CHAPTER 3

Teaching, Learning and Research
An Analysis of the Academic and Political Agenda

Carlinda Leite

Introduction

In academic discourse about teaching it has been argued that teaching only makes sense if it generates learning (Freire, 1972, 1974). In fact, this idea is the basis of criticism of traditional teaching that favours teachers' actions and ignores the role of students as builders and active subjects in their own learning. Recognising that universities are places for production of new knowledge (Lessard & Bourdoncle, 2002; Leite & Ramos, 2010, 2012), the idea here is that teaching must be closely related to that knowledge production. It is on this basis that Cunha (2011) mentions the inseparability of teaching-learning-research recognising that this triad involves a rupture in 'an epistemological condition with an established vision of knowledge, which is common in the positivist scientific conception' (ibid., p. 449). Looked at from the point of view of what is expected from higher education, and having in mind Readings (2002, p. 24) 'is equivalent to thinking about the social articulation of research and teaching in terms of mission', this requires these three key activities to be articulated and integrated on the basis of concrete social situations. Accepting this, the analysis here concerns the academic discourse surrounding these three dimensions of educational action (teaching-learning-research). These perspectives are confronted with a political discourse, especially in the light of the European Bologna Process that, in Portugal, has been undertaken since the start of 21st century. This analysis is structured in order to bring to the debate a set of arguments that make it possible to answer the following questions taken from Balzan (2002, pp. 115–116):

> Is it possible to achieve a good quality education without research? Does the joint-research education constitute a necessary condition for the teaching process to reach a standard of excellence? Can research be a hindrance to good quality education? Does a teacher's success depend on being a good researcher?

Balzan (idem) answers the first two questions, arguing that it is possible to achieve quality education without research. However, these are rare cases and require the presence of other features and conditions for teaching, because the most common situation is that where there is 'teaching excellence', there is also a relationship between teaching and research. Regarding the last two questions, Balzan recalls that, in fact, research can be an obstacle if the teacher is too focused on this. He also reminds us that, although the success of a teacher does not depend on he or she being a good researcher, it is hard to accept teaching without it being associated with the latest knowledge being produced and that corresponds to a continuous extension of 'knowledge borders'.

On this same question, it is worth appealing once more to Cunha (2011, pp. 455–456) when she reminds us that there is 'the unquestioned assumption that the research qualifies the teaching ...' and when she questions: 'Is this relationship done linearly? Whenever there's research there will also be quality education? When and under what conditions ... is (that) confirmed? Will the knowledge that sustains the research be sufficient for the achievement of significant pedagogical practices?' These questions are also present in the debate circulating around the various movements allied to teaching-research nexus and research-led teaching. Although there are several definitions of these relations, I accept the perspective of Willcoxson, Manning, Johnston, and Gething (2011) when they state that this relationship can occur in two distinct senses: conceiving students as the audience, or seeing them as participants. In the first case, it is a curriculum structured by teaching but based upon research data, or research-oriented in which the emphasis is given to the processes of knowledge construction by students themselves. In the second case, i.e. when the teaching is focused on students and conceives them as agents then the research, according to these authors, develops through a research-tutored logic. For example, students base the curriculum on construction of essays and papers, or it emphasises students undertaking inquiry-based learning.

The intention here is to deepen the debate around these relationships and also to contribute to an agenda where tensions arise from international and national (Portuguese) policies for higher education. That said the text is structured around the following axes: (i) what has been mentioned in academic discourse about the teaching-learning-research relationship; (ii) what has been stated in political discourse about the teaching-learning-research relationship; (iii) what would constitute a future agenda for the teaching-research relationship? Some final reflections are then woven through these points.

What Has Been Mentioned in Academic Discourse

Criticism of the curricular guidance founded on academic rationalism (Leite, 2002) has stressed the importance of learning (Almeida, 2002; Ausubel, Novak, &

Hanesian, 1980; Beauclair, 2007). This concept requires a separation from activities that focus on repetition, memorisation and acquisition of knowledge that is regarded as unique and obtained through a single logic. Learning is not intended to be a mere acquisition of information; it assumes that there is the involvement from the person who is learning, through processes of reflection that promote the transformation of information into knowledge. In other words, it requires intellectual activity where, from the information received, students establish relations and new knowledge is built. Based on this idea, Masetto (2011) states that learning is not about replicating the solutions given by teachers to problems. This implies that the class stops 'being the space and time for the teacher to convey information to students' (ibid., p. 599). In fact, in higher education, this orientation relies on creating situations in which students are not relegated to the position of listeners, but are challenged to establish relationships and interactions essential for the construction of knowledge. This is the perspective that supports the idea that teaching must be oriented in order to 'teach learners to learn'.

At its base, this concept is in line with those who consider that a university must prepare students for the complexity of the issues affecting the world, and go where matters are not completely predictable. This complexity requires master skills to identify problems and, based on this identification, create strategies for delineation and solution. This is also Barnett's position (2000, p. 140) when he says that 'the demands of today's society require higher education to open up to creative solutions to the generation and acquisition of new kinds of knowledge; to new kinds of thinking. It is within the framework of this concept that this chapter reflects on the relationship between teaching, learning and research and considers that these three activities, in the context of university education, are inseparability'.

Another argument justifying the need for this issue to be part of the academic debate in higher education is that, at this level of education, besides being researchers, they are also teachers. In this sense, as reminded by Zabalza (2011), all teachers are didacts and, while being didacts, they need to have competence in promoting the learning of students with whom they work and involve them in activities that enable and deepen the knowledge they already have. In short, teaching to promote meaningful learning implies: breaking with the memorising and repetitive education teaching; knowing students' prior knowledge; creating situations that allow students to relate the new knowledge with the knowledge they already have; involving students in studies related to societies and real life. To put it another way, and in line with the position expressed here, this assumes the inseparability of teaching, learning and research. Some studies (Brew & Boud, 1995; Brew, 1999, 2010; Cunha, 2006, 2011; Leite & Fernandes, 2010, 2011; Horta, Dautel, & Veloso, 2012;

Robertson, 2007; Simons & Elen, 2007; Zabalza, 2004, 2011) have pointed to the importance of teaching with research (i.e. through research) and not just performing research to produce knowledge to transmit (Leite & Ramos, 2007, 2012; Mayson & Schapper, 2012). In a way, this idea supports Shulman and Shulman (2004) when they mention a 'community of teachers as learners', that is, the communities of teachers and students collectively involved in building knowledge through research.

Clarifying the position taken in relation to teaching-learning processes, it is necessary to note that this does not reject the need for information and basic knowledge. These are starting points for the development and construction of new knowledge. That is, the reason for which we consider them necessary is profoundly distinct from what justifies a traditional orientation, where they are designed as an end in themselves. The teaching activity in this conception has the function of supporting the construction of bases that allow students who are learning to build knowledge, particularly involving them in research processes that challenge the new interpretations.

As has been mentioned, the relationship between teaching and research has sparked a debate in favour and disfavour, depending on the meanings assigned. Karagiannis (2009) refers to these conflicts and sees the devaluation of those teachers who focus on teaching and who, on many occasions, also seem to be marginalised compared with those who have research as their main focus. Horta et al. (2012, p. 173) state that, although teaching and research are regarded as a university's core mission, the 'status quo among organisational and individual peers is usually enhanced by research visibility, since research is perceived as an activity that brings higher returns in terms of prestige and reputation as compared to teaching' (idem). Using other scholar's investigations, these authors argue that in universities where faculties dedicate less time to research, the teaching is of better quality, while those that neglect it have a higher quality of research. Not ignoring that situations like these might occur, in particular from work overload, which higher education teachers are subject to and often forced to neglect some of these tasks, it should be highlighted here the importance of using university teaching processes that are based on the inseparability between teaching-learning-research.

As is well known, the Humboldtian University model (created in Berlin, XIX) is based on engaging students in an atmosphere marked by the pursuit of knowledge. However, in this model education was the source by which investigation was enabled. On the contrary, from the perspective of the inseparability of teaching-learning-research, research creates learning conditions that favour the construction of knowledge, but at the same time the construction of this knowledge generates conditions for new questions and new learning needs.

This concept of research based on the relationship of inseparability with the activities that allow it and, at the same time, trigger it, is not found in some interpretations, especially in the logic of productivity measured by the number of articles published. On the contrary, and not rejecting the importance that knowledge construction has to be disclosed, the position that is being expressed here is that research is the source that allows an understanding of the social and real situations and, in this sense, provides an ethical commitment, as well as the dissemination of the knowledge produced. Visser-Wijnveen, Van Driel, Van der Rijst, Verloop, and Visser (2009), in a study that analysed the relationships between knowledge, academic research and teaching, concluded that there is a strong relationship between knowledge and research. Willcoxson et al. (2011) maintain that it is more common for the research to be used to inform teaching than the other way around. Whatever the case, it is evident that an involvement in research is not possible without basic knowledge to begin with, that supports the interpretation of the data being collected. In this sense, and once again, the inseparable relationship between teaching and learning and research is strengthened.

Another aspect to consider in this reflection is that the complexity that goes through real situations requires increasingly interdisciplinary knowledge, which can be favoured by having a problem based learning teaching approach. This teaching based on problems (Hung et al., 2008) orientation is characterised by teaching with research that fosters the development of reflection, analysis, articulation of ideas and argumentation skills, as well as organisational and creative thinking.

In summary, the position here is that the university, while being a knowledge-producing institution, has the social responsibility to participate in positive change in society and that this is favoured when there is an emphasis on the real situations studied, like the relationship presented here. The university, as stated by Zabalza (2004), cannot only transmit science, but rather creates science through the relationship between teaching and research. On the other hand, it must assume real life situations as study objects. In this case, the teachers' tasks and the university mission are designated by extension. It is through this process that higher education institutions meet their academic and social mission contributing to knowledge evolution configured in a society where better living conditions are expected.

Returning to the relationship between teaching and research that supports the analysis that is being taken as a focus of this text, and accepting in part Georgen (2002, p. 24) idea that 'the research seeks to develop new knowledge while teaching conveys the knowledge set and introduces students to the practice of research', it can be assumed that none of them is justified without the other, i.e., it is not possible to investigate without possessing basic knowledge, but also it does not make sense to produce new knowledge if the teaching is not trimmed. On the other hand, and as it is supported by Cunha (2011, p. 452), 'in theory, research makes better teachers because it helps them to think, to question, to understand and these are important qualities in teaching', that is, it even helps teachers to carry out in a more effective manner their role in teaching.

Nóvoa (2012) has focused on various changes in higher education in Portugal, notably those arising from the Bologna Process, which has established the need for teaching, to follow an orientation that is based on the involvement of students in research and study procedures. In an interview, he stated:

> We must think of Bologna from the appreciation of the study, that is, the ability to organize the University work around reading and the use of libraries, experimentation and attending laboratories, research practices, self-study and supervised study (mentoring, supervision, among others). To put it another way: we must go beyond logic and rigid curriculum structures, valuing the study, in its various dimensions, as the main reference of the University work. (Nóvoa, 2012, p. 639)

The fact that inseparability between teaching and research is only proclaimed in relation to higher education, leads us to assume that it is this feature that gives the University's main work the specificity that it has in the entire education system. This same position is assumed by some authors for whom a university constitutes higher education because it teaches what it investigates (Barnett, 1994; Magalhães, 2004, 2006). That is, the investigation is part of the mission at this level of education and comprises the heritage of its composing institutions.

What Has Been Stated by Political Discourse and its Institutions?

Ten years after the World Conference on Higher Education in 1998, at the World Conference on HE held in 2009 in Paris under the auspices of UNESCO, a news release was approved which, among other aspects, stated that:

1. Pertaining to higher education's 'social responsibility', higher education is a public service and the superior education institutions, through their main functions (research, teaching and community service), should increase the interdisciplinary focus and promote critical thinking and active citizenship;
2. Pertaining to 'access, equality and quality', the quality criteria should guide all of the higher education goals and of students, critical and

independent thinking, stimulating innovation and diversity. It is also stated that to ensure the quality of higher education requires recognition to attract a team who is committed, talented and qualified;

3. Pertaining to the 'internationalization, regionalisation and globalization' it is mentioned that international cooperation in higher education should be based on solidarity and mutual respect, in addition to the humanistic values and intercultural dialogue. In this sense, it is pointed out that the research partnerships and exchanges promote international cooperation;

4. With respect to 'education, research and innovation' and considering the growing need for research and development funding it is mentioned that it would be important to find new ways, through public-private partnerships and including small and medium-sized enterprises. It is also mentioned that there is an increasing difficulty to maintain a balance between basic and applied research, as well as the challenge of connecting knowledge with local problems. In this sense, it is stated that research systems should be organized in order to promote science and interdisciplinary at society's service.

Analysing this political discourse infers the existence of some contradictions. On the one hand, an approach that appeals to the critical spirit and the exercise of active citizenship and, on the other hand, what some critics consider as adherence to neo-liberal principles. In fact, at this Conference, UNESCO incorporated and accepted, higher education, principles that place tension in education as a human right and, simultaneously, as a commercial service. It is in this critical sense that Dias Sobrinho (2005), relying on the concept of higher education's social responsibility, proposes for 'the University not to give reason to the market [... and] for it not to be an engine of globalization of the market economy, but instead be the globalization of human dignity' (ibid., p. 172).

Having these policy orientations as a reference in Europe, with the signing of the Bologna Declaration (1999), signed at the time by the Ministers of Education from 29 countries, a process began that strongly marked higher education, in particular in the implementation of what is called the European Higher Education Area. These political commitments, in Portugal's case, led to a reform in higher education (Leite & Fernandes, 2012) justified by the comparability of academic degrees, the promotion of student and teachers mobility, and teaching quality improvement. This reform legislated in 2006 (Decree-Law No. 74/2006 of 24 March) entailed changes in the organisation of courses and in their modes of operation. In this sense, and in which teaching and research are concerned, the legislation stated that the 'transition from a system of education based on knowledge transfer to a system based on the development of skills by the students is a critical issue in Europe, with a particular expression in Portugal'. It also stated that, 'identifying the skills, developing appropriate methodologies to achieve it, and putting the new model of teaching in practice, are the challenges faced by higher education institutions'. In summary, a key issue was enunciated in the Bologna Process to

> Change the paradigm of teaching of a passive model based on the acquisition of knowledge for a model based on skills development where it's included both the generic nature-interpersonal and systemic instrumental-specific nature associated with the training area, and where the experimental component and design play an important role. (Decree-Law 74/2006 – Introduction)

From this political discourse, it must be acknowledged that the legislation establishing the suitability of these European commitments indicates a separation from the academic rationale logic (Leite, 2002) – that makes students mere receivers of information that was not built by them – replacing it by a paradigm that values learning and students' involvement in its construction. Therefore, in training activities and in the planning of the study plans the students work time is contemplated. This is the reason behind the ECTS system (European Credit Transfer System) in which in addition to the contact time with teachers, the time students' spend on autonomous study activities, fieldwork, training course and evaluation, among others, is also counted.

As can be seen, this recognition that training through the involvement of students in the dynamics which involve them actively in the construction of their learning can be a promoter for the use of research, in line with what was mentioned above and calling on Nóvoa (2012, p. 639) proposal on how to implement the Bologna speech. As stated throughout this text, a paradigm focused on learning and the students' action as constructors of that learning can and should include a strong research connection. It should then not be a study directed towards memorisation of the information provided, but the establishment of relations between that information and data collected from real life situations that allow knowledge construction. This was the concept that guided the arguments presented here around the inseparability in teaching-learning-research. It is in reference to this that a future agenda for the debate could be presented focused on this theme.

What Could a Future Teaching-Learning-Research Relationship Agenda Constitute?

As stated elsewhere (Leite, 2007), the Bologna Process, when resorting to a speech that pointed out the need to replace school-based teaching for teaching based on learning, had as a consequence the recognition that in higher education there is also a need to learn how to be a teacher. In fact, several studies have pointed to the knowledge required to practice teaching (Gauthier et al., 1998; Perrenoud, 2000; Day, 2001; Leite & Ramos, 2007). All these studies show that, in addition to the specific knowledge areas that each teacher is bound to, pedagogical knowledge that allows the establishment of educational and personal relationships that create conditions for the implementation of a wider scientific knowledge is also needed. At the same time, the establishment of situations capable of creating environments that encourage the willingness to learn should also be developed.

Another aspect to keep in mind is the University Mission, which in the case of higher education has been the subject of some debate in the past years. The Bologna Process, in its goal to make Europe the most competitive region, and the education policies that followed, pointed in the direction of instrumental and economic orientation. As referred by Amaral, Correia, Magalhães, Rosa, Santiago, and Teixeira (2002), higher education is led by the economy. Given this situation, it is urgent to continue to reflect on how teaching-learning-research can identify the right conditions for its success and how that contributes to the teaching and learning improvement in higher education as well as the social utility research can have. Without falling into the 'there's nothing we can do', it is important to question: what position to take in teaching, research and social intervention in order to induce other reconfigurations that positively resume the social responsibility of higher education? Will research just be confined to post-graduate programmes? What possibilities are being offered, in higher education, for a teaching exercise that meets the principle of teaching-learning-research-extension inseparability? What consequences will research have if it's done only by some higher education institutions?, that is, if there is a separation between Teaching Universities and Research Universities? Is the manner in which research is assessed looking for ways to legitimize this scenario? What possibilities do current pressure to publish in English and in journals indexed in ISI Web Science offer to promote a socially committed science (Sousa Santos, 2004)? These are urgent issues for a future agenda of debate focused on this theme. As it was concluded by Brew's (2010) study, 'the aspiration to integrate research and teaching is not well translated into practical strategies for implementation' (ibid., p. 139) due to the fact that the government by separating funding from research and teaching discourages integration.

References

Almeida, L. S. (2002). Facilitar a aprendizagem: Ajudar os alunos a aprender e a pensar. *Psicologia Escolar e Educacional, 6*(2), 155–165.

Amaral, A., Correia, F., Magalhães, A., Rosa, M. J., Santiago, R., & Teixeira, P. (2002). *O ensino superior pela mão da economia*. Matosinhos: CIPES, Fundação das Universidades Portuguesas.

Ausubel, D., Novak, J. D., & Hanesian, H. (1980). *Psicologia educacional*. Rio de Janeiro: Editora Interamericana.

Balzan, N. (2002). Indissociabilidade ensino-pesquisa como princípio metodológico. In I. Veiga & M. E. Castanho (Eds.), *Pedagogia Universitária: A aula em foco* (3rd ed., pp. 115–136). Campinas: Papirus.

Barnett, R. (1994). *The idea of higher education: The society for research into higher education*. Buckingham: Open University Press.

Beauclair, J. (2007). (A)cerca do aprender e do ensinar: Fios, teias e redes como metáforas em subjetividade, aprendizagem e psicopedagogia. *Revista Psicopedagogia, 24*(75), 260–271.

Brew, A. (1999). Research and teaching: Changing relationships in a changing context. *Studies in Higher Education, 24*(3), 291–301.

Brew, A. (2010). Imperatives and challenges in integrating teaching and research. *Higher Education Research & Development, 29*(2), 139–150.

Brew, A., & Boud, D. (1995). Teaching and research: Establishing the vital link with learning. *Higher Education, 29*(3), 261–273.

Cunha, M. I. (2006). A didática como construção: Aprendendo com o fazer e pesquisando com o saber. In M. Morosini (Ed.), *Professor do ensino superior: Identidade, docência e formação* (pp. 79–92). Brasília: Plátano Editora.

Cunha, M. I. (2011). Indissociabilidade entre ensino e pesquisa: A qualidade da graduação em tempos de democratização. *Perspectiva, 2*(29), 443–462.

Day, C. (2001). *Desenvolvimento profissional de professores: Os desafios da aprendizagem permanente*. Porto: Porto Editora.

Decree-Law 74/2006, 24 March 2006, Ministério da Ciência.

Dias Sobrinho, J. (2005). Educação superior, globalização e democratização: Qual universidade? *Revista Brasileira de Educação, 28*(10), 164–173.

Freire, P. (1972). *Pedagogia do oprimido*. Porto: Ed. Afrontamento.

Freire, P. (1974). *Uma educação para a liberdade* (4th ed.). Porto: Edição Textos Marginais.

Gauthier, C., Martineau, S., Desbiens, J. F., Malo, A., & Simard, D. (1998). *Por uma teoria da pedagogia: Pesquisas contemporâneas sobre o saber docente*. Ijuí: Unijuí.

Georgen, P. (2002). A instituição Universidade e a sua responsabilidade social: Anotações críticas. *Quaestio: Revista De Estudos De Educação, 4*(1), 1–25.

Horta, H., Dautel, V., & Veloso, F. M. (2012). An output perspective on the teaching–research nexus: An analysis focusing on the United States higher education system. *Studies in Higher Education, 37*(2), 171–187.

Hung, W., Jonassen, D., & Liu, R. (2008). Problem-based learning. In J. M. Spector, J. G. van Merrienboer, M. D. Merrill, & M. Driscoll (Eds.), *Handbook of research on educational communications and technology* (pp. 486–506). Mahwah, NJ: Erlbaun. Retrieved from http://faculty.ksu.edu.sa/Alhassan/Hand%20book%20on%20research%20in%20educational%20communication/ER5849x_C038.fm.pdf

Karagiannis, S. N. (2009). The conflicts between science research and teaching in higher education: An academic's perspective. *International Journal of Teaching and Learning in Higher Education, 21*(1), 75–83.

Leite, C. (2002). *O currículo e o multiculturalismo no sistema educativo português*. Lisboa: Fundação Calouste Gulbenkian/FCT.

Leite, C., & Fernandes, P. (2010). Bolonha e os processos de ensino-aprendizagem no ensino superior universitário em Portugal: Uma análise a partir do recurso aos fóruns de debate online. In *La docencia en el nuevo escenario del espacio Europeo de educación superior: Vicerreitoría de formación e innovación educativa* (pp. 135–138). Vigo: Universidade de Vigo.

Leite, C., & Fernandes, P. (2011). Inovação pedagógica: Uma resposta às demandas da sala de aula universitária. *Perspectiva, 29*(2), 507–533.

Leite, C., & Fernandes, P. (2012). Curricular studies and their relation with the political agenda for education. *Transnational Curriculum Inquiry, 2,* 35–49.

Leite, C., & Ramos, K. (2007). Docência universitária: Análise de uma experiência de formação na Universidade do Porto. In M. I. Cunha (Ed.), *Reflexões e práticas em pedagogia universitária* (pp. 27–42). Campinas: Papirus.

Leite, C., & Ramos, K. (2010). Questões da formação pedagógico-didática na sua relação com a profissionalidade docente universitária: Alguns pontos para debate. In C. Leite (Ed.), *Sentidos da pedagogia no Ensino Superior* (pp. 29–43). Porto: Livpsic/CIIE.

Leite, C., & Ramos, K. (2012). Formação para a docência universitária: Uma reflexão sobre o desafio de humanizar a cultura científica. *Revista Portuguesa de Educação, 25*(1), 7–27. Retrieved from http://www.scielo.gpeari.mctes.pt/pdf/rpe/v25n1/v25n1a02.pdf

Lessard, C. (2002). Qu'est-ce qu'une formation professionnelle universitaire? Conceptions de l'université et formation professionnelle. *Revue Française de Pédagogie, 139,* 131–154.

Magalhães, A. (2004). *A identidade do ensino superior: Política, conhecimento e educação numa época de transição*. Lisboa: Fundação Calouste Gulbenkian.

Magalhães, A. (2006). A identidade do ensino superior: A educação superior e a universidade. *Revista Lusófona de Educação, 7,* 13–40.

Masetto, M. (2011). Inovação na aula universitária: Espaço de pesquisa, construção de conhecimento interdisciplinar, espaço de aprendizagem e tecnologias de comunicação. *Perspectiva, 29*(2), 597–620.

Mayson, S., & Schapper, J. (2012). Constructing teaching and research relation from the top: An analysis of senior manager discourses on research-led teaching. *Higher Education, 64*, 473–487.

Nóvoa, A. (2012). Entrevista com o Prof. António Nóvoa. *Educação & Sociedade, 33*(119), 633–645.

Perrenoud, P. (2000). *10 novas competências para ensinar*. Porto Alegre: Artmed.

Readings, B. (2002). *Universidade sem cultura?* Rio de Janeiro: Ed. da UERJ.

Robertson, J. (2007). Beyond the 'research/teaching nexus': Exploring the complexity of academic experience. *Studies in Higher Education, 32*(5), 541–556.

Shulman, L., & Shulman, J. (2004). How and what teachers learn: A shifting perspective. *Journal of Curriculum Studies, 36*(2), 257–271.

Simons, M., & Elen, J. (2007). The 'research-teaching nexus' and 'education through research': An exploration of ambivalences. *Studies in Higher Education, 32*(5), 617–631.

Sousa Santos, B. (2004). *A universidade no século XXI: Para uma reforma democrática e emancipatória da universidade*. São Paulo: Cortez.

UNESCO. (1998). *Declaración mundial sobre la educación superior en el siglo XXI: visión y acción*. Paris: UNESCO. Retrieved from http://www.Unesco.org/education/educprog/wche/declaration_spa.htm#marco

UNESCO. (2009). *Conferência Mundial sobre ensino superior 2009: As novas dinâmicas do ensino superior e pesquisas para a mudança e o desenvolvimento social*. Paris: UNESCO. Retrieved from http://www.aplicweb.feevale.br/site/files/documentos/pdf/31442.pdf

Visser-Wijnveen, G. J., Van Driel, J. H., Van der Rijst, R. M., Verloop, N., & Visser, A. (2009). The relationship between academics' conceptions of knowledge, research and teaching: A metaphor study. *Teaching in Higher Education, 14*(6), 673–686.

Willcoxson, L., Manning, M. L., Johnston, N., & Gething, K. (2011). Enhancing the research-teaching nexus: Building teaching-based research from research-based teaching. *International Journal of Teaching and Learning in Higher Education, 23*(1), 1–10.

Zabalza, M. (2004). *O ensino universitário: Seu cenário e seus protagonistas*. Porto Alegre: Artmed.

Zabalza, M. (2011). Nuevos enfoques para la didáctica universitária actual. *Perspectiva, 29*(2), 387–416.

CHAPTER 4

The Advent and Implications of SoTL
Overview of the Initiation and Development of SoTL Internationally

Vaneeta D'Andrea

History of SoTL within the Teaching and Research Nexus Debate

The research/teaching nexus in higher education has been the focus of numerous debates and concerns for many decades. Essentially the crux of this debate centres on how academics engage with the expectations of their dual role to teach and do research in higher education. It concerns whether these roles complement or conflict with each other. More to the point, the core issue surrounding the enactment of these roles centres on the differential rewards within academe for carrying out each of these role sets. Furthermore, in modern universities research activities have been given greater recognition and consequently greater status and monetary rewards. In previous publications (D'Andrea, 2007, 2010, 2014; D'Andrea & Gosling, 2005) I have discussed these differential rewards and their effects on teaching and learning in higher education. This chapter will not rehearse these earlier discussions but rather it will focus on developments in academe that have concerned the promotion of the scholarship of teaching and learning (SoTL) which is being used as a lever for changing this hierarchical research/teaching paradigm and the differential recognition and reward structures attached to each.

One of the earliest challenges to the research privileging paradigm of scholarly activities was the work of the American educator Ernest Boyer. He noted this dilemma in his 1987 publication, *College: the undergraduate experience in America*. In it he argued that not all academics should be publishing researchers but should in all cases be 'first rate scholars'. In 1990 his book, *Scholarship Reconsidered: Priorities of the Professoriate*, he developed a more detailed argument for scholarly activities and challenged the hierarchy of research and teaching. In this fruitful piece he outlined an argument for four forms of scholarship that were each seen as equally valuable to the higher education enterprise. This four-fold model includes: scholarship of discovery, scholarship of integration, scholarship of practice, and scholarship of teaching. The work of Rice (1992) further clarified this model by elaborating on how each contributed to academic work. In his view the scholarship of discovery, or what has been known as 'original' or 'blue-skies' research, is an anchor for all other scholarships. He saw the scholarship of integration as the process that kept scholarly work from becoming fragmented and providing the basis for finding new relationships between the parts and the whole of scholarly knowledge. Rice noted that the scholarship of practice was inspired by the history of the development of the American higher education system which had included practical higher education in agriculture, science, military science and engineering offered at national government funded 'land-grant universities' (https://en.wikipedia.org/wiki/Land-grant_university). The scholarship of teaching, from Rice's point of view, was made up of the other three scholarships with an 'integrity' of its own. In his view it draws together and provides coherence within a field of study and transcends any split between disciplinary content knowledge and knowledge transfer, and helps to understand the relationship between knowledge and the meanings inherent in learning. (See D'Andrea & Gosling, 2005, Chapter 7, which includes a more fulsome discussion of Rice's explanation of this model.)

By defining research in terms of forms of scholarship, research work itself could no longer be understood as only one type of activity. Thus, Boyer's model challenged the status quo in higher education around the recognition and rewards for certain types of scholarship and created the narrative for the Scholarship of Teaching and Learning (SoTL) movement. As might be expected in an academic context, a debate developed around how to define the term scholarship of teaching, and studies were carried out to determine how it was understood in academe (Elton, 1992; Healey, 2001, 2003; Hutchings, 2000). The debates extended to how SoTL related to other key related areas such as pedagogical research (PedR) (Yorke, 2001; D'Andrea, 2000) and pedagogical development (PedD) (D'Andrea & Gosling, 2003, 2005). Clarification of the understanding and use of these various terms in higher education was the focus of the UK Higher Education Funding Council for England (HEFCE) scoping study, commissioned on the state of the art of SoTL (Gordon et al., 2002). Other distinctions between the scholarship of teaching and scholarly teaching (Richlin, 2001) and research-led teaching or teaching-led research (Griffiths, 2004) were also considered in this developing literature.

In addition to defining and situating SoTL within policy agendas and the literature on higher education, discussions of the meaning of the scholarship of teaching and its relationship to other forms of academic work were taking place in the United Kingdom (Elton, 1992; Healey, D'Andrea, & Gosling, 2005), Australia (Brew & Boud, 1995; Brew, 1999; Trigwell et al., 2000; Trigwell, 2001) and Canada (Consolo, Elrick, Middleton, & Roy, 1996; Kreber & Cranston, 2000). The first attempts to engage academe in the processes of re-valuing the scholarship of teaching took hold in North America in the mid 80 s and then over several decades spread around the English-speaking world and eventually further afield. These developments are discussed briefly below.

Developments to Promote SoTL

Any social change is dependent both on organisational structures and bespoke processes to support the intended change. For the SoTL movement, these activities and their related programmes began to appear in quick succession in many of the English-speaking countries around the world. A literature on SoTL including books and journals was soon evident. Higher education conferences started to feature SoTL and national programmes to support the development of SoTL in universities were started (Hutchings & Shulman, 1999). In the beginning, depending on the country in question, the SoTL movement was well supported by either private higher education philanthropic organisations and/or government funding. A few examples are described below.

National Programmes to Promote SoTL

In 1986, ahead of Boyer's publication in 1990, Canada led the SoTL movement through the creation of the 3M Teaching Fellowships. The funding for this programme comes from 3M Canada Inc and the Fellowships have been administered by the Society for Teaching and Learning in Higher Education (STLHE). 'The criteria for the award are those to assess scholarship: the faculty member questions, makes interpretations based on evidence, draws conclusions which she or he makes available to colleagues for their critical assessment' (Consolo et al., 1996, p. 44). Ten Fellows are selected each year and to date there have been a total of 290 Fellows. This year, 2016, will mark the 30th consecutive year for this programme (STLHE website, n.d.). Similarly in 1997 Australia started a national teaching award programme that is still ongoing, though the name has changed over the years. The Australian programme awarded 22 Fellowships in 2015 (Australian Government website, 2015).

Following Boyer's publication, work by organisations focused on higher education issues in the United States of America (USA) also influenced the SoTL movement in a number of specific ways. Soon after the appointment of Lee Shulman (who succeeded Ernest Boyer) as President of The Carnegie Foundation for the Advancement of Teaching in 1997, a three-part programme to support the development of SoTL activities was established. The Carnegie Academy for the Scholarship of Teaching and Learning (CASTL) programme included: (1) the Pew National Fellowship Programme for Carnegie Scholars (started in 1998), (2) the Teaching Academy Campus Programme [managed by the American Association for Higher Education (AAHE) until its dissolution] and (3) work with scholarly and professional associations (who nominated Carnegie Scholars). It worked at the individual academic level, the institutional level and the professional organisation level (Cambridge, 1999).

> With the Carnegie Academy for Teaching and Learning (or CASTL) we are trying to take an aspect of academic work that was never thought of as scholarship and persuade others that it is (a) indeed scholarship and (b) that it ought, therefore, to be recognized and rewarded, and (c) that they ought to be doing it. (interview with Shulman in Hutchings, 1999, p. 7)

Over six cohorts, there were 161 Carnegie Scholars from 22 subject disciplines (Huber, 2016). One hundred twenty Teaching Academy Campus programmes were in place by 1999 (Hutchings & Shulman, 1999) and the work of 38 of these Academies was reported in the book, *Campus Progress: supporting the scholarship of teaching and learning* (Cambridge, 2004). Following the retirement of Lee Shulman, in 2008, the Carnegie Foundation formally ended support for these programmes. Nevertheless the programme still has continuing impact on higher education in the USA through the work of the individual Carnegie Scholars, the universities where the Teaching Academies are ongoing and through the commitment of professional organisations that had been involved in a variety of ways.

The UK followed suite in 1999. In England and Northern Ireland the National Teaching Fellowship (NTF) programme was established (Wales joined in 2010). Similar to the CASTL programme in the USA, the NTF programme was part of a three pronged initiative to enhance teaching and learning in higher education in parts of the UK. Like the Carnegie work it addressed SoTL issues at the individual level (NTFs), project-based work with the Fund for the Development of Teaching and Learning (FDTL) and at the disciplinary level through the Learning and Teaching Subject Networks (LTSNs) (D'Andrea & Gosling, 2002). The NTF is ongoing and awarded 739 National Teaching Fellowships between 2000 and 2015. It started with twenty awards per year and had as many as fifty-five in 2014 with the number varying both more and less over the fifteen years it has been in operation (HEA NTF website).

Other countries have similar awards, for example: New Zealand has awarded Tertiary Teaching Excellence Awards since 2001 and Sweden established the Society of Living Pedagoges in 1990, though no longer in existence, it did last sixteen years. Ahead of the Carnegie Scholars programme, the USA started the University Professor of the Year awards in 1981. However, it should be noted that the only award programmes that were directly linked to the SoTL were the Carnegie Scholars and the original National Teaching Fellows programmes because each recipient was required to complete a SoTL project with the funds awarded to them (see comparison chart in D'Andrea, 2007).

SoTL Conferences

Another structural dimension that supported the SoTL change agenda was the development of a series of international conferences held between SoTL researchers from the United Kingdom (UK) and the USA. Known as the UK International SoTL conferences, they were started in 2001. These conferences continued for ten years.

The first conference matched a Carnegie Scholar with a NTF who shared their work on SoTL topics of common interest. This was a first step in internationalising SoTL. After the first three years the organisers of the UK International SoTL conferences presented a paper at the Society for Research in Higher Education (SRHE), which analysed the topics of the papers for the first three SoTL conferences. This paper reported that the vast majority of papers were concerned with SoTL and the term itself was used more often than Ped(R) or Ped(D). More than 90% of the papers were identified as SoTL work. Thus it was clear that the use of the term SoTL was beginning to be used by those engaged in pedagogic scholarship. In addition, participants from several countries became involved (see Table 4.1). A conclusion of this investigation was that SoTL was becoming 'a nascent field of academic inquiry'.

TABLE 4.1   Summary of number of presentations at UK international SoTL conferences 2001–2003 by overall topic, type of scholarship and country of origin

Year of conference	2001	2002	2003	Total
Overall topic	In%	In%	In%	In%
SoTL	92 (26)	98 (47)	79 (30)	90 (103)
Ped R	8 (2)	2 (1)	13 (5)	7 (8)
Ped D	0	0	8 (3)	3 (3)
Type of scholarship				
Discovery	0	0	3 (1)	1 (1)
Integration	21 (6)	19 (9)	26 (10)	22 (25)
Application	21 (6)	27 (13)	29 (11)	24 (27)
Teaching	57 (16)	54 (26)	42 (16)	42 (48)
Country				
UK	82 (23)	65 (31)	71 (27)	71 (81)
USA	18 (5)	29 (14)	16 (6)	22 (25)
Other: Australia, Canada, Sweden	0	6 (3)	13 (5)	7 (8)

SOURCE: D'ANDREA AND GOSLING (2003, P. 5)

Over time the conference papers became more and more analytically focused on the topics explored and soon critiques of the SoTL movement were the subject of papers presented. At the Third International Conference on the Scholarship of Teaching and Learning held in 2003 Kreber's paper 'Peer Review and the Scholarship of Teaching: SoTL as critical inquiry' began to re-focus the agenda. The paper argued 'for the need for a much more political understanding of the potential of SoTL drawing on works in postmodernism and critical theory'. It further argued, 'that we need to think about the political purposes of learning and not simply regard learning to be a taken-for-granted good' (Gosling, 2003). Kreber concluded that SoTL: 'could be a vehicle to promote social change', and it 'could go beyond teaching the subject ... to include the dimension for empowerment, emancipation and social responsibility' (Kreber, 2003, p. 18).

SoTL Journals

Numerous journals that centred on teaching and learning in higher education had been around in the USA since the 70 s. Most of these were discipline based. By the early 90 s lists of these journals and analyses of their content were being published (Cashin & Clegg, 1993; Weimer, 1993). Cashin and Clegg listed 128 journals publishing articles on pedagogy in 69 disciplines. In addition they also mentioned 45 other journals that published work on university teaching more generally.

So how would the SoTL movement add or change this rich landscape of scholarly activity on teaching and learning? As early as 1998, Indiana University in the USA published a special issue on the scholarship of teaching in its journal, *Research and Creative Activity*. The Internet added to the impact of the dissemination of SoTL work when a number of e-journals were established. *Inventio: creative thinking about learning and teaching* based at Georgetown University started in 1999 was one of these early additions to the SoTL literature and featured 'scholarship of teaching' in its first issue. *The Journal of the Scholarship of Teaching and Learning* (JoSoTL) followed in 2001 and *Mountain Rise* 2006 (restructuring since 2014). Each of these outlets for teaching scholarship added opportunities for this form of scholarship to be recognised as a legitimate scholarly activity.

Early in the development of the SoTL literature *JoSoTL* analysed the work it published in its first three volumes up through October, 2003. There were 11 (38 percent) articles using classroom action research, 10 (34 percent) concerned with issues relating to defining and refining the idea of SoTL, and 8 (28 percent) carrying out traditional pedagogic research (JoSoTL website). *Inventio* had not categorised the 61 articles published between the autumn of 1999 and spring of 2003, however using the same operational definition as applied to the SRHE study cited above, most titles over those five years 39 (63 percent) were on the SoTL, 15 (25 percent) were on Ped(R), 4 (less than 1 percent) were on Ped(D) and the remaining were unclassifiable by title (D'Andrea & Gosling, 2003). If the first two categories of the JoSoTL study were collapsed into the broader category labelled SoTL, the total in the SoTL category would be 72 percent. This closely reflects both the Inventio study and the UK International SoTL conference study. Thus, it would appear that the trend towards more SoTL papers and publications in the early years of the SoTL movement closely resembled each other.

Other outlets for SoTL work have continued to be developed in the last decade and have included: the International Journal for the Scholarship of Teaching & Learning (2006), *The Canadian Journal for the Scholarship of Teaching and Learning* started in (2009), and *Teaching and Learning Inquiry* (2012) the official journal of International Society for the Scholarship of Teaching and Learning (IS-SoTL) (more on this organisation below). The current IS-SoTL site http://issotl.com/issotl15/node/21 also lists the range of current journals, and other publication avenues for SoTL work.

International Developments IS-SoTL

By 2004 the international SoTL movement was being supported by another structural component. A professional association of academics committed to SoTL founded the International Society for the Scholarship of Teaching and Learning (IS-SoTL). A Founding Conference was held that year in the USA and IS-SoTL conferences have been held annually from this date onwards (it essentially replaced the UK International Conference on SoTL). The structure of the organisation and the location of its conferences began to help the SoTL movement become more responsive to international needs. Nevertheless the locations of the conferences have mainly been in North America. Eleven of the fourteen have been in the US or Canada and the rest in other English-speaking countries, with two in Australia and one in the UK in Europe (IS-SoTL website). IS-SoTl also has a website and its own journal (see above), monthly newsletter, social media networks, a blog and an awards programme in addition to the annual conference.

SoTL Now and in the Future

Where is SoTL now? As noted above there are a few of the original structures in place and there are a number of new initiatives. The work started early on in Australia, Canada, the USA and the UK still have many outcomes of note, even for those no longer funded. These are particularly evident in the increasing number of thriving SoTL conferences and journals.

More specifically, IS-SoTL continues to work actively for the promotion of SoTL at large and it has created a number of internal organisational structures for doing this. In an interview for this chapter, the past president of IS-SoTL, Joelle Fanghanel, noted that there were three primary foci for the work of IS-SoTL at this time including: promoting the involvement of students in SoTL, international writing groups that support the preparation of papers for the annual IS-SoTL conference and the use of technologies as SoTL work, particularly online teaching and learning, mobile applications and social networks – such as blogging and tweeting. IS-SoTL is also concerned with extending the international dimension of its work and involving students more directly in its organisational structure by including them on the Board of IS-SoTL.

Another indicator of the health of this movement is a major initiative being taken forward by the Higher Education Academy (HEA) in the UK. Entitled: Defining and Supporting SoTL in Higher Education, it was launched in January 2016. Its main aims are to: (1) update the international literature on SoTL, (2) chart the way SoTL is defined, supported and embedded in institutional policy in the UK, (3) provide institutions with resources for their reward and promotion processes, and (4) indentify ways to engage students in SoTL. The project outputs include: discipline case studies in the creative arts, sciences and humanities; international exemplar case studies from Australia, Europe and the USA; thematic case studies on SoTL as a discipline, engaging staff in SoTL, loci, processes; and activities for institutions, promotion criteria, supporting the dissemination of SoTL research, the benefits of SoTL, understandings of SoTL, the UK Professional Standards Framework (UKPSF); student engagement case studies on practice examples of involving students with SoTL, student engagement leaders' perspectives, students' perspectives; and reports: a literature review, an executive summary and a survey; an audit tool; and additional resources (HEA SoTL site: http://sotl.eu/). Although a national initiative, this is a rich resource for SoTL researchers both in the UK and in other areas of the world for now and in the foreseeable future[1].

Australia, too, has just initiated a new National Institute for Learning and Teaching that replaces the Office for Learning and Teaching. It will officially open in July of 2016. One of its underlying principles is to: "assist in raising the recognition of learning and teaching in the higher education sector and beyond" (Milbourne, 2015, p. 3). This harks back to Boyer's concern for the improvement of the status of teaching in higher education and the concomitant support for SoTL.

In the USA, it is noteworthy that the Carnegie Foundation for the Advancement of Teaching and Learning is working to create an archive of the materials produced during the CASTL programme years. Though slow-going it is in train. In addition Hutchings et al. (2011) report that there are:

A growing set of international conferences, disciplinary interest groups, journals, speaking engagements, consultancies, and initiatives [that] have enriched the professional lives of scholars of teaching and learning everywhere, and helped increase the circulation of pedagogical ideas across national boundaries .... There are many sources of commentary on the movement to establish a scholarship of teaching and learning. Among the most important are reports by campus leaders at institutions involved in the work, leaders who are often well attuned to tensions and shortcomings. Some of these reports are publicly available.

Furthermore numerous surveys have been conducted to attempt to determine the future of SoTL and it seems the future has an expanding SoTL agenda (see Hutchings et al., 2011, for a list of recent surveys).

So, what is the future of this movement? The infrastructure in the English-speaking countries that led in its development is clearly still supporting new developments and adding the work of IS-SoTL to this, it appears the SoTL movement will remain a major force for future developments in higher education. Although this social movement, like most others, requires the ongoing commitment of its advocates, it remains a collective attempt to bring about a change in higher education as a social institution. Until research and teaching are given equal status and equal rewards the work the SoTL movement, prompted by Boyer's work, will not be over.

Notes

1   Elton (1992) cites earlier discussions of the issues surrounding the definition of scholarship for defining types of research; including: Goodlad (1976) and Carter (1980).
2   I am grateful to Joelle Fanghanel, Research Project Leader, for bringing this initiative to my attention.

References

Bok, D. (1992). Reclaiming the public trust. *Change, 24,* 13–19.

Boyer, E. L. (1987). *College: The undergraduate experience in America.* New York, NY: Harper & Row.

Boyer, E. L. (1990). *Scholarship reconsidered: Priorities of the professoriate.* Princeton, NJ: The Carnegie Foundation for the Advancement of Teaching.

Brew, A. (1999). Research and teaching: Changing relationships in a changing context. *Studies in Higher Education, 24*(3), 291–391.

Brew, A., & Boud, D. (1995). Teaching and research: Establishing the vital link with learning. *Higher Education, 29*, 261–273.

Cambridge, B. L. (1999, December). The scholarship of teaching and learning: Questions and answers from the field. *AAHE Bulletin*.

Cambridge, B. L. (Ed.). (2004). *Campus progress: Supporting the scholarship of teaching and learning*. Washington, DC: American Association of Higher Education.

Carter, C. (1980). *Higher education for the future*. Oxford: Blackwell.

Cashin, W. E., & Clegg, V. L. (1993). *Periodicals related to college teaching* (Idea Paper No. 28). Manhattan, KS: Kansas State University.

Cunsolo, J., Elrick, M., Middleton, A., & Roy, D. (1996). The scholarship of teaching: A Canadian perspective with examples. *The Canadian Journal of Higher Education, 26*(1), 35–56.

D'Andrea, V. (2000, November 16). *Comments on questions for pedagogical research conference*. Pedagogical Research in Higher Education, An Invitational Workshop, Coventry, London.

D'Andrea, V. (2007). National strategies for promoting excellence in teaching: A critical review. In A. Skelton (Ed.), *International perspectives on teaching excellence in higher education* (pp. 169–182). Abingdon: Routledge.

D'Andrea, V. (2010). Rewarding teaching: Lessons from the faculty roles and rewards movement. In C. Howery & T. Van Valey (Eds.), *Peer review of teaching*. Washington, DC: American Sociological Association.

D'Andrea, V. (2014). Engaging the international scholarly and policy community though active dialogue on the research-teaching nexus. In P. John & J. Fanghanel (Eds.), *Dimensions of marketization in higher education*. Abingdon: Routledge.

D'Andrea, V., & Gosling, D. (2002, September). *The research and teaching nexus and managing change in higher education: A comparison of two national initiatives*. The European Association for Institutional Research, Prague, Czech Republic.

D'Andrea, V., & Gosling, D. (2003, December). *The discourse of scholarship of teaching and learning: A case study of the international SoTL conference*. Symposium on the Scholarship of Teaching, Society for Research in Higher Education Annual Conference, London.

D'Andrea, V., & Gosling, D. (2005). *Improving teaching and learning: A whole institution approach*. Maidenhead: McGraw Hill.

Elton, L. (1992). Research, teaching and scholarship in an expanding higher education system. *Higher Education Quarterly, 46*(3), 252–268.

Goodlad, S. (1976). *Conflict and consensus in higher education*. London: Hodder & Stoughton.

Gordon, G., D'Andrea, V., Gosling, D., & Stefani, L. (2003). *Building capacity for change, research on the scholarship of teaching, review report for the HEFCE*. Retrieved from http://heer.qaa.ac.uk/SearchForSummaries/Summaries/Pages/RES02.aspx

Gosling, D. (2003, July 17). *Email message, subject: RE: Scholarship of teaching*.

Griffiths, R. (2004). Knowledge production and the research-teaching nexus: The case of the built environment disciplines. *Studies in Higher Education, 29*(6), 709–726.

Healey, M. (2001, June). *The scholarship of teaching: A disputed concept*. Paper presented to the First Annual International Conference on the Scholarship of Teaching and Learning.

Healey, M. (2003). The scholarship of teaching: Issues around an evolving concept. *Journal on Excellence in College Teaching, 14*(1–2), 1–22.

Heberle, R. (1968). Social movements. *International encyclopedia of the social sciences*. Retrieved March 28, 2016, from http://www.encyclopedia.com

Huber, M. T. (2014). *Personal email communication*.

Hutchings, P. (Ed.). (1999, May 7–8). Scholarship is the big picture. *National Teaching and Learning Forum/Carnegie Chronicle*.

Hutchings, P. (Ed.). (2000). *Opening lines: Approaches to the scholarship of teaching and learning*. Palo Alto, CA: The Carnegie Foundation for the Advancement of Teaching.

Hutchings, P., Huber, M. T., & Ciccone, A. (2011). *The scholarship of teaching and learning reconsidered*. San Francisco, CA: Jossey-Bass.

Hutchings, P., & Shulman, L. (1999). The scholarship of teaching: New elaborations, new developments. *Change, 31*(5), 11–15.

Inventio: Creative Thinking about Learning and Teaching, February 1999, Volume 1: 1.

Journal of Scholarship of Teaching and Learning (JoSoTL), April 2000, Volume 1:1.

Kreber, C. (2003, May 29–31). *Charting a critical course on the scholarship of university teaching movement*. Paper presented at the Annual Meeting of the Canadian Society for the Study of Higher Education, Dalhousie University, Halifax.

Kreber, C., & Cranton, P. A. (2000). Exploring the scholarship of teaching. *The Journal of Higher Education, 71*(4), 466–495.

Milbourne, R. (2015). *A new national institute for learning and teaching: A report to the department of education and training*. Retrieved from http://www.olt.gov.au/system/files/news/New%20Institute%20for%20Learning%20and%20Teaching%20Report%20FINAL%2017%20August.pdf

Rice, R. E. (1992). Toward a broader conception of scholarship: The American context. In T. G. Whiston & R. L. Geiger (Eds.), *Research and higher education: The United Kingdom and the United States* (pp. 117–129). Buckingham: Open University Press.

Richlin, L. (2001). Scholarly teaching and the scholarship of teaching. In C. Kreber (Ed.), *New directions in teaching and learning*. San Francisco, CA: Jossey-Bass.

Trigwell, K. (2001). Scholarship of teaching: An Australian perspective. *Institute for Learning and Teaching in Higher Education.* Retrieved from https://www.ilt.ac.uk/portal [This site is no longer available]

Trigwell, K., Martin, E., Benjamin, J., & Prosser, M. (2000). Scholarship of teaching: A model. *Higher Education Research &Development, 19*(2), 156–168.

Weimer, M. (1993, November–December). The disciplinary journals on pedagogy. *Change, 25*(6), 44–51.

Yorke, M. (2000). A cloistered virtue? Pedagogical research and policy in UK higher education. *Higher Education Quarterly, 54*(2), 106–126.

Websites Cited

Australian Government Department of Education and Training: https://www.education.gov.au/news/2015-australian-awards-university-teaching (accessed 6 March 2016).

HEA NTF site: https://www.heacademy.ac.uk/recognition-accreditation/national-teaching-fellowship-scheme-ntfs (accessed 24 March 2016).

HEA SoTL site: http://sotl.eu/ (accessed 20 March 2016).

IS-SoTL site: http://issotl.com/issotl15/node/21 (accessed 6 March 2016).

JoSoTL site: http://titans.iusb.edu/josotl_database/papers_published BY_ISSUE.html (accessed 10 December 2003).

Land Grant Universities: https://en.wikipedia.org/wiki/Land-grant_university (accessed 24 March 2016).

STLHE site: http://www.stlhe.ca/awards/3 m-national-teaching-fellowships/ (accessed 4 March 2016).

CHAPTER 5

A University Learning and Teaching Unit
Work in Practice

Fiona Denney

Introduction

University learning and teaching units, also known as educational development units and referred to as EDUs in this chapter, are now commonplace in the UK higher education sector. They occupy a sometimes uncomfortable middle ground between supporting and developing academic staff, conducting scholarly activity into learning and teaching, devising and implementing policies relating to educational enhancement and encouraging engagement with accredited, often mandatory, pedagogical training. A review has been undertaken on behalf of the UK Heads of Educational Development Group (HEDG) to map the work that is done by EDUs (Jones & Wisker, 2012) and we also have a similar picture from work done by Holt, Palmer, and Challis (2011) in Australian universities, which are usually slightly ahead of the UK in their educational support. It is clear from both reports that the environment within which educational developers work has changed considerably since the turn of the 21st century, and that there are certainly plenty of debates and dilemmas encountered by EDUs every day!

As disciplinary boundary-crossers and strategic change agents, educational developers work in a complex operational zone – between discipline specificities and generic knowledge about teaching practice; about enhancement and control; and at the interface of theory and practice – educational development has become a complex function that is handling an increasingly broad portfolio that includes professional development for both new and experienced academics; curriculum and quality enhancement; innovation and technology; the interface of education with work and industry; learning support and research and scholarship into higher education (Jones & Wisker, 2012, p. 4).

I came to head up the newly-created Brunel Educational Excellence Centre (BEEC) in 2014, amidst many changes both at Brunel and across the UK higher education sector more widely. The common theme for most university EDUs is how to cope with significant change and continue to support academic staff and contribute to educational enhancement whilst everyone feels that they are on shifting sands. My experiences and those of BEEC are not intended to be exemplary, but more illustrative of the challenges and opportunities that we encounter. BEEC has made good progress to date, and the work is always on going.

This chapter explores the different roles that EDUs can take in universities as structures and remits vary across the sector. I also look at the challenges of leadership and working in such a unit. Last, I have refocused on what I see as being the key mission of EDUs – to contribute to the development of the current and future generation of effective academics and academic leaders and I have included details of some research in this area.

Background, Structures and Remits

Background

EDUs were in their infancy in universities when I started as an academic in 1996. At that time, the way in which academics learned to teach largely consisted of "see one, do one", if they were given that opportunity at all. When it came to assessment, I remember asking a colleague for some guidance on grading the first assignments I marked. He replied (in jest, I'm sure!) that I should stand at the top of the stairs and nominate steps at the bottom A, B, C, D etc., drop the assignments down the stairs and grade them according to the step that they had landed on. Needless to say, I did not follow his advice but I remember feeling quite desperate that I needed to know *how* to teach, mark, design modules etc. and that I was somehow a real amateur as a lecturer without this guidance.

I was clearly not alone. Gibbs et al. (2000) identified four discrete phases in the development of the enhancement of learning and teaching in UK universities, of which the first three were prior to the time when I started as an academic but had, at the time, not had a significant impact:

1. Prior to the 1980s it was left to the individual to improve as they saw fit – perhaps in discussion with enlightened colleagues and/or heads of department.
2. During the 1980s where polytechnics and colleges (now the post-1992 universities) set up educational development departments in their response to rapid changes
3. Late 1980s–mid 1990s where the Enterprise in Higher Education initiative firstly led to around 50 HEIs being funded to develop a greater focus on student employability and then secondly led to these enterprise departments becoming educational development units once the funding had ceased.

I felt that I had a very difficult first year in teaching but shortly after this baptism of fire, the university I was working for at the time developed an introductory teaching programme for new academic staff and PhD students. This was fairly innovative at the time – Gibbs and Coffey (2004) note that these courses were not commonplace for new academic staff until the early 2000s. I was fortunate to find a well-thought through programme run by an experienced academic who understood and related to the concerns and issues we raised. This was also the case when I had the opportunity to pursue a postgraduate certificate in university teaching at the next university I moved to. I was technically exempt from this – I had been teaching for 5 years by this point and had achieved membership of the Institute for Learning and Teaching in HE (now the Higher Education Academy), but I had a sense that the wind was already blowing in the direction of teaching qualifications being a requirement for career progression, and I decided that doing one at an early stage would be a good idea. And so it has largely been the case – the requirement for academics to receive certified or accredited pedagogical training is largely mandatory in most UK universities unless the academic can claim exemption. This reflects the fourth phase identified by Gibbs et al. (2000):

1. The 1990s where, in response to increasing student numbers, the introduction of modules and semesters, the Research Assessment Exercise and the Teaching Quality Assessment exercise, universities found they needed to be more strategic in their planning for learning and teaching. This was the era of significant growth in EDUs as part of this more complex set of changes.

As I progressed in my career, the option of working in an EDU seemed very attractive and I moved to the Educational and Staff Development Unit at Queen Mary, University of London (QMUL) in 2003, headed by Dr Steve Ketteridge. This was a time when pedagogic teaching qualifications were coming into their own and were becoming compulsory and linked to probation requirements for new members of staff (Gibbs & Coffey, 2004). Some EDUs, such as that at QMUL, were also focusing on how to support other groups of staff (e.g. researchers) and other academic activities. We developed, for example, an early leadership programme for Principal Investigators and senior academic staff and Steve was influential, along with other colleagues, in developing doctoral supervisor training and considering the support needed for academic staff in the various roles they take on during their career lifecycle.

Nomenclature

For EDUs, what the department is actually called is an area of some debate in the sector. The 2012 HEDG survey (Jones & Wisker, 2012) found that, out of a total of 39 respondents:

1. 5 respondents included "educational development" in their department name
2. 5 had "academic development"
3. 6 had "learning development"
4. And 12 centres referred to "learning and teaching".

The decisions on nomenclature reflect the orientation that the University wants to give to what the department does and are, to some extent, important in terms of how the department is perceived across the organisation. 'Academic development' and 'educational development' are more flexible than "learning and teaching" and allow for pedagogical and evidence-based research, and potentially a wider range of activities. References to teaching can be contentious – as academics sometimes do not like to perceive themselves as 'teaching' *per se*. This attitude, I feel, will change as a result of current policy changes on tuition fees and the Teaching Excellence Framework (TEF).

BEEC's name – the Brunel Educational Excellence Centre – is therefore unusual. What is most important, however, is that the name, BEEC, is now recognised across Brunel, and that academic staff know that this is where they come for their development and engagement with the UK Professional Standards Framework (UKPSF), and that students come to BEEC for support with their academic skills. The key is to ensure high quality support.

BEEC has both student-facing and staff-facing services and the structures and remits of EDUs do vary across the UK sector. We not only offer academic staff development – we also have responsibility for providing academic skills and English language support for students, along with digital education support for both staff and students. In the truest sense of the Quality Assurance Agency's definition of enhancement: "taking deliberate steps at provider level to improve the quality of learning opportunities" – this is very much what BEEC is about, but it is apparent from conversations across the sector that it is relatively unusual for a learning and teaching unit to include student-facing academic support and English language support along with academic staff development. It also presents some challenges in identifying how the teams best need to work together and complement each other without creating competition for resource. This is one of a number of challenges and opportunities that we face and I discuss later in this chapter.

Structure

I am fortunate to have worked in EDUs that have been, or still are, centrally based in the University and not subsumed into another directorate such as Human Resources (HR). HR departments perform many critical functions within universities – but they can lack an understanding of the academic world and EDUs are, in my view, better headed up people who are active academics, or who have been at one point in their career. The academic role is a particular one and I have found on many occasions in the 20 years that I've worked in universities that an understanding of what academics do, the demands placed upon them and the way in which they like to work is essential for getting them onside when it comes to their professional development. To some extent, this is unusual in the pre-1992 university sector in the UK. Data from the HEDG report in 2012 showed that a larger number of EDUs in the pre-1992 sector became subsumed into larger central university departments and this led to a perceived loss of autonomy and status as a result. Interestingly, post-1992 universities seemed keener to keep their EDUs as separate entities, which the HEDG report suggests may be linked with an increase in status of educational development in an environment where there is a high teaching focus, as opposed to the pre-1992 universities which tend to be more research-focused (Jones & Wisker, 2012). This may change in the TEF environment.

In addition, and part of being seen as important within the University structure, the role of using and creating an evidence-base is crucial. There is a critical balance to be struck between being "academic enough" to have credibility with academic colleagues as a learning and teaching unit, and being "too academic" and insufficiently focused on supporting staff in their day-to-day practicalities. It is important for academics to understand the pedagogical research that is carried out, and to see where the evidence for the things we recommend comes from, but it is also important to have discussions and offer guidance on the very practical issues such as how to deal with disruptive students and competing demands on time.

Challenges and Opportunities

Keeping up with Policy Changes

Universities in the UK have to respond rapidly to changing government priorities. We are largely funded by public money and there have been increasing levels of government initiatives in UK universities over the 20 years since I have been working in the sector. Every time the government changes, there are new policies, new government departments (or re-badged old ones), changes to funding streams and new information that has to be absorbed and implemented in every university in the land. It often feels like a full-time job in keeping up with the changes and understanding the implications for the large, complex organisations we work in. It is the role of EDUs to understand the changes fully so that we can communicate them to our colleagues in workshops that we run and to influence our own university's strategies and policies. Academic colleagues should be given the information in order to understand the wider reasons for changes in rules and policies that universities make. Sometimes the response to such changes from academics is a resistance to a perceived increase in bureaucracy because the university has not communicated well that the drivers for such changes come from government legislation or changes in policy in the macro-environment. Understanding the macro-environment and the impact of changes is therefore crucial to the EDU although keeping up with an increasing pace of legislative changes can be hard work. Currently there are enormous changes within the HE sector and we have only partly absorbed these to date – changes to student funding and the implications of the Teaching Excellence Framework and an Office of Students, as proposed in the Green Paper, may significantly change our relationships with students, curriculum development and the extent to which the university takes teaching quality seriously. All of these impact on the core business for educational developers.

One of the things I like best about working in an EDU is leading on different university initiatives directly as a result of the changes in the macro-environment – it adds to the variety of work that we do and is often the area that makes us feel as though we are making a real contribution to the staff and students of the institution. Some of the initiatives that BEEC has been involved in since its creation have included:

1. The introduction of Peer Assisted Learning Schemes (PALS) to support students supporting each other in their learning
2. Obtaining funds from the Higher Education Academy to conduct a project to support students better in their transition from school/college to university
3. Obtaining funds from the Leadership Foundation for Higher Education to do some research and produce guidance on how to develop the next generation of research and academic leaders (mentioned later in this chapter).

Projects of this sort enable us to build networks across the organisation and engage with staff and students at the coalface. We, as a unit, learn more from these interactions about what support we need to provide than in almost any other way. This enables us to 'take the temperature' of the organisation which gives us information on what we think will be well received by the academic community and what might need a bit more work before we can introduce it. We also build effective relationships with colleagues through project and working groups and therefore know who to approach as "champions" for our work in the student community and academic departments, which can help enormously with breaking down barriers and creating supportive partnerships.

Leading Different Teams

When I took on the position of Director of BEEC, I realised that one of the biggest challenges I would face would be to bring together the existing different teams into one cohesive unit. It is also a huge privilege to support colleagues in supporting each other and working collaboratively as it can be very exciting to see the innovations that come out of this but there are a number of reasons for this being a challenge – as well as an opportunity.

As previously mentioned, BEEC combines both student-facing support and staff-facing support and in this regard it is unusual in Brunel and the sector more broadly. The problem with this is that we sometimes get forgotten by working groups focusing on one or the other (it happens both ways!) and we have to remind people that we are involved in supporting both staff and students and need to be included in any work that goes on for either. It is my belief that BEEC is better for the fact that staff- and student-facing services are brought together – particularly with regards to developing students' academic skills. The drive from Government and the UK higher education sector over the past five years has been very much around rationalisation and cost-cutting and offering greater value for money. Along with this, students' needs have changed in terms of how and where they want to learn with increases in part-time, flexible and distance learning provision; they have a greater sense of a global marketplace of higher education and their learning experiences on entry to higher education have also changed. We need to be able to support staff in embedding support for students in this new world into the curriculum and classroom, as well as providing standalone support functions for students. I am therefore of the belief that the learning environment at Brunel is enhanced by the closer engagement of academic staff and student support functions within BEEC.

Each team in BEEC has its own specialism and although it is easy enough to stand back and identify the synergies, on a day-to-day basis it is much harder to think about how to work together and I am constantly reviewing how team interactions can be improved for the benefit of enhancing the educational environment at Brunel.

Each team, however, maintains its own specialism and therefore its own priorities. The priorities are driven firstly by the macro-environment, the University's Education Strategy in response to that and then BEEC's objectives taken from all of this. From my perspective, what this can mean is an attempt to become an expert in all four areas, and certainly I have to have a good understanding and overview of what each team does on a day-by-day basis. More importantly though, it has been crucial to recruit and develop experts who head up each team and to give them the opportunity to develop their leadership skills and I trust these colleagues to advise me in the specialist areas of knowledge that they have. Interestingly, however, I have recently had a number of conversations with fellow heads of EDUs across the sector that leads me to conclude that the UK is sadly not awash with excellent people aspiring to work in these roles, and we could do more ourselves in terms of talent management and succession planning for the EDUs of the future.

Whilst challenges and opportunities abound in the daily life of an EDU and require a certain amount of resilience on the part of the staff, there are lots of positive aspects to working in an EDU.

Integration with Academic Departments

It has been inferred that EDUs are sometimes viewed with hostility in universities. There are a number of reasons for this – including the credibility of EDU staff as I referred to earlier. Academics are regarded as experts in their discipline – and do not take too kindly to being told that 'professional development' in the arena of teaching practice is required in order to progress with their career! It is therefore often the case that integration of activities with academic departments can be difficult and universities approach this in different ways, including have learning and teaching representatives or champions who are academics based in their department but who are invited to lead on learning and teaching developments and also represent their department's interest to the EDU and related strategic committees.

At Brunel, we have departmental Directors of Learning and Teaching, who are excellent and provide very useful liaison for us. We have also introduced a new academic contract type in the past two years, which is intended to help the integration a stage further. 'Academic Education Contract Staff' are not expected to produce research to be included in the university's Research Excellence Framework submission, but they are expected to do pedagogical research – especially in their discipline area – and to provide BEEC workshops with insights from different disciplines. They are also expected to work with the Directors of Learning and Teaching to champion the importance of teaching in the department – particularly when it may be in conflict with research for resource allocation and regard.

So far we have around 20 staff that has been appointed on Academic Education Contracts. Although they are not 'traditional' academic contracts in the sense of being REF-able, they are expected to lead on research into teaching in their areas and projects to improve the academic student experience and to raise the value of teaching in the university and they provide an excellent disciplinary-based pedagogical link for BEEC.

Research v. Teaching

Brunel is a research-intensive university. This is the first thing that people are usually told about the university, and in the UK higher education sector, this sets it in a certain context. It also doesn't help the profile of teaching in the institution because staff often, erroneously, believe that as long as they are producing 'good' research, they can get away with 'bad' teaching – or teaching that is not sufficiently student-centred – and research gets most of the prestige and focus. This is not an easy culture to change. We are fortunate in having a Vice-Chancellor who states publicly and clearly that teaching is of equal importance to research in the university, but it is still the case that there is a 'Research v. Teaching' culture in UK higher education. Currently some academics sadly view teaching as taking resource and time that could be given over to research. And it is still the case that research brings more kudos for the individual and the department. Career progression is still dominated by research success – publications and grant income mainly – although teaching accolades are entering the promotions lexicon. Teaching accolades, however, are few and far between – when compared with the rampant prestige of publishing and grant applications.

There is no easy solution to this – the introduction of student fees has not yet helped the situation to the extent that I expected – or hoped – it would do. And academics transmit their attitudes and assumptions to students implicitly – even if they do not usually state their preoccupations with research explicitly, students are well aware that they are not top priority.

None of this helps EDUS. We do not particularly want to deal with academics who are reluctant to engage in professional development of their academic practice – we would like enthusiastic colleagues who want to develop. We would also like a culture where resources were not begrudged to learning and teaching units and prioritised to research. Many units such as ours struggle to get the basics such as dedicated, suitably-equipped, training rooms and reasonable office space, allocated to them, whereas by contrast, funding for laboratories and vast buildings for large-scale engineering research, as examples, seems to be more easily found.

In addition, we still have to fight to ensure that introductory teaching programmes (the very basics of what we can offer) are included as mandatory probationary requirements and the resistance of the staff who attend them, *and* their heads of department who have to release them for that amount of time can be immense. And it is only the most enlightened of universities that link to the various recognition categories of HEA Fellowship as relevant to career progression and promotion. The reality is that we can do so much more in our

EDUs, if the culture were more conducive to it but we spend huge amounts of time and energy fighting battles that really we should not have to.

It is my belief that universities would benefit enormously if we were able to support academic staff in their development progression far more than we currently do – if for no other reason than we should be investing in the development of the next generation of academic leaders, taking an integrated approach in supporting research, teaching and management, administration and leadership to enable our staff to do the best that they can. Our universities depend on us doing a good job – and our students and the development of disciplines depends on it too.

Developing the Next Generation

This section of the chapter summarises a study to identify the kinds of things we should be incorporating in training the next generation of academic and research leaders. This study came about because I started to ask those in current leadership positions in UK universities what they wish they had known before they took on their first leadership role. The purpose behind this was the thought that if we could identify from the benefit of hindsight what would have been useful then we could shape this into something more meaningful to support academics at various stages of their career life-cycle.

Theoretical Framework

Although much exists in the education literature and wider management and leadership literature about the qualities of 'good' or 'effective' leaders there is little that considers the experience of leaders in the academic field (Peters & Ryan, 2015). Those in academic leadership positions are interesting to study, however, because they have usually reached their leadership position as a result of being highly successful in their discipline area – particularly with regards to research – but not necessarily because they exhibit the characteristics or skills necessary for their leadership role. Research on the role that prestige plays in academic progression (Blackmore, 2015; Kandiko-Howson & Coate, 2015, for example) indicates clearly that prestige is important for progression to an academic leadership position but that the role itself may require the individual then to prioritise other aspects besides those which traditionally contribute to prestige (obtaining grants, writing papers etc.) which can cause identity conflict and dissatisfaction and may be in tension with the efficiency and effectiveness agenda in UK universities.

The Leadership Foundation's Higher Education Leadership and Management Survey (HELMS) conducted in 2014 found that the majority of respondents felt that the leadership skills and abilities required in UK higher education differed from those required for leadership and management in other sectors (Peters & Ryan, 2015). In other words, that the context has a significant impact on the ability of the leader to be effective. Given this, it would be reasonable to assume that the process of identifying, selecting and training successors would have a more prominent role in UK HEIs but in spite of developments in some UK universities, this is not the case universally.

Several UK universities are developing variations of leadership training for those already in key positions – (for example, the HeadStart Programme at King's College London for new Heads of Department and UCL's leadership and management programmes for staff at certain grades and those with line management responsibilities). Whilst these interventions are positive developments to support those already appointed to leadership positions, they do not help early career researchers and academics in identifying what they need to do in order to progress (besides developing the prestige markers) and, more importantly, to be better equipped for the challenges of an academic leadership role.

Our research identified 8 key themes and additional information about the context within which the interviewees are leading. These themes have been developed into training materials that are available across the UK HEI sector. The research provides an evidence-base for focusing training and developing the next generation for the challenges of leadership ahead of them actually attaining a leadership position, and takes the literature beyond prestige factors to encompass the other aspects that aspiring leaders need to consider in their career planning.

Methods

This project was funded from the UK LFHE's fund for Innovation and Transformation and included Vitae, a national organisation supporting researcher development as a key partner.

We identified and approached 18 academics in various leadership positions across 5 universities who all agreed to be interviewed. The universities were from different areas of the UK higher education sector – 3 were from the elite, large research intensive 'Russell Group'; one was a 'post-1992' new university, smaller and more teaching focused and the fourth was a 'plate glass university', founded in the mid-1960s, smaller and research-intensive. There were no refusals and considerable interest in the project was shown. Ethics approval for the project was obtained at the lead partner institution – Brunel University London – and then at the other universities. We guaranteed our interviewees complete anonymity and all identifying comments have been redacted from the analysis of the interview transcripts.

We were keen that our 18 academic leaders were reflective of the spread of leadership roles, disciplines, ages and genders across the Universities and Table 5.1 shows these details.

Prior to the interviews, we agreed an initial set of questions (see Table 5.2) and that further probing would be allowed. The lead researcher at each institution conducted their university's interviews. All interviews lasted approximately one hour in duration and were audio-recorded and were then transcribed and uploaded to NVivo™ for analysis.

The questions were key issues that we wanted to know about – in particular around lessons that our leaders had learned along the way and what they wished they had known before they took on their leadership role. This provided us with insights on topics that could be focused on when developing the next generation of academic leaders.

The questions therefore gave us *a priori* codes which we used when analysing the transcripts and we also coded anything additional that we thought was insightful or potentially useful. The coding was done by 1 person initially and then reviewed by 2 other people as a "sense check". These were developed into 8 core themes.

TABLE 5.1   Interviewee data

Title/position/role	Number
Dean or Head of School	2
Dean or Director of Research	3
Vice, Deputy or Associate Dean	5
Senior Lecturer or Reader	2
Vice Principal, Pro Vice Chancellor, Deputy Vice Chancellor	4
Head of Department or Department Lead	2

Gender	Number
Male	10
Female	8

Discipline	Number
Arts and Humanities	5
Social Sciences	4
Engineering and Physical Sciences	4
Biological and Biomedical Sciences	5

TABLE 5.2 Interview questions

1. Please give a brief description of your backgrounds and how you came to be at this current point in your career?
2. What do you consider to be the key decision-points in your career journey? What factors at the time prompted you to make the decisions that you did?
3. What lessons have you learned in your position(s) of leadership?
4. What do you wish you had known before you moved into a position of leadership? What would have helped you in your journey?
5. What 3 pieces of advice would you give to an early career researcher (post-doc/PhD student) who wants to develop their career in academia and become a research leader?
6. What do you do to enhance the performance of your researchers?
7. If you designed leadership training for academics/Early Career Researchers (ECRs), what would be the top 5 topics that you would include and prioritise?

Findings and Conclusions

The 8 themes that emerged were further divided into two groups as follows:

1. Aspects that help career progression:

Career Advancement and Planning

Using appraisals and taking the time to think and plan ahead, being resilient and being clear about the importance of values in career planning amongst other aspects.

Mentoring and Role Models

The pivotal roles that effective mentors and role models had played in helping the interviewees to develop; and also the role for them as leaders, to act as role models for the people that they lead.

Building Networks

The importance of building and maintaining networks, including making effective use of conferences and using networking as a career and professional development opportunity.

Building a Research Profile

The prestige factors – the importance of doing the 'business' of research in order to progress with their career as academic leaders – publishing, getting funding and demonstrating impact.

2. Aspects of leadership that were found to be challenging:

Balancing Work and Life
The challenge of putting appropriate boundaries in place to stop work from consuming everything. Interviewees shared specific tools that they had tried.

Impact of Culture and Environment
Interviewees indicated that academia has undergone considerable cultural and business change in recent decades and this has had consequences in terms of work-life balance, management, leadership and the balance of teaching and research.

Working with Others
The importance of working with other people to being able to achieve goals in an academic environment. The ability to interact with others in a way that achieves things positively is seen as a key aspect of working in modern universities.

Challenges of Management and Leadership
The testing nature of managing and leading within a higher education environment, including the complexity of meeting organisational goals, working with staff with differing contributions and motivations alongside developing research.

The 'challenging' findings gave us a clear steer on the kinds of things that academic leaders would have found useful prior to taking on leadership positions. Most of the people we spoke to felt under-prepared for their first leadership role – they didn't know how to deal with the people issues that would arise or navigate the institutional politics. And they certainly felt under-prepared for the multiple demands on their time. This information is useful across the UK higher education sector because it provides an opportunity to broaden the topics that EDUs cover and to provide universities with the opportunity to focus on succession planning in a meaningful way.

Conclusions

Heading up a university EDU is both a huge privilege and a huge challenge. Structurally there are some things that are unique about Brunel's Educational Excellence Centre but most of the challenges and opportunities I have discussed here are common across the sector and indeed in other areas of the world. Australia is more developed than we are in the UK in terms of their pedagogical support and Holt et al.'s (2011) analysis of the changing nature of EDUs in Australian universities is interesting because of the similarities that can be drawn from the UK standpoint. They refer to 10 'leverage points' (Senge, 2006) where EDUs could or should be making a strategic contribution in the university and I leave you at the end of this chapter with these points for you to consider in your own institution. I have found them to be a useful 'roadmap' for identifying our areas for development within BEEC:

1. Contributing to new visions/new plans – around where the institution wants to be with regards to teaching, learning and the student academic experience;
2. Preparation of new continuing academic staff – the discussion by Holt et al. (2011) is framed around the specific Australian context where a compulsory Graduate Certificate of Higher Education has been introduced for new continuing teaching staff. The article refers to the need for flexibility within this framework for universities to apply it appropriately and the fact that EDUs lead the development of institutional approaches of how these are appropriately implemented – a significant point of leverage in engaging staff with academic development opportunities consistently across the entire institution (Holt et al., 2011, p. 11).
3. Compulsory casual teaching development programme – the special development needs of casual staff. A problem for most UK universities – how do we develop the not-insignificant numbers of hourly paid visiting lecturers when they are often not paid to attend staff development workshops but impact significantly on the student experience?
4. Just-in-time professional development – the pressing needs of providing online professional development in geographically dispersed universities – I would add in the additional challenges of ensuring that staff are able to access help and development when they need it – not just when we want to run it – regardless of whether they are geographically dispersed or not
5. The development of communities of practice – both virtual and face-to-face. This is one of the key ways in which cultural change in universities can be achieved and the more communities of practice there are around enhancing learning and teaching, the better and more rapid the changes are likely to be
6. Strategic funding for development – stimulus funding/pump-prime funding and then publication and sharing of findings. Many UK EDUs have some form of grants that can be applied for to encourage innovation in learning and teaching
7. Supporting teaching excellence through awards and fellowships – showcasing excellence to help inspire others
8. Disseminating exemplary practices online – which can contribute to 4) above as they help to provide a database of resources and advice that can be referred to at any point in time

9. Recognition and use of education 'experts' – a resource bank of potential mentors and expert educators. At Brunel, we are seeking to develop our staff appointed on Academic Education Contracts as potential mentors and expert educators – along with those who obtain recognition as Senior or Principal Fellows of the Higher Education Academy
10. Renewing leadership – The contribution of research and work to support the development of academic leaders – such as that carried out by myself and colleagues above. In particular, Holt et al. (2011) reference the development of special leadership programmes for people in positions such as Head of Department, Associate Deans etc but I would advocate that we start to do more in identifying and developing leadership skills in those who aspire to progress – not just those who already have.

I certainly do not feel that we have met all 10 areas yet at Brunel, but I am pleased that we are some way on with this "work in progress".

References

Blackmore, P. (2015). *Prestige in universities: In tension with the efficiency and effectiveness agenda?* Paper presented at the Society for Research into Higher Education Annual Research Conference, Newport.

Gibbs, G., & Coffey, M. (2004). The impact of training of university teachers on their teaching skills, their approach to teaching and the approach to learning of their students. *Active Learning in Higher Education, 5*(1), 87–100.

Gibbs, G., Habeshaw, T., & Yorke, M. (2000). Institutional learning and teaching strategies in English higher education. *Higher Education, 40*(3), 351–372.

Holt, D., Palmer, S., & Challis, D. (2011). Changing perspectives: Teaching and learning centres' strategic contributions to academic development in Australian higher education. *International Journal for Academic Development, 16*(1), 5–17.

Jones, J., & Wisker, G. (2012). *Report for the Heads of Educational Development Group (HEDG)*. Retrieved from http://www.hedg.ac.uk/documents/

Kandiko-Howson, C., & Coate, K. (2015). *The prestige economy and mid-career academic women: Strategies, choices and motivation.* Paper presented at the Society for Research into Higher Education Annual Research Conference, Newport.

Peters, K., & Ryan, M. (2015). *Leading higher education: Higher Education Leadership and Management Survey (HELMs)* (1st ed.). London: Leadership Foundation for Higher Education.

Senge, P. M. (2006). *The fifth discipline: The art and practice of the learning organization.* New York, NY: Crown Publishing Group.

CHAPTER 6

Challenging Physics Lectures through Questioning and Collaborative Work

Research Developed in Portuguese Higher Education Institutions

Nilza Costa

Introduction

In an expanding global technology society there is an ever increasing need for well qualified professionals, like engineers, this being one of the reasons why Higher Education Institutions (HEI) have been criticized by several sectors due to the high levels of engineering student's failures, drop outs and graduation rates (Karimi, Manteufel, & Peterson, 2015; Marra et al., 2012; Watkins & Mazur, 2013). Despite the complexity of this phenomenon, introductory Physics courses in students' curriculum path have been pointed out as a barrier for engineering student's success (Jiang & Freeman, 2011). Several studies show that engineering students consider Physics as a difficult subject and much too abstract (e.g. Ornek, Robinson, & Haugan, 2008), and do not often see its relevance for their study programme and future profession (Booth & Ingerman, 2002; Marques, 2011; Smaill et al., 2012). Adding to that, research also indicates that one of the most important factor for the delay in graduation rates in engineering courses, is the failure and withdrawal from a course (Physics, for example) and that one of the reason to drop out of HE engineering programs is poor teachings (Watkins & Mazur, 2013). So, universities should focus on the effectiveness of the teaching and learning (T&L) process (Karimi, Manteufel, & Peterson, 2015), namely in the first or second year of the study programs, in which the majority of failure cases occur. Introductory Physics courses in engineering degrees are exactly one of these cases and our main challenge has been to search for ways to overcome the obstacles mentioned above and so to promote academic success.

The aim of this chapter is to present and discuss the research developed, in the last 10 years, by a team of researchers, coordinated by its author, focused on ways to promote engineering students learning in introductory Physics classes, mainly in Portuguese educational settings. The research undertaken was developed in two stages. The first one included studies with an action-research design, where the researcher was mainly the teacher in his own classroom

(Chivangulula, 2014; Oliveira, 2009). In order to increase the impact of the research results, and also to contribute to HE staff development, the second stage involved studies where the researcher worked collaboratively with teachers from the Physics Department (Oliveira, 2011).

The conceptual framework underlying the didactical approach used in the T&L process in the Physics classrooms was based on the instructional model developed since the late 1990s of the 20th century by the American researcher, Eric Mazur, also known as *peer instruction* (PI) *method*, and in which the cornerstone is the conceptual question. Besides PI method, the framework also included the principles and guidelines of *active learning*, which have been developed for several years in the field of engineering education (Prince, 2004). In stage 2, the conceptual framework was adapted from the rationales underlying the studies developed at the University of Aveiro (Portugal) by Pedrosa-de-Jesus and her team (e.g. Pedrosa-de-Jesus & Silva Lopes, 2012; Watts & Pedrosa, 2006), namely the concept of scholarship of T&L (SoTL) with respect to collaborative work. The work developed in the classroom was sustained by the same framework of stage 1.

This chapter is structured in the following way: after this Introduction, it summarizes the main features and results of the studies carried out on in each stage of the research. At the end, final considerations, the main constrains and challenges that the research team is facing today are presented, since they may be seen as priority topics for a research agenda in the area under study.

Physics Lessons through Questioning (Stage 1)

The studies carried out on in stage 1 had as their main goal to investigate how to improve engineering students' learning and motivation in introductory Physics lessons, namely in HEI in Portugal. Notice that this goal has a particular importance in Portugal due to the fact that HE lessons, namely lectures, are still often characterized by the teacher delivering information to learners through passive learning aimed at knowledge acquisition (Cravino, 2004; Marques, 2011). In accordance to these authors, this didactic approach is one of the reasons for the high rates of failure and the lack of motivation of engineering students in their introductory Physics classes.

As referred above the theoretical framework underlying our studies was based on Mazur's model – *peer instruction* (PI) *method*, including also the principles and guidelines of *active learning* (AL) developed for several years in the field of engineering education (Prince, 2004). Two cornerstones

characterize both approaches, the conceptual question (PI) and the studented-centred-instruction (AL). PI includes a didactic sequence in a lecture with the main following steps (adapted from Litzinger et al., 2011):
- the lecture is divided into a set of short presentations by the teacher (around 15 min), each focused on a central physics concept/theory;
- after each short presentation, students are given a conceptual question in order to test their understanding of the physics concept/theory presented (see an example in Figure 6.1);
- students are given a few minutes to answer individually and then they are asked to explain and discuss their answer to the other students sitting around them. The teacher encourages students to provide the reasoning behind their answers;
- the students give their answers to the class;
- according to the students' answers the teacher decides what to do next (for example, moves to the next topic if the majority of the answers are correct).

Notice that, according to the literature, a conceptual question usually is a short, conceptual multiple choice question (not involving mathematical calculations), and is "targeted to address students difficulties and promote student thinking about challenging concepts" (Watkins & Mazur, 2013, p. 37). Given the lack of motivation and interest in studying Physics, in particular by Portuguese engineering students (Marques, 2011), namely given its abstract nature and the non-exiting articulation with real life and students future

What happens to a bright and sonorous alarm clock when we put it in a bell vacuum?

A) it rings, but doesn't flash

B) it flashes, but doesn't ring

C) it doesn't rings and doesn't' t flash

E) it flashes and rings normally

FIGURE 6.1 Example of a conceptual question in a physic class (adapted from Oliveira et al., 2009, p. 99)

profession, the conceptual questions addressed in our empirical studies were also focused on concrete situations, close to everyday life situations, and whenever possible close to phenomena from the area of expertise of their future profession.

Three empirical studies were developed by our research team, consisting in the design, implementation and evaluation of lessons following a didactic strategy similar to the one summarized above, although with some variations (Oliveira, 2011; Oliveira, 2009; Oliveira & Oliveira, 2013) in introductory Physics courses for engineering students. Due to differences in the contexts where the studies occurred the conceptual questions (CQ) were not always asked in the same moments of the lessons (see Table 6.1).

Data was collected through questionnaires and interviews applied to students and also, in one case (Oliveira, 2011), through an interview carried out on with the physics teacher who participated in the study. Quantitative data was statistically analyzed using SPSS®, and qualitative data submitted to content analysis using N'Vivo 7®. Table 6.1 summarizes the context and the participants of the studies.

The results from the questionnaires applied to the students at the end of the courses showed that (a) the arguing and discussing in the classes helped the learning process and (b) the conceptual questions (CQ) were a motivator factor for physics learning. However, the percentage of students answering in this way was bigger in study A (more than 80%, against 60% in studies B and C). This difference may be explained by the more frequent use of CQ during the class in study A. In this study CQ were used not only during the class (every 15 min in average, but also at its beginning). In study B and C, and due to the teacher' option the CQ were only used at the end of each class and students' answers discussed in the following lesson.

The students interviewed in both studies, as well as the teacher, corroborated the role of the CQ in the improvement of the learning process and to motivate students to learn Physics. Also some students that were interviewed mentioned the characteristics of the questions formulated, which were close to real situations and therefore made them understand the importance of Physics. In synthesis, the students interviewed mentioned the following advantages of the use of CQ. CQ made them (a) think and understand better the contents taught and (b) apply Physics to the real world. As the use of CQ promoted discussions between students and between students and the teacher, they also allowed to (c) clarify doubts and (d) verify what they knew (or not knew) and (e) enhance the interaction with the teacher.

To illustrate what has been said, we present below same examples of interviews transcriptions:

TABLE 6.1 Context and participants of the studies carried on in stage 1

Study (reference)	HEI	Date	Role of the researcher	CQ asked ...	Data collection	Data analysis	Participants
A (Oliveira, 2009)	Instituto Superior de Engenharia/ Porto	2006/2007	Teacher/ researcher	– at the beginning of the class – every 15 min	Questionnaires and interviews to students	Statistical analysis (SPSS) Content analysis (NVivo 7)	40 students
B and C - (Oliveira, 2011)	Universidade de Aveiro/ Aveiro	2007/2008 2008/2009	Collaboration with a Physics teacher who implemented the strategy	– at the end of the class (discussion took place at the beginning of the following class)	Questionnaires and interviews to students and interview to the teacher	Statistical analysis (SPSS) Content analysis (NVivo 7)	76 students (38 in each year) 1 teacher

It is a motivational component because it causes discussion and everything that causes discussion promotes learning. These questions have made the lessons more dynamic and this is a motivating factor. (Study A – student interview 2; Oliveira & Oliveira, 2013, p. 420)

These questions motivated me to attend the classes and to clarify my doubts. (Study A – students, interview 6; ibid.)

... the questions were unusual ... these questions did not require calculations like normal exercises, but knowledge of concepts. (Study B – students, interview 6; ibid.)

they were interesting as we could apply what we were learning to more real life situations. (Study C – student, interview 4; Oliveira, 2011, p. 154)

the conceptual questions promote reflection ... they consolidate knowledge ... also they are interesting questions as usually they are about concrete things, everyday life aspects .... (Study B – teacher interview; Oliveira, 2011, p. 186)

The results achieved are in agreement with others studies (e.g. Watkins & Mazur, 2013), namely by giving evidence that the use of conceptual questions in introductory Physics lessons promotes learning and motivation. The discussions generated among students when CQ are presented, in particular if they are asked during the lessons, uncover their (mis)conceptions and guide the teacher in conducting the lesson in accordance with students' knowledge. Notice that this procedure is in line with up-to-date learning theories. Also, the characteristic of the questions (often focused on concrete and everyday life situations, not involving mathematical calculations) may be a reason to motivate students to learn Physics as they may help to overcome some obstacles: the abstract nature of Physics and its apparently distant relation to real life (Marques, 2011; Ornek, Robinson, & Haugan, 2008; Smaill, 2012).

More recently the author of this chapter supervised a Master Dissertation consisting in an exploratory study in Republic of Angola developed by one teacher (Chivangulula, 2014), aiming to characterize engineering students' difficulties in learning introductory Physics and make proposals to minimize them. The theoretical framework of the study was mainly the same of the project team presented here. It is interesting to notice that similar results have been found in terms of engineering students difficulties in Physics and a good receptivity from the teacher/researcher involved, and his colleagues, towards the alternative T&L strategy concerning active learning and the use of conceptual questions. On-line communication is continuing with the teacher/researcher from Angola (the last one on 8th June 2016) which indicates that he is now implementing the proposal in his Institution. For example, the teacher said in the last exchange of mails: "during my classes I continue to use conceptual questions" and "I continue to talk with my colleagues who teach physics about the importance of the use of conceptual questions as they promote active learning".

However, some constrains and challenges occurred in the scope of this extension of our work. As the context of this study is different from all the others carried on by the research team (Geology Engineering in Africa) the teacher ("researcher") feels a lack of concrete material, namely examples of conceptual questions, relevant for his context. Also the process of collecting data from his classes, fundamental to understand the impact of his practices and to give evidence about the effectiveness of the strategy used, has been poorly given. In other words, so far the teacher has not been providing us with compelling evidence about what is happening in his practices. Lack of time for doing it is the main reason given by the teacher, who has indeed other responsibilities in his Institutions apart from teaching. However, making changes to teachers' practices is very complex and challenging (Pedrosa-de-Jesus & Silva Lopes, 2012) and so requires continuous support. The presence of an educational researcher, working collaboratively with this teacher in Angola, could overcome such difficulties (see next section).

Challenging Physics Lessons through Collaborative Work (Stage 2)

The majority of teachers teaching Physics to engineering students are not educational researchers and so they are not most probably familiar with the new strategies of T&L suggested in the literature. In order to tackle this issue, and so looking for the enhancement of the impact of the use of such strategies into practices, our research team decided to pursue with another line of research (stage 2). The aim of the research to be carried on was how to develop a collaborative way of work with Physics teachers in order to make them change their practices, now sustained on suggestions from the literature. This means, in our case, practices guided by the framework, guidelines and practical examples derived from the work done in stage 1.

In this stage we focused our theoretical framework in literature based on collaborative work and staff developmental in HE, much oriented by the research work developed at the University of Aveiro (UA)/Portugal under the coordination of Maria Helena Pedrosa–de-Jesus (see for example, Watts & Pedrosa, 2006; Pedrosa-de-Jesus & Silva Lopes, 2010). One of the central concepts taken on board from this work was the concept of Scholarship of Teaching and Learning in HE (SoTL). Despite the different meanings it assumes in the literature, we adopted the concept proposed by Maria Helena Pedrosa-de-Jesus and her team, that is: the concept of SoTL concerns the *improvement of the quality of HE* and in particular of the *T&L process* through *academic growth* through the integration of *teaching and research*. The SoTL is operationalised by the development of *supportive educational communities* (with practioners and educational researchers) for *changing practices* by making *teachers more critically reflective*, namely by *exploring students' learning*.

In what empirical approaches are concerned, the research team started at this stage to look for collaborators in the Physics Department of the UA: teachers who were experienced lectures of Introductory Physics courses to engineering students interested in improving their practices. The study to be presented here was developed by Oliveira (2011), a researcher in Didactics of Physics, and involved a Physics teacher of the Physics Department/UA. The empirical work lasted for two years long. The context and the participants of the study are presented in Table 6.2.

The collaborative work with the physics teacher was developed according to the general plan presented in Figure 6.2. Besides the work with the teacher in several meetings, the research had also a classroom component where the teacher, supported by the researcher, implemented and evaluated the new teaching practices.

As one can see in Figure 6.2, the collaborative work started with a common aim: both teacher and researcher wanted to improve student's motivation and learning in Physics classes. The researcher, however, also aimed to develop knowledge about this collaborative work.

After a kick off meeting, mainly focused on the negotiation of the project to be developed together, and which occurred at the beginning of the collaborative work and before the beginning of the academic year, several regular meetings (usually before and after each class) happened. In these meetings, some more formal than others, the main proposes were (a) to design the teaching approach, (b) to discuss materials to be used with students, (c) to discuss instruments for the collection of evidence about the progress of students learning and (d) discussion of classes observations and results obtained along the implementation of the teaching strategy. The role of the researcher and the teacher were not the same but in a sense they were complementary. The researcher mainly (a) introduced the knowledge produced about ways to improve engineering students' learning in Physics classes, some of them

TABLE 6.2   Context and participants of the studies carried on in stage 2

Study	HEI	Date	Role of the researcher	Data collection	Data analysis	Participants
Oliveira, 2011	Universidade de Aveiro/Aveiro	2007/2008 2008/2009	Collaboration with a Physics teacher	– Records of meetings with the teacher – Class observations – Interviews (informal and formal) with the teacher – Questionnaires and interviews to students	Statistical analysis (SPSS) Content analysis (NVivo 7)	1 Physics Teacher (15 years of experience) 76 students (38 in each year)

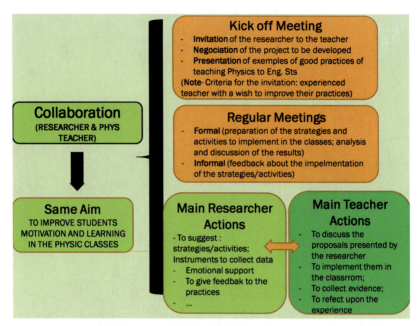

FIGURE 6.2   General description of the work developed by Oliveira (2011)

unfamiliar to the teacher, (b) presented examples of materials used in some empirical students (for example, conceptual questions), (c) introduced proposals of instruments to collect data from the students so that teacher could reflect about the students' learning process, (d) provided feedback from classrooms observations and (e) supported the teacher emotionally when she felt that she was having too much work with this experience or when students did not seem to react as positive as she expected. The teacher mainly (a) discussed the proposals presented by the researcher and adapted them to her classes, (b) implemented and evaluated the proposals in the classrooms and (d) reflected upon this implementation. Notice that, due to time consuming, the researcher often needed to help the teacher, for example in analyzing the data collected from the students.

The researcher (Oliveira, 2011) gathered data through field notes – from the meetings with the teacher and class observations, and from a semi-structured interview done with the teacher at the end of the collaborative work. Students were also interviewed at the end of each course about the strategies used and the quality of the teaching process and the teacher.

The results of the study show that the teacher considered the collaborative work with the researcher as a contribution to her professional development, and the improvement of her practice, referring the following four main characteristics of the profile of the researcher to this effectiveness: the physics background of the researcher; the didactic of physics background of the researcher, namely in the domain of T&L Physics for engineering students; the researcher's availability and her personal competences (the kind of relationship established). In fact, the support of the researcher, for example in helping the teacher to select conceptual questions for the different Physics topics and to analyze students responses collected during the classes were very important as these were very time consuming tasks for the teacher. The two transcriptions from the final interview done with the teacher illustrate those results (Oliveira, 2011):

> ... the talks we had, where we discussed your proposals about these new methodologies, for example the conceptual questions (...), your availability to analyze students answers to the conceptual questions (...) because without it, it would be impossible for me to do all the work (...) also the proposals you gave me about examples of conceptual questions to use for particular topics, and so I didn't need to spend time on that and many others ideas you gave me were very important. Besides it was good to have somebody, with your profile, observing my classes, seeing things in a different perspective and helping me to interpret what is going on .... (p. 198)

> From my point of view, as a teacher, this collaboration made me think about some aspects of my practice which I had never thought. This collaboration was not good only for my students, but also for me. Actually I became aware of some important elements of the teaching and learning process ... the conceptual questions, practical things, questions related with daily life which are fundamental and also related with the student's field of study ... students saw the importance of the course for they study program. (p. 199)

The students also recognized the quality of the teacher, as illustrated in the following transcription:

> the quality of the teacher, in a scale of o to 10 ... I would give 8,5 or 9 because the teacher corresponded to my expectations and even overcome them ... and that what was taught in the course may be important for my future profession. (Student interview 4, Oliveira, 2011, p. 198)

One aspect which also seems important to note is that the work developed by the teacher, in collaboration with the researcher, did not only impact on her professional practice, but was also disseminated in a joined written academic book chapter where the teacher and the researchers involved in the work were the co-authors (Oliveira et al., 2009).

Another contribution of this study was the enlargement of the concept of Scholarship of Teaching and Learning in HE (SoTL), which we initially integrated in our theoretical framework. From the initial definition given above, SoTL focused on the contribution of *supportive educational communities* (with practioners and educational researchers) for *changing practices* by making *teachers more critically reflective*. From the work developed by our team in collaboration with teachers, one has no doubt that the gains were not only for teachers (in the sense that they became *more critically reflective* and *innovative* in their *practices*) but they were also for educational researches. To have the opportunity to discuss our knowledge with experienced teachers and be able to overcome challenges they put to us (for example, to think about what is involved in the conceptualization of conceptual questions in quite different cultural contexts, such as Angola) enhances our competences as researchers.

Final Considerations

Although one cannot statistically generalize the results from our studies about the positive impact of the strategies used in the enhancement of engineering students learning introductory Physics as well as the increasing of their motivation for the subject, given the methodologic approach used, the results are aligned with other studies (see for example Freeman et al., 2014). By researching in new educational contexts, our studies reinforce the important role of the use of conceptual questions in Physics lessons in line with what Pedrosa-de-Jesus and Silva Lopes (2010) say "(…) students' questions can trigger their thinking process and generate opportunities for the identification of incorrect conceptions and main obstacles for concepts' understanding" (p. 34). The use of conceptual questions in lectures also promotes, as seen, students-centered-instruction, that is active learning, which increases students' performance in engineering (Freeman et al., 2014). This performance was not only related with conceptual knowledge but also to changes in students' attitudes towards Physics. Perhaps because of the kind of specific situations our conceptual questions were focused on, our students become more motivated to study Physics as they saw its relevance to real world and to their future profession.

However, our work also shows that teachers need to have support to innovate their practices (Costa et al., 2012). Evidence is given to say that collaborative work in designing and adopting new practices, between Physics teachers and educational researchers (in Didactics of Physics), is a promising way towards innovation, to increase its impact and also to staff development. Also, as referred, this collaborative work is an added value to researchers' competences. However, introducing new T&L methodologies and materials, as those required by the approaches used (e.g. conceptual questions for several physics topics) requires, at least, time (e.g. for designing conceptual questions) and support (e.g. teachers in changing their practices).

Deriving from that, the research team is facing today the following two main challenges: how to transform the knowledge so far developed in materials which can be used by teachers in their practices (for example, list of conceptual questions for different Physics topics, engineering degrees and even cultural contexts). Notice that this material will not have the desired impact if it will not be incorporated in a new approach of T&L. Therefore, together with the material produced there must be a set of dissemination strategies of these materials so that teachers will see them as part of a different didactic approach. The second challenge concerns the complexity of changing teachers practices namely in HE. The challenge concerns the need to deepen the understanding on how to create sustained collaborative communities to support such changes, for example to assure the long term continuity of a community created in the context of a funded project after its end.

References

Booth, S., & Ingerman, Å. (2002). Making sense of physics in the first year of study. *Learning and Instruction, 12*(5), 493–507.

Chivangulula, F. (2014). *Ensino e Aprendizagem da Física para Futuros Engenheiros: O caso do Curso de Engenharia em Geologia do Instituto Superior Politécnico da Huíla* [Teaching and Learning of Physics for future engineers: The case of the graduation course in geologic engineering from the Instituto Superior Politécnico da Huíla] (Unpublished master thesis). Instituto Superior de Ciências da Educação da Huíla, Lubango.

Costa, N., Oliveira, P., & Oliveira, C. (2012). O Ensino da Física em Cursos de Engenharia: Elementos Potenciadores do Sucesso dos Estudantes [The teaching of Physics in Engeenring Courses: Potencial Elements of Students' sucess]. In J. E. Fuentes Betancour, A. P. Perdomo, & O. A. Calzadilla Amaya (Eds.), *Proceedings of Taller Iberoamericano de la Enseñaza da la Física Universitaria*. Havana: CdRom.

Cravino, J. (2004). *Ensino da Física Geral nas Universidades Públicas Portuguesas e sua Relação com o Insucesso Escolar* [The teaching of general physics at Portuguese Public Universities and its relation to academicunsucess] (Unpublished PhD thesis). Universidade de Trás-os-Montes e Alto Douro, Vila Real.

Freeman, S., Eddy, S. L., McDonough, M., Smith, M. K., Okoroafor, N. H., Jordt, H., & Wenderot, M. P. (2014). Active learning increases student performance in science, engineering, and mathematics. *PNAS, 111*(23), 8410–8415.

Jiang, X., & Freeman, S. (2011). *An analysis of the effect of cognitive factors on students' attritions in engineering: A literature review.* Proceedings of the American Society for Quality STEM Agenda Conference, University of Wisconsin – Stout, Menomonie, Wisconsin. Retrieved May 10, 2015, from http://rube.asq.org/edu/2011/07/engineering/an-analysis-of-the-effect-of-cognitive-factors-on-students-attrition-in-engineering-a-literature-paper.pdf

Karimi, A., Manteufel, R., & Peterson, L. (2015). *Reasons for taking students too long to complete engineering degrees.* Proceedings of the 2015 ASEE Gulf-Southwest Annual Conference, American Society for Engineering Education. Retrieved May 8, 2015, from http://engineering.utsa.edu/~aseegsw2015/papers/ASEE-GSW_2015_submission_108.pdf

Litzinger, T., Lattuca, L., Hadgraftt, R., & Newstetter, W. (2011). Engineering education and the development of expertise. *Journal of Engineering Education, 100*(1), 23–150.

Marques, J. (2011). *O Ensino e a Aprendizagem da Física em Engenharia: Um estudo de caso no ensino politécnico* [The teaching and learning of Physics in Engineering: A case study from polytechnic teaching] (Unpublished PhD thesis). Universidade de Évora, Évora.

Marra, R., Rodgers, K., Shen, D., & Bogue, B. (2012). Leaving engineering: A multi-year single institution study. *Journal of Engineering Education, 101*(1), 6–27.

Oliveira, C. (2011). *Ensino da Física em Cursos de Engenharia: Percursos Colaborativos no Ensino Superior* (Unpublished PhD thesis). Universidade de Aveiro, Aveiro.

Oliveira, C., Costa, F., Costa, N., & Neri de Souza, F. (2009). O Ensino Introdutório de Física em Cursos de Engenharia: Estratégias Promotoras de uma Aprendizagem Activa [The introductory teaching of Physics in engineering Courses: Strategies promoting active learning]. In I. Huet, N. Costa, & J. Tavares e A. Baptista (Eds.), *A Docência no Ensino Superior: Partilha de Boas Práticas* (pp. 95–107). Aveiro: Universidade de Aveiro.

Oliveira, P. (2009). *Ensino da Física num Curso Superior de Engenharia: Na Procura de Estratégias Promotoras de uma Aprendizagem Activa* [The teaching of Physics in na academic course of engineering: Looking for strategies promoting active learning] (Unpublished PhD thesis). Universidade Aveiro, Aveiro.

Oliveira, P., & Oliveira, C. (2013). Using conceptual questions to promote motivation and learning in physics lectures. *European Journal of Engineering Education, 38*(4), 417–427.

Ornek, F., Robinson, W., & Haugan, M. (2008). What makes physics difficult? *International Journal of Environmental & Science Education, 3*(1), 30–34.

Pedrosa-de-Jesus, M. H., & Silva Lopes, B. (2010). Classroom questioning and teaching approaches: A study with biology undergraduates. In G. Cakmakci & M. F. Taşar (Eds.), *Contemporary science education research: Scientific literacy and social aspects of science* (pp. 33–40). Ankara: Pegem Akademi.

Pedrosa-de-Jesus, M. H., & Silva Lopes, B. (2012). Exploring the relationship between teaching and learning conceptions and questioning practices, towards academic development. *Higher Education Network Journal, 5*, 37–52.

Prince, M. (2004). Does active learning work? A review of the research. *Journal of Engineering Education, 93*(3), 223–231.

Smaill, C. R., Rowe, G. B., Godfrey, E., & Paton, R. O. (2012). An investigation into the understanding and skills of first-year electrical engineering students. *IEEE Transactions on Education, 55*(1), 29–35.

Watkins, J., & Mazur, E. (2013). Retaining students in Science, Technology, Engineering, and Mathematics (STEM) majors. *Journal of College Science Teaching, 42*(5), 36–41.

Watts, M., & Pedrosa, H. (2006). *Enhancing university teaching through effective use of questioning.* London: SEDA Special 19.

CHAPTER 7

Using an Understanding of Cognitive Styles to Enhance Pedagogy

Carol Evans

Introduction

Enhancing the quality of learning and teaching in higher education (HE) is of international concern. There has been considerable debate about what constitutes "high impact pedagogies" (Gibbs, 2012; Kuh, 2008) and teaching excellence within HE contexts (HE) (Evans, Muijs, & Tomlinson, 2015; Gunn & Fisk, 2013; Land & Gordon, 2015). However, little attention has been given to how an understanding of cognitive styles can contribute to enhancing pedagogy even with the increasing emphasis on quality and equity within HE (Department for Business, Innovation and Skills, 2015). This omission of cognitive style is surprising given that it is "an adaptive system that moderates the effects of both an individual's predispositions [both innate and learned] and the external environment" (Kozhevnikov, Evans, & Kosslyn, 2014, p. 22). However, the application of such information in the form of explicit guidance on how an understanding of cognitive styles can be applied to learning and teaching in HE has been relatively limited (Evans, Muijs, & Tomlinson, 2015; Evans & Waring, 2012).

We know that cognitive style does matter (Zhang & Sternberg, 2009); it impacts on how individuals interact with the learning environment and an understanding of this is crucial in developing teaching expertise (Evans, 2015b, 2015c; Waring & Evans, 2015; Zhang, Sternberg, & Rayner, 2012). In attending to the sustainable lifelong learning agendas of higher education institutions Sadler-Smith (2012) contributes to this debate by arguing that it is impossible for learners to adopt a metacognitive approach without an informed awareness of their own habitual and information processing preferences.

There has been considerable development in our understanding of cognitive styles with research demonstrating integration of education, neuroscience, and cognitive psychology perspectives (Kozhevnikov et al., 2014), along with evidence of enriched cognitive styles pedagogies (Evans, 2013a, 2015c). Evans (2013, 2015c) in defining what is constituted by an enriched cognitive styles pedagogy places emphasis on the existence of an integrated approach in the consideration of: (a) theoretical frameworks from a range of disciplines (education, psychology, neuroscience); (b) a focus on overarching principles of styles applications to practice; (c) specialist development of knowledge and skills as well as the importance of supporting adaptation and transfer of learning to new contexts; (d) building on the strength of learner attributes; (e) use of methodologies appropriate to context (quantitative and qualitative); (f) teacher and learner perspectives; (g) understanding of learners' cognitive styles profiles; (h) the role of other individual difference and contextual variables in addition to cognitive styles; (i) focus on the requirements of a specific learning task and overall learner development; (j) relationship between learning context and broader contexts (institution, society); (k) learning within the immediate context and wider networks (academic and social).

In practice, styles pedagogy involve consideration of current research-informed understandings of style (Kozhevnikov et al., 2014). A styles pedagogy acknowledges the importance of the context in shaping and being shaped by the process of learning (Sharples et al., 2015). Cognitive styles are implicated in how individuals' perceive and interact with the learning environment to shape both their own brains and their learning environments. Key issues to consider in teaching when developing a styles pedagogy include the following (see Evans, 2015b, 2015c; Waring & Evans, 2015):

1. The student should be at the centre of the learning process.
2. Pedagogy should emphasize the development of self-regulatory skills through a focus on *how to learn*, and by identifying effective learning strategies to support learner autonomy. Linked to self-regulatory development is the importance of exploring learner beliefs, values, and expectations about learning to include motivational and emotional aspects of self-regulation.
3. Cognitive style is about how an individual processes information and this can have significant implications on learning outcomes in relation to the effective completion of certain tasks.
4. All learners have a styles profile, and what is of significance is that they can develop their styles. The learning environment should, therefore, provide sufficient challenge, exposure to new ways of doing, insights into understanding one's own learning, and promote the 'best ways' to achieve specific outcomes to promote such style flexibility.
5. Learners vary in their levels of flexibility, therefore, it is important to emphasize metacognitive development to enable students to develop strategies to overcome style rigidity if and when it presents as a problem within a specific context.

6. The emphasis in teaching should be primarily on ensuring the most appropriate representation of material in relation to the requirements of a task rather than attempting to match learners' styles. Therefore, such environments should enable opportunities for students to develop their styles; to enable learners to navigate their learning environment in different ways (i.e. adaptive rather than adapted environments).
7. The focus in learning should be on discipline-specific core concepts that serve as essential building blocks and threshold concepts (those that are most likely to cause potential stumbling blocks for learners).
8. What a deep approach looks like within a discipline should be made clear in terms of what constitutes good and what it is to be a learner within a specific disciplinary community.
9. The learning environment should be accessible to all learners. This should be facilitated through the provision of explicit guidance in how to navigate opportunities within the learning environment (e.g. clarifying the role of the learner in the process; how a programme fits together; what are the principles underpinning it; ensuring access to resources; networks of support).
10. Supporting learners to be able to navigate different learning contexts to build connections between existing and new knowledge, to transfer, and adapt learning from one context to another is vitally important.
11. Active engagement in learning is defined as students doing something with the information, which could be an individual and/or group endeavour. The 'doing' is about manipulating information; presenting and processing in different ways.
12. In supporting learning autonomy and connectivity, ensuring both a range of assessment opportunities, and students' negotiated choice in assessment focus are paramount.
13. Students need to be supported in order to effectively self-manage the requirements of assessment including self-monitoring, and feedback.
14. Assessment needs to be perceived as meaningful and relevant by students. A key issue is in promoting the rationale behind the assessment design openly with students to build understanding of relevance and value.
15. The notion of partnership needs clarification and authenticity involving an honest dialogue between learners and teachers to support both independence and co-construction in learning.

The Personal Learning Styles Pedagogy

The Personal Learning Styles Pedagogy (Evans & Waring, 2014) is an example of an inclusive participatory cognitive styles pedagogy acknowledging the multifaceted nature of cognitive style working at different levels of cognitive functioning and in relation to different style families (Kozhevnikov et al., 2014). The PSLP framework has been successfully applied across a range of HE contexts (institution; discipline). It combines cognitivist and socio-cultural theoretical perspectives (Cobb, 1994; Packer & Goicoechea, 2000; Saxe, 1991; Tynjälä, 1999), and social critical theory (Butin, 2005). The framework is the outcome of evidence-based research and practice in naturalistic settings over the last fifteen years, including the systematic analysis of 707 full peer-reviewed journal articles from a total of 9073 articles (Evans, 2013a; Evans & Waring, 2012). It comprises five interrelated components of educational practice which together provide the holistic framework essential to the design of effective learning and teaching in higher education.

In summary, the PLSP is about promoting self-regulation in learning through an understanding of styles. As already noted, a number of core principles underpin the PLSP; in summary these comprise: the importance of guided and informed choice for learners; the centrality of the learner in the process; recognition of the unique starting points of learners; the importance of explicit guidance; the need for concrete and appropriate exemplars to contextualize learning events; the need for reinforcement and transference of ideas to new contexts.

PLSP Components

The five components of the framework are: (A) Exploration of learners and teacher beliefs/modelling and support; (B) Careful selection and application of models to suit the requirements of the learning context; (C) Optimising conditions for learning; (D) Design of learning environments – to promote an integrated approach to the application of cognitive styles to learning and teaching; (E) Supporting learner autonomy: choices in learning and learner voice (see Table 7.1).

The PLSP is a flexible framework; it can be used in the implementation of specific innovations or can serve as an overarching holistic framework. The PLSP has been used to inform holistic assessment practice (Evans & Waring, 2015). It has also been used to develop a resilience framework to support learner development in the workplace (Evans, 2015d). Using this framework

TABLE 7.1   Components of a Personal Learning Styles Pedagogy (Evans & Waring, 2014)

Exploration of Student and Teacher Beliefs / Modelling and Support

12. Focus on the learning histories of student and teacher.
13. Holistic understanding: Consideration of the whole experience of the learner.
14. Exploration of learner (student and teacher) beliefs about learning (e.g., ability, self-efficacy, identity and sense of fit within learning contexts).
15. Enhancing learner awareness and application of styles as part of ongoing instruction on individual learning differences. Understanding of individual differences central to the design of learning environments.

Design of Learning Environments

1. Housekeeping attended to (organisation of resources; information for students and lecturers etc).
2. Teaching methods informed by an understanding of cognitive styles and attuned to the requirements of the content and context (constructive alignment).
3. Aimed at supporting learners in developing understanding of learning to think within a specific discipline and to be become part of that community.
4. Judicious use of accommodation of cognitive styles and the concept of matching.
5. Judicious approach in promoting development of the most appropriate cognitive styles for specific contexts.
6. Teaching strategies aimed at stretching the student through careful addition and removal of scaffolding and sufficient constructive friction: Aimed at developing and broadening cognitive styles and strategies as and when appropriate.
7. Designs focused on encouraging learners to adopt deeper and more self-regulated/directed approaches to learning (constructivist approaches with a strong emphasis on the development of metacognitive skills).Supporting learners to reflect critically on the learning process to include self- and co-regulation. Appropriate use of tools to support process.
8. Maximising learning opportunities: Design of learning environments focused on enhancing awareness of different learning strategies through explicit guidance and exposure to diverse learning experiences: Different ways of seeing and doing, observation, modelling, practice, application, reinforcement, and transfer.
9. Authentic and appropriate assessment designs to support the development of deep approaches to learning.
10. Appropriate use of technology to support learning.

Optimising conditions for learning: Sensitivity to learner context

26. Sensitivity to needs of the learner: Recognising unique starting points. Addressing the emotional dimension of learning; Working with students to ensure readiness (will and skill).
27. Enabling a positive learning environment: Focusing on supporting students during important transition points in their learning.
28. Care afforded to how new ideas introduced as to the level of cognitive complexity in order to support learner flexibility.
29. Supporting learners' integration into communities of practice.
30. Attention given to learners' networks of support and development of identity within academic context.

Careful Selection of Instruments

16. Judicious and informed use of instruments /styles models.
17. Critical analysis of styles as part of instruction on individual learning differences. Appropriate application of styles models: Instruments used as metacognitive tools to support understanding of the learning process.
18. An integrated approach: Awareness of the interdependence of cognitive style and other individual learning differences – role of cognitive style as a moderator variable.
19. Development of cognitive styles as an integral element of culturally responsive pedagogies.

Supporting learner autonomy: Choices in learning / student voice

20. Focus on the centrality of the learner as a co-constructor of knowledge.
21. Focus on the role of the student in managing the learning process. Learners as co-designers of their learning experience(s).
22. Learner control afforded through design of curriculum (content, process, product) including e-learning possibilities.
23. Flexible designs facilitated through, for example, organisation of resources to maximise access; choices in pathways through programmes; nature of assessment.
24. The importance of guided/informed choice for learners.
25. Informed and responsible use of groupings individual and group work. Collaborative learning opportunities informed by understanding of styles (e.g., dangers/limitations of labelling, justification for groupings).

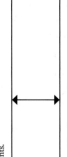

to address Goswami's (2006) concern about making ideas accessible to practitioners it is possible to highlight key messages for learning and teaching; selected examples will be provided for each component of the PLSP (for a fuller elaboration, please see Waring & Evans, 2015, where explicit elaboration of each component and subcomponent is provided).

Exploration of Learners and Teacher Beliefs/Modelling and Support
It is fundamental to attend to learner beliefs and perceptions about learning in order to effect positive change (Pilitsis & Duncan, 2012). There is a need for explicit discussion of underpinning principles of the pedagogy being enacted so that students are able to contextualise the requirements within the discipline. Positive perceptions of the learning environment lead to the adoption of a deep approach to learning, higher levels of learner engagement with programmes of study (Ullah, Richardson, & Hafeez, 2011), better engagement with assessment (Segers, Gijbels, & Thurlings, 2008), and higher levels of learner retention (Van Bragt, Bakx, Teune, Bergen, & Croon, 2011). Failure to explain the rationale of new learning designs aimed at promoting deeper approaches to learning can have significant unintended negative side effects, with learners adopting more surface approaches to learning (Balasooriya, Tetik, & Harris, 2011).

Careful Selection and Application of Models to Suit the Requirements of the Learning Context
How and indeed whether cognitive style instruments need to be used are fundamental questions for teachers to address. Such tools, where applied, should be used as teaching tools to promote understanding of learning processes rather than as labelling tools (Yates, 2000). Using tools requires an understanding of the hierarchical, multidimensional, pejorative nature, and relative flexibility of cognitive style. If cognitive tools are required, emphasis must be on the appropriate use of robust, reliable, and valid tools that are appropriate for use within the specific context (Evans & Waring, 2012). What is important is an understanding of the different cognitive style constructs and their relevance to specific dimensions of learning (Waring & Evans, 2015). The mapping of empirically derived cognitive style families (*perception, concept formation, higher order cognitive processing, and metacognitive processing*) to four different levels of information processing (*context-dependency vs. independency, rule-based vs. intuitive processing, internal vs. external locus of control, and integration vs. compartmentalization*) (Kozhevnikov et al., 2014) enables learners (students and teachers) to identify those styles that might be particularly useful in the completion of specific learning tasks.

Optimising Conditions for Learning
It is important to acknowledge that there are many potential cultural layers that impact on the development of an individual's cognitive styles profile; from the micro (individual) to macro level (society). Of high interest is how an individual's involvement in many different cultures existing at all levels (individual, family, education, professional, society, ethnicity) impacts on the development of his/her cognitive styles profile. How an individual filters information, and moves between different cultures reinforcing or adapting his/her cognitive styles profile is important in seeking to understand and support learner development especially within 21st century learning environments (Signorini, Wiesemes, & Murphy, 2009; Zhang, 2013).

Attending to the relational dimension of learning is important in order to support learners to navigate effectively the many different communities of practice (academic and social) in which they participate and to choose their level of membership and engagement in different communities. Of particular importance is the nature of the relationship between learners' cognitive styles, their perceptions of the environment, identity development, and self-efficacy in their membership of different learning communities within and across different learning environments. A high sense of membership within an academic community along with active engagement in learning has been found to be related to the adoption of deep approaches to learning (Kek & Huijser, 2011), and to completion rates (Bluic et al., 2011).

While cognitive style is a relatively flexible construct some individuals are capable of greater style flexibility than others. It is also evident that exposure to different roles, experiences, and cultures can promote style flexibility (Zhang, 2013). The key issue for teachers is in providing sufficient challenge, appropriate addition and timely removal of support; this requires accurate and early assessment of student's needs. Some learners may be particularly vulnerable at key learning transition points (Choi, Lee, & Kang, 2009) and will require additional scaffolding to be able to adapt ways of learning to suit a specific context. Three broad recommendations have been made to address both learner variations in cognitive style flexibility and the potential impact of the learning environment to reinforce or ameliorate potential style flexibility in learners: (i) reduce the complexity of the learning environment in order to reduce cognitive overload in learners (Kyndt, Dochy, Struyven, & Cascallar, 2011); (ii) enhance learner strategy development – e.g., working with learners to improve the efficiency of working memory and development of long-term memory (Minear & Shah, 2006); (iii) use of a reflective and critical approach whereby teachers are encouraged to consider how their approach to planning could assist/restrict learner learning and to consider alternative learning and teaching approaches to assist style flexibility within their learners to encourage independence and not dependence on a particular mode of delivery (Renzulli & Sullivan, 2009; Waring & Evans, 2010).

Design of Learning Environments – Promoting an Integrated Approach to the Application of Cognitive Styles to Learning and Teaching

The PLSP approach advocates implementing overarching principles of effective learning for all learners rather than individual instruction for each and every learner. It is concerned with empowering learners to take responsibility for their own learning through an informed understanding of cognitive style. In order to support the development of learner self-regulatory skills, housekeeping issues are of fundamental importance (provision and organization of resources and teaching, explicit guidance, timing of assessment, authentic assessment; development of blended learning environments) see Evans and Waring (2009) and Waring and Evans (2015) for an overview.

The PLSP approach acknowledges the pejorative nature of cognitive styles in that certain cognitive styles may be more useful and fruitful in the completion of specific tasks in specific contexts (Zhang & Sternberg, 2009); the role of the teacher should be to actively promote learner development of certain cognitive styles and to actively discourage the development of other styles to meet the requirements of specific contexts (Fan, Zhang, & Watkins, 2010). Caution regarding the value of trying to match learner and teacher styles is advocated given that each learner has a cognitive styles profile comprising different layers of the cognitive style hierarchy and different cognitive styles families (Kozhevnikov et al., 2014; Nosal, 2009), and has capacity for style flexibility.

In supporting learning the focus should be on developing ways to encourage learners to adapt to different learning environments rather than to design adaptive systems (Choi et al., 2009). Emphasis should be placed on supporting learners' development of self-regulation skills; an important area of this is acknowledging the role of cognitive styles on learners' abilities to access, make sense of, and give feedback. Understanding how learner's access and process information and facilitating them to map their feedback networks can be highly effective in identifying and supporting learners with impoverished feedback profiles (Evans, 2013b; Evans & Waring, 2015); in this way learners can be supported to maximize feedback opportunities as part of sustainable learning.

Effective e-learning environments informed by a cognitive styles perspective also promote adaptive rather than adapted systems. Given that learners styles profiles are complex and changeable it is important that an e-learning environment enables flexibility in how learners can engage with it. An enriched e-learning pedagogy is about more than matching pedagogical preferences or increasing awareness of different styles. It is about an integrated understanding of learning drawing on research about deep learning, diversity, authentic learning with IT and the relationship of these elements with the personalising learning process (Jones & McLean, 2012). Effective cognitive styles mediated e-learning environments promote sustained interactivity (Samah, Yahaya, & Ali, 2011) in meaningful activities (Evans et al., 2015). Developing e-learning environments that 'discourage the 'grab-and-go' strategy associated with surface learning, and encourage the more explorative and interactive strategies associated with deep and active learning', is identified by Knight (2010, p. 74) as key to increasing learner understanding and potential performance. In summary, cognitive styles mediated e-learning pedagogies incorporate key elements of good design that are applicable to all learners regardless of their styles (Chen & Liu, 2011). Adaptive environments as defined in the PLSP emphasise the importance of using principles of good practice for all learners predicated on an informed understanding of styles where the organization and provision of resources and activities enables choice for the learner in how they engage with the learning environment. There are other definitions of adaptive environments that focus on the potential of computer applications to respond to the way a learner uses a learning environment that are able to adapt the context to suit the specific characteristics of the learner (Sharples et al., 2015).

Supporting Learner Autonomy: Choices in Learning and Learner Voice

It is important to acknowledge the centrality of the learner within the learning process as a co-constructor of knowledge mindful of the fact that learners vary considerably in their ability, readiness and willingness to engage within learning environments (abilities – e.g., self-regulatory capacity, cognitive style flexibility, subject knowledge, and personal learning histories). Curriculum design should support informed choice for learners especially in relation to group and individual activities (Renzulli & Sullivan, 2009). Exposure to a broad range of learning experiences and the opportunities afforded to deepen understanding by leading on projects of interest and participating in authentic assessment are important (Renzulli & Sullivan, 2009). Such approaches require careful scaffolding and training given the varying levels of self-regulation among learners. Judicious and effective training in the use of cognitive styles to support learning can enable learners to be more autonomous in their control over their learning over a sustained period of time (Mayfield, 2012) and specifically in making more informed and effective choices in learning (Leithner, 2011).

To support learner autonomy learners need support in managing their learning transitions. Supporting learner transitions requires (i) empathetic awareness of the fact that individuals learn in different ways (Campbell, Smith, Boulton-Lewis, Brownlee, Burnett, Carrington, & Purdie, 2001); (ii) clarifying with learners that cognitive styles are just as important as abilities are in their learning in order to support them in developing more adaptive attributions (Zhang, 2010); (iii) supporting students' basic psychological needs which are linked to intrinsic motivation (Devi, 1971) to enhance satisfaction and adoption of deeper approaches to learning (see Betoken & Artiga, 2011); (iv) supporting students to develop different/more appropriate frames of reference for new learning environments (Yang & Tsai, 2010); (v) working with students to enhance cognitive flexibility (Vitiello, Greenfield, Munis, & George, 2011); (vi) ensuring coherent programme design (Wilson & Fowler, 2005); (vii) explicit introduction, and induction into the requirements of new learning environments and purposes of specific learning activities (Karagiannopoulou & Christodoulides, 2005).

The cognitive styles perspective as articulated in this chapter and associated literature base provides an important tool for teachers to consider in reviewing how they can use and develop their practice by integrating a cognitive styles approach within instruction. The PLSP is an example of an inclusive participatory pedagogy but what separates it from other models of differentiated instruction is its focus on cognitive styles. The cognitive styles emphasis as a fundamental element in developing learner self-regulatory practice should be an essential feature of any differentiated instruction to maximise the potential and efficacy of learning environments for all learners and teachers in order "to take the best of what theories have to offer and apply the concepts in artistic ways within the [learning context]" (Minter, 2011, p. 8).

References

Balasooriya, C. D., Tetik, C., & Harris, P. (2011). Why is my design not working? The role of student factors. *Research Papers in Education, 26*(2), 191–206.

Betoret, F. D., & Artiga, A. G. (2011). The relationship among student basic need satisfaction, approaches to learning, reporting of avoidance strategies and achievement. *Electronic Journal of Research in Educational Psychology, 9*(2), 463–496.

Bliuc, A.-M., Ellis, R. A., Goodyear, P., & Hendres, D. M. (2011). Understanding student learning in context: Relationships between university students' social identity, approaches to learning, and academic performance. *European Journal of Psychology Education, 26*, 417–433.

Butin, D. (Ed.). (2005). *Service-learning in higher education: Critical issues and directions.* New York, NY: Palgrave Macmillan.

Campbell, J., Smith, D., Boulton-Lewis, G., Brownlee, J., Burnett, P. C., Carrington, S., & Purdie, N. (2001). Students' perceptions of teaching and learning: The influence of students' approaches to learning and teachers' approaches to teaching. *Teachers and Teaching: Theory and Practice, 7*(2), 173–187.

Chen, C.-J., & Liu, P.-L. (2012). Comparisons of learner-generated versus teacher-provided multimedia annotation. *Turkish Online Journal of Educational Technology (TOJET), 11*(4), 72–83.

Choi, I., Lee, S. J., & Kang, J. (2009). Implementing a case-based e-learning environment in a lecture-oriented anaesthesiology class: Do learning styles matter in complex problem solving over time? *British Journal of Educational Technology, 40*(5), 933–947.

Cobb, P. (1994). Where is the mind? Constructivist and sociocultural perspectives on mathematical development. *Educational Researcher, 23*(7), 13–20.

Deci, E. L. (1971). Effects of externally mediated rewards on intrinsic motivation. *Journal of Personality and Social Psychology, 18*, 105–115.

Department for Business, Innovation and Skills (BIS). (2015). *Fulfilling our potential: Teaching excellence, social mobility and student choice.* Sheffield: Higher Education Directorate, Department for Business, Innovation and Skills.

Evans, C. (2013a, June 18–20). *Styles in practice: A research perspective.* Presentation at ELSIN Conference, Legoland, Billund.

Evans, C. (2013b). Making sense of assessment feedback in higher education. *Review of Educational Research, 83*(1), 70–120.

Evans, C. (2015, July 29–30). *Making sense of cognitive styles to promote an inclusive and pragmatic pedagogy: An evidence-based approach: What we know about learning from integrating education, neuroscience and cognitive psychology perspectives.* Presentation at Teach First Impact Conference, Leeds Beckett University, Leeds.

Evans, C. (2015a). Exploring students' emotions and emotional regulation of feedback in the context of learning to teach. In V. Donche, S. De Maeyer, D. Gijbels, & H. van den Bergh (Eds.), *Methodological challenges in research on student learning* (pp. 107–160). Garant: Antwerpen.

Evans, C. (2015b, July 29–30). *A styles pedagogy: In making sense of cognitive styles to promote an inclusive and pragmatic pedagogy. An evidence-based approach: What we know about learning from integrating education, neuroscience and cognitive psychology perspectives presentation.* Presentation at Teach First Impact Conference, Leeds.

Evans, C. (2015c). *Innovative pedagogical practices: The personal learning styles pedagogy.* York: Higher Education Academy.

Evans, C., Muijs, D., & Tomlinson, D. (2015). *Engaged student learning: High impact strategies to enhance student achievement.* York: Higher Education Academy.

Evans, C., & Waring, M. (2009). The place of cognitive style in pedagogy: Realising potential in practice. In L. F. Zhang & R. J. Sternberg (Eds.), *Perspectives on intellectual style* (pp. 169–208). New York, NY: Springer.

Evans, C., & Waring, M. (2012). Application of styles in educational instruction and assessment. In L. F. Zhang, R. J. Sternberg, & S. Rayner (Eds.), *The handbook of intellectual styles* (pp. 297–330). New York, NY: Springer.

Evans, C., & Waring, M. (2014). The personal learning styles pedagogy implementation framework. In M. Waring & C. Evans (Eds.), *Understanding pedagogy: Developing a critical approach to teaching and learning* (pp. 187–214). Abingdon: Routledge.

Evans, C., & Waring, M. (2015). Using an informed understanding of styles to enhance learning and teaching in 21st century learning environments. In R. Wegerif, J. Kauffman, & L. Liu (Eds.), *Handbook of research on teaching thinking* (pp. 137–150). London: Routledge.

Fan, W., Zhang, L.-F., & Watkins, D. (2010). Incremental validity of thinking styles in predicting academic achievements: An experimental study in hypermedia learning environments. *Educational Psychology, 30*(5), 605–623.

Gibbs, G. (2012). *Implications of 'dimensions of quality' in a market environment.* York: Higher Education Academy.

Goswami, U. (2006). Neuroscience and education: From research to practice. *Nature Reviews Neuroscience, 7*(5), 406–413.

Gunn, V., & Fisk, A. (2013). *Considering teaching excellence in higher education, 2007–2013.* York: Higher Education Academy.

Jones, M. M., & McLean, K. (2012). Personalising learning in teacher education through the use of technology. *Australian Journal of Teacher Education, 37*(1), 75–92.

Karagiannopoulou, E., & Christodoulides, P. (2005). The impact of Greek university students' perceptions of their learning environment on approaches to studying and academic outcomes. *International Journal of Educational Research, 43*(6), 329–350.

Kek, M., & Huijser, H. (2011). Exploring the combined relationships of student and teacher factors on learning approaches and self-directed learning readiness at a Malaysian university. *Studies in Higher Education, 36*(2), 185–208.

Knight, J. (2010). Distinguishing the learning approaches adopted by undergraduates in their use of online resources. *Active Learning in Higher Education, 11*(1), 67–76.

Kozhevnikov, M., Evans, C., & Kosslyn, S. (2014). Cognitive style as environmentally sensitive individual differences in cognition: A modern synthesis and applications in education, business and management. *Psychological Science in the Public Interest, 15*(1), 3–33.

Kuh, G. D. (2008). *High impact educational practices: What they are, who has access to them, and why they matter.* Washington, DC: American Association for Colleges and Universities.

Kyndt, E., Dochy, F., Struyven, K., & Cascallar, E. (2011). The perception of workload and task complexity and its influence on students' approaches to learning: A study in higher education. *European Journal of Psychology of Education, 26*(3), 393–415.

Land, R., & Gordon, G. (2015). *Teaching excellence initiatives: Modalities and operational factors.* York: Higher Education Academy.

Leithner, A. (2011). Do student learning styles translate to different "testing styles"? *Journal of Political Science Education, 7*(4), 416–433.

Mayfield, L. R. (2012). Nursing students' awareness and intentional maximization of their learning styles. *Learning Assistance Review, 17*(1), 27–44.

Minear, M., & Shah, P. (2006). Sources of working memory deficits in children and possibilities for remediation. In S. J. Pickering (Ed.), *Working memory and education* (pp. 274–298). London: Elsevier.

Minter, R. L. (2011). The learning theory jungle. *Journal of College Teaching and Learning, 8*(6), 7–15.

Nosal, C. S. (2009). The structure and regulative function of the cognitive styles: A new theory. *Polish Psychological Bulletin, 40*(3), 119–127.

Packer, M. J., & Goicoechea, J. (2000). Sociocultural and constructivist theories of learning: Ontology, not just epistemology. *Educational Psychologist, 35*(4), 227–241.

Pilitsis, V., & Duncan, R. G. (2012). Changes in belief orientations of preservice teachers and their relation to inquiry activities. *Journal of Science Teacher Education, 23*(8), 909–936.

Renzulli, J. S., & Sullivan, E. E. (2009). Learning styles applied: Harnessing students' instructional style preferences. In L. F. Zhang & R. Sternberg (Eds.), *Perspectives on the nature of intellectual styles* (pp. 209–232). New York, NY: Springer.

Sadler-Smith, E. (2012). Metacognition and styles. In L. F. Zhang, R. J. Sternberg, & S. Rayner (Eds.), *The handbook of intellectual styles* (pp. 153–172). New York, NY: Springer.

Samah, N. A., Yahaya, N., & Ali, M. B. (2011). Individual differences in online personalized learning environment. *Educational Research and Reviews, 6*(7), 516–521.

Saxe, G. B. (1991). *Culture and cognitive development: Studies in mathematical understanding.* Hillsdale, NJ: Lawrence Erlbaum Associates.

Segers, M., Gijbels, D., & Thurlings, M. (2008). The relationship between students' perceptions of portfolio assessment practice and their approaches to learning. *Educational Studies, 34*(1), 35–44.

Sharples, M., Adams, A., Alozie, N., Ferguson, R., Fitzgerald, E., Gaved, M., McAndrew, P., Means, B., Remold, J., Rienties, B., Roschelle, J., Vogt, K., Whitelock, D., & Yarnall, L. (2015). *Innovative pedagogy 2015.* Milton Keynes: The Open University.

Signorini, P., Wiesemes, R., & Murphy, R. (2009). Developing alternative frameworks for exploring intercultural learning: A critique of Hofstede's cultural differences model. *Teaching in Higher Education, 14*(3), 253–264.

Tynjälä, P. (1999). Towards expert knowledge? A comparison between a constructivist and a traditional learning environment in the university. *International Journal of Educational Research, 33*, 355–442.

Ullah, R., Richardson, J. T. E., & Hafeez, M. (2011). Approaches to studying and perceptions of the academic environment among university students in Pakistan. *Compare: A Journal of Comparative and International Education, 4*(1), 113–127.

Van Bragt, C. A. C., Bakx, A. W. E. A., Teune, P. J., Bergen, T. C. M., & Croon, M. A. (2011). Why students withdraw or continue their educational careers: A closer look at differences in study approaches and personal reasons. *Journal of Vocational Education and Training, 63*(2), 217–233.

Vitiello, V. E., Greenfield, D. B., Munis, P., & George, J. L. (2011). Cognitive flexibility, approaches to learning, and academic school readiness in head start preschool children. *Early Education and Development, 22*(3), 388–410.

Waring, M., & Evans, C. (2010, June 28–30). *A consideration of physical education student teachers' feedback-seeking behaviours from a cognitive styles perspective.* Paper presented at the 15th European Learning Styles Information Network (ELSIN) Conference, Aveiro.

Waring, M., & Evans, C. (2015). *Understanding pedagogy: Developing a critical approach to teaching and learning.* Abingdon: Roultedge.

Wilson, K., & Fowler, J. (2005). Assessing the impact of learning environments on students' approaches to learning: Comparing conventional and action learning designs. *Assessment and Evaluation in Higher Education, 30*(1), 87–101.

Yang, Y.-F., & Tsai, C.-C. (2010). Conceptions of and approaches to learning through online peer assessment. *Learning and Instruction, 20*(1), 72–83.

Yates, G. C. R. (2000). Applying learning style research in the classroom: Some cautions and the way ahead. In R. J. Riding & S. G. Rayner (Eds.), *International perspectives on individual differences, cognitive styles* (Vol. 1, pp. 347–364). Stamford, CT: Ablex.

Zhang, L.-F. (2010). Do age and gender make a difference in the relationship between intellectual styles and abilities? *European Journal of Psychology of Education, 25*(1), 87–103.

Zhang, L.-F. (2013). *The malleability of intellectual styles.* New York, NY: Cambridge University Press.

Zhang, L.-F., & Sternberg, R. J. (Eds.). (2009). *Perspectives on the nature of intellectual styles.* New York, NY: Springer.

Zhang, L.-F., Sternberg, R. J., & Rayner, S. (Eds.). (2012). *Handbook of intellectual styles: Preferences in cognition, learning and thinking.* New York, NY: Springer.

CHAPTER 8

The Effects of Collaborative Learning on Students' Achievements and Skills According to Their Learning Styles within an E-Learning Environment
Qatar University

Aisha Fadl A. A. Al-Kaabi and Sarmin Hossain

Introduction

In the modern world, technology plays a significant role in facilitating many actions in diverse areas of life. Since education plays such a fundamental role in development in different fields, new applications have been adopted to enhance levels of education. In general, education tools and items can be allocated for each student and adapted depending on their field of study as well as their intellectual interests (Marshall, 2002). Furthermore, the recent development of distance education programmes has been reinforced through the growth of technology and the Internet. Online education seems to have the ability to alter the educational landscape. Technological innovation is essential to improving distance education, but it is not enough to ensure that distance education is effective. Students' study preferences in terms of learning styles differ: some may learn better by listening and watching, others by doing and moving in a hands-on environment, while others prefer reading. Thus, teachers who know about differences in learning styles are more capable of changing their teaching techniques and strategies in online education (Zapalska & Brozik, 2006).

It is important to understand that different learning contexts help shape the relevance of specific learning styles. For instance, the appointment of various learning contexts such as perception, concept formation, higher order cognitive processing, and metacognitive processing lead to four different levels of information processing, namely context-dependency vs. independency, rule-based vs. intuitive processing, internal vs. external locus of control, and integration vs. compartmentalization, which enable the use of different learning styles (Evans, 2015).

The research discussed here aims to examine the effect of including collaborative learning in an online research methods course at Qatar University (QU) on the achievement and skills of students who display different learning styles. Accordingly, this empirical research sets out to achieve the following sub-objectives, to examine the effect of:

1. Collaborative/group work on students' achievements in an e-learning environment.
2. Collaborative/group work on students' skills in an e-learning environment.
3. Learning styles on students' achievements, regardless of whether or not collaborative learning is used.
4. Learning styles on students' skills, regardless of whether or not collaborative learning is used.

The participants used in the present study were divided into three teaching classes, as outlined below:
1. Control class: In this randomly chosen category, the students were placed in a group to work separately and not collaborate together: in other words, each student worked alone.
2. Teamwork class: in this randomly chosen category, the students were placed in teams to work collaboratively with each other. In other words, these students were chosen randomly without knowing their learning style or classifying them in terms of how they prefer to work.
3. Teamwork class: in this class, the students were placed in a group in which members assisted and supported each other as one body. In other words, teamwork took place, but at the same time, unlike the previous group, the education style favoured by students within this category was taken into consideration.

Thus, the core of this research has been to examine the extent of the benefits of collaborative learning within the environment of e-learning, in light of the role played by learning style as an effective factor. The study has examined the following main hypotheses, that there is a significant difference in the:
1. Achievements and skills of students who work individually in an e-learning environment in a control group and those who collaborate in an e-learning environment in the first experimental group.
2. Achievements and skills of students who engage in collaborative learning in an e-learning environment due to their learning style.
3. Students' achievements and skills depending on whether or not collaboration is used in the three groups due to learning style.

Qatar Context

Arguably, decision makers and administrators in educational institutions in Qatar, just like those in other Arab regions, regardless of their level (schools, colleges and universities), consider education as the main foundation for future social, political, and economic progress. In other words, they believe that a country's capability to survive in the global economy and enable its individuals to utilise all advantages of technological advances depends on ensuring that its curricula are aligned with national priorities and global developments (Zellman et al., 2009).

Qatar's National Vision is founded on sound policies for the country's leadership, via a set of guidelines from the Qatari Constitution and broad-based national consultations. In addition, Qatar's National Vision is based on four areas: social development, environmental development, economic development, and human development. The most essential part of these areas is human resource development including education, health, manpower development, and training (Al-Sulaiti, 2011). Thus, in 2001, Qatar initiated large reform efforts to improve and adjust the system in line with the country's developing social, economic and political ambitions. The aim of this reform was to make Qatari students better prepared for career centres (Stasz, Eide, & Martorell, 2008).

For instance, in summer 2001, Qatar's leadership entrusted the RAND Corporation to test the K–12 (kindergarten through grade 12) schools' system in Qatar. The leadership took many concerns into consideration, since the president of the RAND Corporation was of the view that the system was not producing high-quality results for students in terms of academic achievements, college attendance and success in the labour market. In light of this, the RAND report analysed and determined the main advantages and disadvantages of the current education system and concentrated on two basic efforts and endeavours for reform: enhancing the education system's main elements among standards-based reform and devising a system-changing plan to deal with the system's shortages and insufficiency (Zellman et al., 2011).

Finally, this shift and development includes changing the centralized, rigid, and low performing education system into a decentralized (self-managed), modern and effective one. The two fundamental components of this reform initiative are establishing annual student evaluation and views to assist monitoring student performance and learning, and constructing new government-funded Independent Schools. Every Independent School must make curriculum standards in Arabic, science, maths and English fit with periodic financial demands (Yamani, 2006).

Collaborative Learning

People vary in their ways of learning, which produce various levels of success, and these varied ways of learning preferred by students are usually known as learning styles. Xu (2011) defines learning styles as the special methods in which students orientate to problem-solving. In other words, learning styles include the emotional and cognitive practices that act as fixed pointers of how students imagine, communicate with and respond to the learning environment. Learning style is also known as the comprehensive model that provides an overall trend for learning behaviour and practices, so learning style is group of biologically and developmental characteristics that make the same teaching methods useful for some and counterproductive for others (Felder & Brent, 2005).

According to Evans (2015), improving the quality of learning and teaching is considered as an international concern. There has been considerable debate about what constitutes 'high impact pedagogies' and teaching excellence within the learning context. However, close attention must be paid to how an understanding of learning styles can contribute to enhancing pedagogy even with the increasing emphasis on quality and equity within various education levels.

It can be concluded that learning style can be defined as the varied ways or means by which students learn, and the ways in which students begin to focus on, process and remember new information or knowledge, and tackle learning tasks. Furthermore, teachers can depend on different learning styles, and they might prefer and focus on several types of information, tending to operate on perceived information in many ways. Thus, teachers should select the style that best serves to reduce attrition and enhance skill, and to meet the needs of students whose learning styles are neglected by traditional styles. One of these styles is collaborative learning.

In general, the term 'collaborative learning' covers a range of approaches to learning which include two or more students learning or trying to learn something together. The components of this concept may be translated in many ways: into a small group, a class of 20–30 subjects, hundreds or thousands of learners, or even society, which includes several thousands or millions of people, while *"together"* may be translated as several classes of interaction: synchronous or asynchronous, face-to-face, frequent in time or not, computer mediated, true common effort or in projects that are separated systemically (Dillenbourg, 1999).

Moreover, collaborative learning employs small groups of students in the teaching process in order to encourage them to strengthen and increase their own knowledge and each other's culture. Maesin, Mansor, Shafie, and Nayan (2009) indicated that collaborative learning needs elements of individual responsibility, face-to-face encouraging interaction, positive interdependency, and proper utilization of collaborative skills and group processing. Arguably, collaborative learning employs small groups of students in the teaching process in order to encourage them to strengthen and increase their own knowledge and each other's culture.

Actually, this includes different educational approaches that need to combine deep effort by learners, or both learners and teachers. Learners work in groups of two or more, trying to recognize solutions or meanings, or establishing a product. Consequently, collaborative learning activities obviously differ from other styles of learning, and are mainly dependent on learners' exploration or application of the curriculum, not simply the teacher's presentation or explication of it (Laal & Laal, 2011).

Moreover, collaborative learning is considered as an important change from the ordinary teacher-centred or lecture-centred environment in school classrooms. This means that in collaborative learning, teachers who rely on such learning styles in their classrooms must try to consider themselves less as expert transmitters of information to students, and more as expert designers of experiences for students – as coaches of a more emergent learning process (Smith & MacGregor, 1992).

Collaborative learning is closely allied to the theory of social constructivism, which means that knowledge is built and translated through students. The learning process must be realized as something learned through activation of the existing cognitive structures or building new cognitive structures that adapt new input. Learners do not passively acquire knowledge from the teacher, but learning becomes a deal between all the students and teachers in the learning process (Hassan, Fong, & Idrus, 2011). Individual learning enables students to interact at their own pace: this has advantages and disadvantages. Some students will complete their work rapidly and will either feel wonderful or stressed in the classroom. Other students may not complete the task in the classroom at all and may decide to finish at home (which may or may not happen). Also, individual learning imposes the need for learners to control their time, and some students may not do this well. Teachers should always provide structure with individual learning (Depriter, 2008).

Another learning style, as stated by Evans (2015), is the cognitive learning style, which is characterised by an interest in determining the way in which individuals or learners communicate with the learning environment. The ideal understanding of these styles is considered as a core and critical point in developing teaching expertise. Furthermore, in her study, Evans defines some considerations that must be borne in mind to enrich cognitive style pedagogy. These considerations are outlined below:

1. Theoretical frameworks of several disciplines (education, psychology, neuroscience).

2. Concentration on general principles of styles' applications to practice.
3. Specialist development of knowledge and skills as well as the importance of supporting the adaptation and transfer of learning to new contexts.
4. Focus on the strength of learner attributes.
5. Focus on teacher and learner perspectives.
6. Understanding of learners' cognitive styles profiles.
7. Concentration on the need of a particular learning task and overall learner development.
8. Relations among learning context and broader contexts (institution, society).
9. Learning within the immediate context and wider networks (academic and social).

Methodology

This research was considered to be experimental in nature, since experimental research is defined as a test under controlled conditions that are conducted to prove a popular truth, to investigate the validity of a hypothesis, or to identify the efficacy of something previously untried. True experiments have four elements: manipulation, control, random assignment, and random selection. The most significant of these elements are manipulation and control. Manipulation means that the researcher purposefully changes something in the environment. Control is used to prevent outside factors from influencing the research results (Creswell, 2008). In this study, a mixed method approach has been used to gather data for the main research questions, as well as determining its nature and aims. This approach is represented by questionnaires, students' achievements and interviews.

The sample included 135 students, whose ages ranged between 19 and 22 years at the time of the study and who were registered in the three branches of the Research Methods course at Qatar University. The sample was divided into the three classes, with 45 students in Class 1, 44 in Class 2 and 46 in Class 3: these were named the control class (C), the first experimental class (E1) and the second experimental class (E2) respectively. In the control class, each student worked separately. The first experimental class E1 was divided into small groups of four students, such that every student in the same group had a different learning style. The second experimental class E2 was also divided into four groups but all students in the same group had the same learning style. These two experimental classes followed the course through collaborative learning, in addition to face-to-face learning. The students were asked to complete a questionnaire three times in order to distinguish their learning styles. If any differences emerged in the students' responses or in their learning styles, then their responses were eliminated from the analysis process due to instability in their learning style across the three responses. Finally, from each class, equal numbers represented by the first 27 students' scores were analysed to get accurate results through comparing symmetric groups in terms of the numbers of students in each group.

Getting back to the data collection tools, the first objective of the questionnaire was to divide students according to their learning style. The questionnaire focused on the Kolb Learning Style Inventory, the teaching method of the course and the course content. The following procedures were taken in designing and interpreting the questionnaire:

1. Statements were taken from these questionnaires and were edited to be commensurate with the requirements of the current research.
2. After making the required amendments, the questionnaire consisted of twelve statements spread over the Kolb Learning Style Inventory dimensions.
3. The researcher then translated the questionnaire into Arabic because all 135 course students were Arabs who might face difficulty with filling in the questionnaire in English.
4. To increase the credibility of the study instrument, it was revised through various steps.
5. The researcher chose a Likert-type scale for the questionnaire. This style involves asking the participants to respond to each statement through marking the suitable box from among four choices.
6. The reliability of the questionnaire was verified and Cronbach's alpha was used to test the consistency of the results produced by the scale. According to Sekaran (2004), the values of Cronbach's Alpha for each variable of the questionnaire and for the entire questionnaire should exceed 0.60 in order to consider the result acceptable; in this study it was 85%, which reflects high consistency.

On the other hand, interviews were used to gather more detailed information. The questions and discussions in the interviews refer to learning experiences within this module and seek to identify the difficulties that the students faced, in addition to covering the benefits that they gained and lessons they learned through the stages of this module. Moreover, information about how students view their learning style after finishing this course was gathered. These interviews were carried out with seventy-one students: twenty (28.2%) from the control class, twenty five (35.2%) from the first experimental class (E1), and twenty-six (36.6%) from the second experimental class (E2).

The Research Methods course is compulsory. Thus, it is very important to check the validity and reliability of the exams for this course. Consequently, the following points were checked in advance:

1. The appropriateness and relevance of each question to the goals of the course
2. The appropriateness and relevance of each question to the objectives of the course units
3. The linguistic clarity of each question
4. The correctness of the scientific content of the questions.

Finally, achievement tests (Final) were prepared based on the units' objectives and items, as featured in a book provided by the Department. The tests included many types of questions.

After gathering the data from the study sample, the researcher used the Statistical Package for Social Sciences (SPSS) to analyse the data collected from the questionnaires, and the interview data were analysed using content analysis. The statistical tests that were used in this research are presented below, alongside a brief explanation of each one derived from Walliman and Baiche (2001):

1. Cronbach's alpha can be defined as a coefficient of internal consistency. It is usually used as an estimate of the reliability of a researcher's test for a study sample.
2. Independent sample t-tests were used to test the equality of the experimental and control groups in terms of the control variables.
3. One-way analysis of variance (ANOVA) was used to compare students' achievements due to learning style.

Result and Discussion

This section answers the research questions, confirms their consequences and provides an overview of the main result of the research. Achievements are viewed through final exam scores, while skills are viewed through scores on the proposal and poster task. The following table presents these main results:

Having discussed the three classes' results through their achievements in the exams, posters and proposal task, the qualitative results from interviews are presented below:

TABLE 8.1 The main results of the research

	Hypothesis (1)	Hypothesis (2)	Hypothesis (3)
Poster	There is a significant difference in poster scores between the control class and the first experimental class, as the sigma (2-tailed) is 0.000, which is below the significance level of 0.05. The control class has the higher mean value. Thus, it can be concluded that there is no effect of collaborative learning on the students' poster scores.	There is no significant difference in the students' scores for the proposal due to differences in learning style, as the sigma value is 0.347, which is above 0.05. It can be concluded that difference in learning style has no effect on the students' proposal writing skills in the collaborative learning environment.	There is no significant difference in the students' scores for the poster task due to different learning styles, since collaborative learning has not occurred, as the sigma value is 0.836, which is greater than 0.05. It can be concluded that there is no effect of the difference of learning style on the students' poster skills, as individual learning take place.
Proposal	There is a significant difference in proposal writing skills between the control class and the first experimental class, as the sigma is 0.001, which is below the significance level of 0.05. The E1 class has a higher mean value. Thus, it can be concluded that there is an effect of collaborative learning on the proposal scores of students.	There is no significant difference in students' scores on the proposal due to differences in learning style, as the sigma value is 0.443, which is above 0.05. It can be concluded that learning style has no effect on students' proposal writing skills in a collaborative learning environment	There is no significant difference in the students' scores on the proposal task due to different learning styles, since collaborative learning has not occurred, as the sigma value is 0.842, which is greater than 0.05. It can be concluded that difference in learning style has no effect on the students' proposal writing skills, as individual learning take place.

(Cont.)

EFFECTS OF COLLABORATIVE LEARING ON STUDENTS' ACHIEVEMENTS   97

TABLE 8.1   The main results of the research (*Cont.*)

	Hypothesis (1)	Hypothesis (2)	Hypothesis (3)
Final exam	There is no significant difference in final achievement between the control class and the first experimental class, as the sigma (2-tailed) is 0.031, which is above the significance level of 0.05. This indicates that collaborative learning did not enhance the scores of the E1 class, and thus has no effect on their achievements.	There is a significant difference in the students' achievements in the final exam due to different learning styles, as the sigma value is 0.009, which is below 0.05. Again, the converging learning style has the highest mean score. It can be concluded that learning style has an effect on the students' achievements in the final exam in a collaborative learning environment while this style is used.	There is a significant difference in the students' achievement in the final exam due to different learning styles when collaborative learning has not occurred, as the sigma value is 0.009, which is below 0.05. This difference is due to the assimilating learning style, which has a higher mean value. It can be concluded that learning style has an effect on the students' achievement in the final exam as individual learning take place.

1. Across all three classes, students agreed that they preferred to perform tasks by themselves, as it enabled them to save time and effort and to gain more knowledge.
2. These three classes disagreed with each other, as most of the students from the control class stated that they preferred to perform tasks with their colleagues, while students from group E2 did not. Students from class E1 had a range of opinions: some stated that they preferred to perform tasks with colleagues whilst others did not, and a few stated that they preferred to perform tasks with colleagues on some occasions but not others.
3. Respondents from the three classes agreed that they experienced anxiety when working in groups and did not quickly adapt to teamwork.
4. Students across all three classes described themselves as effective team members through accepting other members' opinions, discussing issues and sharing ideas.

5. Students in the control and E1 classes reported that they were more active with data work than through cooperation with other individuals, but most of the respondents from class E2 disagreed, indicating that they are more active through cooperation with other individuals than with data work.
6. The three classes agreed that the proposal tasks need teamwork to accomplish.
7. These three classes agreed that the biggest challenges in teamwork are coordination, accepting each other's ideas and understanding them.
8. These three classes agreed that the key roles within teams were as follows: (1) researcher, searching for references on specific topics; (2) divider, sharing out roles among team members; (3) leader, coordinating the team; and (4) effective members, sharing and giving information.
9. All three classes agreed that teamwork disrupts or impairs task completion for several reasons, such as lack of cooperation and frequent controversy, lack of responsibility on the part of some students, lack of collaboration and inadequate time commitment.

Conclusions

The main results of the current research can be briefly summarised as follows: there was no effect of collaborative learning on the students' poster skills or in their scores for the final exam. Collaborative learning also had a significant effect on the students' proposal writing scores between the control class and the first experimental class (collaborative without learning style). Moreover, there was no significant difference in the achievements and skills of students who worked individually in the final exam between the control class and the first experimental class, who collaborated in an e-learning environment. This indicates that collaborative learning had no effect on students' scores in these exams. Furthermore, there was an effect on the final exam scores of students engaged in collaborative learning with the same learning style in an e–learning environment due to their learning style. On the other hand, differences in learning style had no significant effect on the achievements of collaborative learners in the proposal-writing task. There was a significant difference in the final exam scores in an e–learning environment due to learning style, since collaborative learning did not occur. This difference was due to learning style, with students with the assimilating learning style doing significantly better. However, there was no significant difference in the students' scores for their proposal in an e-learning environment due to learning style, as collaborative learning did not occur.

It can be concluded from the result above that, first, it is becoming an important step for all Qatari academic institutions to adopt the most suitable approaches to encourage and support students in their learning. As this study has demonstrated, collaborative learning represents one of the effective approaches that should be utilized. However, a suitable environment must be put in place to facilitate this adoption. Culture could play a significant role, as seen in the present study: students in Qatar University see collaborative learning as appropriate for some tasks, but in other contexts they prefer individual work. This is related to culture and the way they have been raised by their families and schools.

Moreover, a suitable learning environment provides an important tool for teachers to use in reviewing how they can use and develop their practice, and to develop learner self-regulatory practice, which should be an essential feature of any differentiated instruction to maximise the potential and efficacy of learning environments for all learners and teachers in order 'to take the best of what theories have to offer and apply the concepts in artistic ways within the [learning context]' (Evans, 2015).

An important conclusion is that the combination of collaborative learning and e-learning environments has a good and positive effect on students, as they become more enthusiastic and interested. This sheds light on the importance of combining technology with modern education strategies. A further element that was observed to have a positive impact and really make a difference in collaborative learning was the students' learning style, which reflects a cornerstone in affecting their behaviour when they work together, and thus affects their achievement. In future, this could be a turning point for e-learning and other learning strategies.

Therefore, the best approach for improvement is to continue to evolve through improving the understanding of such strategies in order to identify the strengths and weaknesses in the application of the collaborative approach. These factors are also important in addressing the contents of the entire system, such as teaching presence, distance education, collaborative pedagogy and critical thinking.

The education sector is considered crucial in achieving sustainable development, which is an essential requirement of any reform process related to upgrading the community and its components, and has become necessary for technology. Thus, the issue is obviously relevant to teachers, researchers, and individuals. To conclude, the education process must be developed in an integrated manner and with a comprehensive outlook, and the search is thus beginning for modern teaching and learning methods. Thus, it is more advantageous to challenge long-term education prospects in order to contribute to the creation of a strategic plan.

Additionally, this study contributes to the development of the educational process, the adoption of modern teaching methods, the accommodation of the steadily increasing numbers of students seeking to obtain a university education and the adoption of the principles of lifelong learning and self-learning. It diffuses the literature on the benefits offered by modern information technologies and the ability to disseminate knowledge among the educated in many ways. By attempting to investigate and discuss the concept of learning styles and their relationships with e-learning, it adds new and valuable information to the literature on this issue. Overall, this research contributes to the growing empirical research on collaborative e-learning and provides rich information about the factors that motivate students in Qatar University and the problems they face in using different learning styles, regardless of whether or not collaborative learning is used.

Finally, in light of the study's results and findings, the following recommendations can be drawn:

1. The attention of decision-makers at universities in Qatar should be drawn to the need to improve educational skills and competencies, including understanding of the use of effective tools such as personal profiles in e-learning systems.
2. E-learning success stories need to be published and communicated. Such stories will help universities to adopt collaborative learning to fight inner hurdles, and help with the reduced societal education, which puts the student in a difficult position between parents and universities.
3. University strategies should be directed towards overcoming any restrictions or weaknesses in the tools used in educational skills and competencies, and towards providing the freedom for students to choose their learning style.
4. Instructors in universities should focus on giving motivational encouragement and support to learners in collaborative learning. This may also help to harbour positive attitudes and allow for more interdependence and social interaction between group members in different styles of e-learning.

References

Al-Sulaiti, H. (2011). *Intervention of the state of Qatar* (4th ed.). New York, NY: Permanent Mission of the State of Qatar to the United Nations.

Creswell, J. W. (2008). *Research design: Qualitative, quantitative, and mixed methods approaches*. Thousand Oaks, CA: Sage Publications.

Creswell, J. W., & Plano Clark, P. L. (2011). *Designing and conducting mixed methods research* (2nd ed.). Thousand Oaks, CA: Sage Publications.

Depriter, T. (2008). *Individual or collaborative learning: An investigation of teaching strategy in the distance learning mathematics classroom* (Doctoral dissertation). Morgan State University, Baltimore, MD.

Dillenbourg, P. (1999). *What do you mean by collaborative learning? Collaborative-learning: Cognitive and computational approaches.* Oxford: Elsevier.

Evans, C. (2015). Using an understanding of cognitive styles to enhance pedagogy. In H. Pedrosa-de-Jesus & M. Watts in collaboration with C. Guerra, B. da Silva Lopes, & A. Moreira (Eds.), *Academic growth in higher education: Questions and answers'.* Rotterdam, The Netherlands: Sense Publishers.

Felder, R. M., & Brent, R. (2005). Understanding student differences. *Journal of Engineering Education, 94*(1), 57–72.

Hassan, M. A., Fong, S. F., & Idrus, R. M. (2011). Impact of e-cooperative learning modules on interpersonal communication skills. *Recent Researches in Education*, 25–30.

Laal, M., & Laal, M. (2011). Collaborative learning: What is it? *Procardia – Social and Behavioral Sciences, 31*, 491–495.

Maesin, A., Mansor, M., Shafie, L. A., & Nayan, S. (2009). A study of collaborative learning among Malaysian undergraduates. *Asian Social Science, 5*(7), 70–76.

Marshall, J. M. (2002). *Learning with technology: Evidence that technology can, and does, support learning* (PhD thesis). San Diego State University, San Diego.

Sekaran, U. (2004). *Research methods for business: A skill building approach* (4th ed.). New York, NY: John Wiley & Sons.

Smith, B. L., & MacGregor, J. T. (1992). *What is collaborative learning?* Olympia, WA: Washington Center for Improving the Quality of Undergraduate Education.

Stasz, C., Eide, E. R., & Martorell, P. (2008). *Post-secondary education in Qatar: Employer demand, student choice, and options for policy.* Santa Monica, CA: Rand.

Walliman, N., & Baiche, B. (2001). *Your research project: A step-by-step guide for the first-time researcher.* London: Sage Publications.

Xu, W. (2011). Learning styles and their implications in learning and teaching. *Theory and Practice in Language Studies, 1*(4), 413–416.

Yamani, S. (2006). Toward a national education development paradigm in the Arab world: A comparative study of Saudi Arabia and Qatar. *The Fletcher School Online Journal for Issues Related to Southwest Asia and Islamic Civilization*, 1–8.

Zapalska, A., & Brozik, D. (2006). Learning styles and online education. *Campus-Wide Information Systems, 23*(5), 325–335.

Zellman, G. L., Karam, R., Constant, L., Salem, H., Gonzalez, G., Orr, N., & Al-Obaidli, K. (2009). *Implementation of the K-12 education reform in Qatar's schools.* Santa Monica, CA: Rand.

Zellman, G. L., Ryan, G. W., Karam, R., Constant, L., Salem, H., Gonzalez, G., & Al-Obaidli, K. (2011). Implementation of the K-12 education reform in Qatar's schools. *QNRS Repository, 2011*(1), 3653.

CHAPTER 9

Promoting University Students' Inquiry-Based Learning through Use of Questioning

Review of Previous Research and Description of New Research in Japan

Yoshinori Oyama and Emmanuel Manalo

Introduction

Higher education provision in Japan needs to adopt alternative ways of teaching, such as reciprocal learning (e.g., Fantuzzo, Riggio, Connelly, & Dimeff, 1989) and the 'flipped classroom' (e.g., Fulton, 2012) approaches, to promote the development of crucial 21st century skills in students. Currently, the majority of university classes still rely on the use of lecture methods, in which students are generally passive in their learning. When students are passive in their learning, they do not learn as effectively (e.g., Benware & Deci, 1984). Hence, teachers need to encourage and facilitate the use of more active learning approaches in their students, such as elaboration and self-questioning (e.g., King, 1992). The aim of the research described in this chapter was to contribute to methods for the development of students' question generation skills and the promotion of university students' inquiry-based learning.

Since questioning is a fundamental skill for learning (e.g., King, 1992), various studies have been undertaken to explore factors relating to learners' questioning behaviour, and to propose pedagogical methods for promoting the development of learners' questioning skills. From a pedagogical perspective, the 1970s was when many research studies focused on the development of questioning skills for reading comprehension. For example, in Frase and Schwartz's (1975) study, participants were asked to generate questions when reading materials they were provided, and the results showed that the 'question generation' group recalled more than a control group that simply studied the materials without generating questions. During the late 1980s and early 1990s researchers introduced the questioning strategy for lecture comprehension. For instance, King (1992) analysed the effect of questioning in a lecture setting. She compared self-questioning, summarising, and note-taking review and reported that students who used self-questioning performed slightly better than the summarisation group, and significantly better than the note-taking review group, in the retention test that followed the lecture learning task.

From a cognitive perspective, Miyake and Norman (1979) analysed the interaction between the difficulty level of the materials-to-be-learned and the knowledge possessed by learners. They found that, for the easier materials, the novice learners asked more questions than the trained learners did. However, for the more difficult materials, the trained learners asked more questions than the novice learners did. They concluded that material difficulty interacts with learners' knowledge level in determining the number of questions that learners would generate. Graesser and Olde (2003) focused more on the processes involved in questioning. They asked participants to study the mechanism of a certain device (e.g., a lock), and then to read a breakdown scenario. The participants generated questions concerning the cause of the device's failure and were instructed to think-aloud. Their results showed that deep comprehension of the mechanism of the device did not always lead to the generation of a larger number of questions, but it related to better quality questions that more precisely identified the possible causes of the break-down of the device. In more recent years, studies that have focused on questioning skills in specific subjects have increased. In a university social studies class, Yeşil and Korkmaz (2010) reported that a teaching method based on student questions better contributed to the development of students' question-asking skills, compared to methods based on teacher questions and on a combination of teacher and student questions.

In Japan, a number of researchers have described strategies they have used to promote their own students' use of the questioning strategy in their courses. Tanaka (1999), for example, described a method that he called 'the question card method'. In the university course that Tanaka was teaching, he decided to base students' course grades entirely on the question cards that they submit at the end of each lecture. In Tanaka's question card method, students first wrote questions on the lecture topics, including some background explanation of why he/she asked the question(s). Second, after the lecture, the instructor (Tanaka) read the students' questions; he then rated their appropriateness from 0 to 1. Irrespective of the number of questions generated, '0' was given to questions unrelated to the lecture topic, 0.5 was given to questions without background explanation, and 1 was given to appropriate questions with sufficient background explanation. Finally, in the next lecture, Tanaka responded to the students' questions – individually or in clusters according to similarity. The students received grades based on the total points they had accumulated for the questions they had written on the question cards. Tanaka's view, expressed in his book, was that through question generation, students thinking skills improved including their ability to see things from multiple perspectives.

In Ikuta and Maruno's (2005) study, questioning skills were taught to pupils in a Japanese elementally school. A three-step approach was used. First, the teacher asked pupils to read the target material and to underline the points they did not understand. Second, the teacher handed out a list of question stems similar to those used by King (1992) to assist the pupils in writing their own questions. Finally, the teacher asked the pupils to verbally report their questions, and to discuss their questions with their classmates – with the aim of improving the quality of those questions. Ikuta and Maruno reported that the pupils' eagerness to learn more appeared to increase following the use of this approach.

Another Japanese researcher, Michita (2011), attempted to develop his own undergraduate university students' questioning skills, not by providing question stems, but through activities they were given to do in their psychology course. One hundred and seventy-three (173) undergraduate students participated in Michita's (2011) study. These students were required to give group presentations on lecture topics of the course. While one group was making their presentation, students in the other groups listened to the presentation and discussed it to generate questions. Afterward, members of the presenting group answered the questions raised by the students in the other groups. Michita (2011) reported that the number of questions the students asked, and their attitudes toward questioning, both improved.

One crucial aspect that previous studies had not thoroughly examined is the longer-term effects of teaching the questioning strategy to students and, more specifically, whether the provision of such instruction promotes student spontaneity in use of the questioning strategy. Therefore, the objective of this paper was to examine the longer-term effect of a method for teaching questioning skills previous studies have used, and to verify if it is appropriate to use for promoting learners' spontaneous generation of questions. Three studies are described. Study 1 sought to find out students' metacognitive skills and beliefs about questioning that might affect their ability to generate factual and thought-provoking questions. Study 2 examined whether the provision of question-stems would improve students' question generation in both the immediate- and the long-term. Finally, Study 3 investigated whether linking course evaluation with the expectation for students to generate questions would increase and maintain their question generation behaviour during the course.

Study 1

Previous studies have suggested that variables such as metacognition and cognitive processing cost could influence students' use of various learning strategies (e.g., Garner, 1990; Sato, 1998). In the use of some learning strategies, such as the construction of diagrams to assist in math word problem solving and to enhance the quality of written communication, a number of studies have already been undertaken to examine the relationships between strategy use and such cognitive factors (e.g., Manalo & Uesaka, 2012; Uesaka & Manalo, 2012; Uesaka, Manalo, & Ichikawa, 2007). However, where student use of the questioning strategy is concerned, the extent to which such cognitive factors exert an influence and what teachers might need to target in classroom interventions to improve strategy use had not been examined. Thus Study 1's primary objective was to find out the possible relationships between variables such as metacognitive skills, perceptions about cognitive processing cost, and the number of questions students generate when engaged in learning tasks. It was hoped that findings would provide suggestions for what teachers ought to focus on when attempting to promote the use of questioning in their students' learning.

Method: Participants and Procedure

The participants were 96 undergraduate students taking a psychology course in one university in Japan. A questionnaire booklet containing the research items was distributed to the students by the course instructor (the first author) at the end of one lecture session. Completion of the questionnaire, and hence participation in the study, was voluntary and students had an option of opting out of completing the questionnaire to undertake some other learning tasks.

Materials

The booklet distributed to the students contained the following items.

Assessment of Meta-Cognitive Skills

Participants' meta-cognitive skills were measured using the Japanese version of Schraw and Dennison's (1994) Metacognitive Awareness Inventory (Abe & Ida, 2010). This inventory assesses students' knowledge about cognition and their regulation of their own cognition.

Question Generation Task

Participants were randomly assigned to read a Japanese version of a short passage describing either "Clouds" or "Dissolved Oxygen", based on Costa's (1997) study (cited in Otero & Graesser, 2001). Half of the participants read the "Clouds" passage and the other half read the "Dissolved Oxygen" one. After reading the passage, they were asked to write questions that occurred to them while reading. After writing the questions, the participants were given four short questions to check their passage comprehension.

Beliefs about the Use of Questions in Learning

Participants' belief about the use of questions in learning were measured by using four items that focused on "cognitive cost of question generation" (*It is hard for me to generate questions*), "recognition of the effect of generating questions" (*Asking questions deepens my understanding*), "easiness of question verbalization" (*I can easily verbalize what I am puzzled about*), and "not knowing how to generate an appropriate question" (*I am at unsure how to ask when I have questions*). They were asked to respond using a six-point Likert-type scale (where 1 = "strongly disagree" and 6 = "strongly agree").

Results

Relationship between Participants' Beliefs about Questioning and the Total Number of Questions they Generated

Based on King's (1995) study, the questions generated by the participants were categorized by two raters as either a "factual" question (e.g., What is a schema?) or a "thought-provoking" question (e.g., How is a schema different from a script?). The inter-rater agreement was considered satisfactory (Cohen's

TABLE 9.1 Examples of questions participants generated

Questions
Cloud Passage
Factual Questions
What is the distance between clouds and the ground?
What are the effects of friction and current in the air?
Thought-Provoking Question
Why do clouds look white?
Why do droplets in the clouds scatter light?
Dissolved Oxygen Passage
Factual Questions
What are oxygen atom and hydrogen atoms?
What are oxygen, nitrogen and carbon dioxide gases?
Thought-Provoking Question
What will happen if water becomes polluted?
Why do oxygen atom and hydrogen atoms have strong bonds?

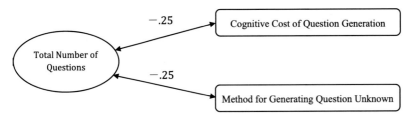

FIGURE 9.1 Correlations between total number of questions, cognitive cost of question generation, and lack of knowledge about question generation

kappa coefficient = .94). Examples of the participants' questions are shown in Table 9.1.

Concerning the relationship between participants' belief about questioning and the total number of questions they generated (i.e., sum of factual and thought-provoking questions), analysis revealed that the total number of questions significantly correlated with participants' cognitive cost of question generation ($r = -.25$, $p < .05$), and question method unknown ($r = -.25$, $p < .05$). Recognition of the effect of generating questions, and easiness of question verbalization, were not significantly correlated with the total number of questions. These results mean that the higher the participants perceived the cost of generating questions, and the more uncertain they were about how to generate appropriate questions, the fewer questions they actually produced. However, their awareness of the benefit of asking questions to deepen understanding, and perceived ability to verbalize questions they want to ask, appeared unrelated to the number of questions they produced.

With regard to the relationship between participants' metacognitive skills and the total number of questions they generated, no correlations were found. Also, participants' total correct score from the four short comprehension questions did not significantly correlate with the total number of questions they produced.

Relationship between the Participants' Beliefs about Questioning and the Factual and Thought-Provoking Questions they Generated

Concerning the relationship between participants' beliefs about asking questions and the number of factual and thought-provoking questions they produced, analysis revealed significant correlations (Figure 9.2) between the number of factual questions and participants' beliefs about the easiness of question verbalization ($r = .29$, $p < .05$), and between the number of thought-provoking questions and participants' cognitive cost of question generation ($r = -.30$, $p < .05$). This means that the higher the participants perceived the cost of generating questions, the fewer thought-provoking questions they produced. In contrast, the easier they considered it was to verbalize questions they want to ask, the more factual questions they produced. No significant

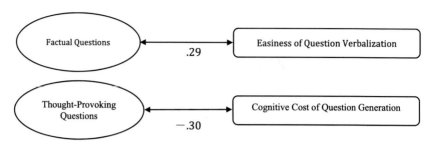

FIGURE 9.2   Correlations between total number of factual questions and easiness of question verbalization, and between total number of thought-provoking questions and cognitive cost of question generation

correlations were found with participants' awareness of the benefit of asking questions to deepen understanding, or with uncertainty about how to generate appropriate questions. Likewise, no significant correlations were found with participants' metacognitive skills or their passage comprehension scores.

Discussion

The findings of Study 1 suggest that when students consider it easy to verbalize the questions they want to ask, they are more likely to generate questions – at least, where factual question are concerned. However, perceptions of difficulties with questioning – such as perceiving the cognitive cost as being high and being unsure about how to make appropriate questions – hindered question generation. It is therefore possible that provision of question stems, like those used in King (1992), could improve students' generation of questions when learning from passages they are provided. Questions stems conceivably could provide hints on how to verbalize questions students might want to ask and reduce uncertainties about how to generate appropriate kinds of questions, and by doing so the provision of question stems could reduce perceptions about the hardships – or cognitive cost – associated with generating questions. Therefore, in Study 2, the effect of an intervention to promote students' spontaneous question generation by providing question stems to lighten their "cognitive cost of question generation", reduce their perceptions of "question method unknown", and ease "question verbalization", was examined.

Study 2

Previous studies (e.g., King, 1992, 1995) have reported positive effects of providing question stems in promoting learners' question generation. However, those studies did not examine the longer-term effects of the intervention and it is not known whether learners continue to spontaneously generate questions even after the training period has finished. Therefore, this study compared three phases (baseline, training, and post-training phases) to examine the longer-term effects of question stems provision.

Method

The participants were 58 undergraduate students taking an introductory psychology course in one university in Japan. Part of the course schedule was divided into three phases: baseline, training, and post-training phases. Each phase had 6 lectures in 3 weeks and, combined, lasted 9 weeks in total. During the baseline phase, the students received no training in generating questions, and a sheet to gather their feedback and spontaneous questions on the lecture topics was distributed at the beginning of every lecture and collected at the end. During the training phase, at the beginning of each lecture, the students were given a "question matrix" (see Figure 9.3). The matrix had six blank spaces, and each had six question stems (i.e., why, relation/influence, advantage/disadvantage, similarity/difference, what if ..., and ... in the first place) that were aimed at assisting in the generation of "thought provoking questions" (King, 1995). During the post-training phase, the "question matrix" was not distributed to the students, and the instructor did not ask or verbally encourage the students to generate questions: only a comment sheet, in the same format as the one handed out during the baseline phase, was given to the students. The generated questions were grouped into two categories by two ratters using King's (1995) "thought provoking questions" and "factual questions" categories.

Why	**Relation / Influence**	**Advantage / Disadvantage**
e.g., *Why are people demotivated?*	e.g., *How is Freud's idea related to Jung's?*	e.g., *What are the main advantages of*
Similarity / Difference	**What if**	**In the first place**
e.g., *What are the similarities and differences between classical and operant conditioning?*	e.g., *What if a child has no parents, would he/she struggle to form attachment to others?*	e.g., *Do intelligence scales really measure intelligence in the first place?*

FIGURE 9.3   Question matrix used during the training phase of study 2

Results

A total of 155 questions (average of 2.67 questions per student) were collected from the students during the three phases of the study. Inter-rater agreement in categorizing the questions was considered satisfactory (Cohen's kappa coefficient = .92). A two-way ANOVA was conducted to analyze the effect of the question matrix on the types of questions the students generated and the three learning phases (baseline, training, and post-training). The results showed significant main effects of the types of questions ($F (1, 57)$ = 9.30, $p < .01$, $\eta^2 = .140$), and learning phases ($F (2, 114) = 15.66$, $p < .001$, $\eta^2 = .215$), and a significant interaction effect between the types of the questions and the learning phases ($F (2, 114) = 3.70$, $p < .05$, $\eta^2 = .06$). Differences in the mean number of two types of questions (factual and thought-provoking) in the three learning phases (baseline, training, and post-training) were assessed using the Bonferroni multiple comparison procedure. The result showed that, in the training phase, the largest number of thought-provoking questions was generated and it was statistically significant when compared to the ones in the baseline and post-training phases. The relative numbers of factual and thought-provoking questions across the three phases of the study are shown in Figure 9.4.

Discussion

This study is the first to examine the long term or maintenance effects of providing question stems on students' question generating behaviour. The findings revealed that, although the number of questions students produced during the training phase increased significantly, this increase was not maintained during the post-training phase. In other words, students did not

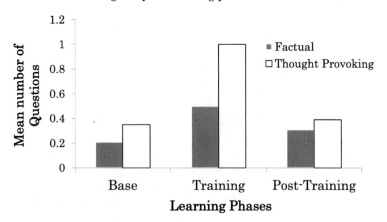

FIGURE 9.4 Changes of number of factual and thought-provoking questions across the phases of the study

continue to generate questions to facilitate more effective learning during the lectures they were attending. This raises the question of how it may be possible to promote spontaneity in students' use of the questioning strategy to enhance their learning. Lack of spontaneity in strategy use is a serious problem (e.g., Borkowski, Carr, & Pressley, 1987; Garner, 1990; Uesaka et al., 2007), not least because it means that students fail to obtain the benefits of using the strategy they have learned in many everyday learning situations where teachers or parents are not present to prompt them to use the strategy. Thus, in the next study (Study 3), one possible way of promoting spontaneity in students' use of the questioning strategy during lectures they attend was explored.

Study 3

The main objective of Study 3 was to examine in a real classroom setting how teachers might be able to promote a certain degree of spontaneity in students' use of the questioning strategy during a learning activity (attending a lecture).

Murayama (2003) reported that evaluation method is a powerful tool that can change students' learning strategy use. In Murayama's (2003) study, students assigned to a "fill-in-the-blank" format test group were found to rely on use of the rote-memorization strategy, but students assigned to a "writing short essay" format test group were found to use deeper and more elaborative learning strategies. Also, Pedrosa-de-Jesus and Watts (2012) pointed out the important role of evaluation in question generation, and they included "evaluation" as an integral part of their proposed question generation process, "CARE" (the construction, asking, reception, and evaluation of a learner's question). Other researchers have likewise emphasized the influence of evaluation method or assessment on students' approaches to learning (e.g., Garner, 1990; Hattie, 2008). Based on this idea, Study 3 tested the hypothesis that if question generation is a part of the grading requirement of a course and term papers are based on the questions students generate, the number of questions students generate would increase and their questioning behaviour would maintain over the course of an entire semester.

Method

Participants were sophomore (i.e., second-year) students in educational psychology courses in one Japanese university during the 2013 and 2014 academic years.

"Control" Class

Students in the 2013 class (91 students) were asked to generate questions concerning the materials covered in the lectures of the course. They were also administered two quizzes (during the 4th and 8th class sessions) for grading during the semester.

"Experimental" Class

Students in the 2014 class (90 students) were asked to generate questions concerning the materials covered in the lectures of the course and were told that the questions they generate would be collected at the end of each lecture and would be part of their course grade (5% of total). The students were also required to submit reports based on the questions they generated in class, and to search for answers to the question they generated (also during the 4th and 8th class sessions).

Results

The total numbers of the questions the students generated per lecture are shown in Figure 9.5.

A two-way ANOVA was conducted to analyse the effect of the two types of evaluation (quizzes or reports) on the students' questioning behaviour. One hundred and thirty-three (133) students completed the course and the number of questions they generated were examined. The result showed significant main effects of the lecture sessions ($F(10, 1310) = 32.21$, $p < .001$, $\eta^2 = .197$) and of the group ($F(1, 131) = 449.39$, $p < .001$, $\eta^2 = .77$), and a significant interaction effect between lecture sessions and group ($F(10, 1310) = 25.49$, $p < .001$, $\eta^2 = .16$). Differences in the mean number of questions generated by students in the

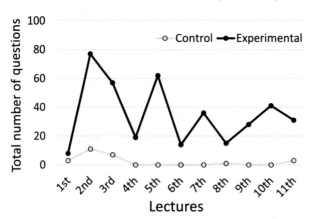

FIGURE 9.5   Total numbers of questions that students in the "control" and "experimental" classes generated

Control and Experimental classes were assessed using the Bonferroni multiple comparison procedure. The result showed that differences in number of questions generated in the Control and Experimental classes were statistically significant in all lecture sessions except the first session, during which only course introduction was provided and no instruction about the evaluation of questions was provided.

Discussion

The findings of Study 3 revealed that a teacher's evaluation of students' question generation increases the number of questions students generate and maintains that increase over the course of an entire semester. This finding confirms the influence of evaluation method or assessment on the strategies students use for learning (cf. Garner, 1990; Hattie, 2008; Murayama, 2003). Although question generation by students in the Experimental class can be considered as 'spontaneous' in the sense that the instructor did not tell the students to generate questions in each lecture session, it was also not truly spontaneous because the generation was in direct response to the instructors' requirements and expectations for the course (i.e., the students had to generate the questions if they wanted the grades allocated for it) – not of the students' own volition.

Future research would need to consider, design, and test other methods of promoting more authentic spontaneity in students' use of the questioning strategy in their learning. It is also possible that the students' belief about question generation differed between the Control and Experimental classes, independent of the manipulation or as a consequence of it – but this dimension was not assessed in this study. Another important aspect that was not considered in this study was the quality of questions that students generated. It could be argued for example that in terms of promoting university students' inquiry-based learning competence, a teachers' role would not be just to assist in increasing students' question generation, but also to evaluate and help improve the quality of questions students generate. It is possible that provision of teacher or peer feedback on how to improve questions generated would help students' learn how to generate higher quality questions. Future studies would need to examine these other important aspects in the promotion of the questioning strategy for student learning.

Summary and Conclusion

Self-generation of questions for the purposes of better learning is an integral part of inquiry-based learning, which in turn is considered one of the essential and most powerful ways to facilitate the development of crucial 21st century skills in students (e.g., Hmelo-Silver, Duncan, & Chinn, 2007). The three studies described in this paper contribute toward better understanding of how it may be possible to promote the spontaneous use of the questioning strategy among students. Study 1 examined students' perceptions and beliefs about questioning that could affect their ability to generate factual and thought-provoking questions. Its findings revealed that perceptions of high cognitive cost associated with formulating questions and uncertainties about how to appropriately ask questions were hindrances to question generation, while perceptions of ease in verbalizing intended questions promoted such generation. Based on these findings, Study 2 examined the effect of providing question stems, similar to those used by King (1992), for students to use: the provision of question stems could conceivably relieve perceptions of high cognitive cost, reduce uncertainties about how to ask questions, and make it easier to verbalize the questions that are intended. The findings of Study 2 revealed however that, although the provision of question stems increased the number of questions the students generated during the training phase (when question stem sheets were provided), the increase failed to maintain through to the post-training phase. Study 2 therefore highlighted an important problem: that of students' lack of spontaneity in using the questioning strategy for their own learning. Study 3 designed and tested one possibly way of promoting student use of the questioning strategy in a university course – by making the questions that students generate a part of their grading and assigning a report based on those questions. An examination of the number of questions students generated during the course of an entire semester showed that the design was effective in getting students to use the questioning strategy during their lectures in the course. However, as noted, such use of the strategy cannot be regarded as truly 'spontaneous' – as it was in direct response to the expectations of the instructor and the grading requirements of the course. Future research will need to formulate and evaluate ways of promoting authentic spontaneity in students' use of the questioning strategy for their own learning. Equally important in future research would be the design and evaluation of methods to enhance the quality of questions that students generate for their own learning purposes.

References

Abe, M., & Ida, M. (2010). An attempt to construct the adults' metacognition scale: Based on the metacognitive awareness inventory [Seijin you meta ninchi shakudo no sakusei no kokoromi: Metacognitive Awareness Inventory wo mochi ite]. *The Journal of Psychology of Rissho University, 1*, 23–34.

Benware, C. A., & Deci, E. L. (1984). Quality of learning with an active versus passive motivational set. *American Educational Research Journal, 21*, 755–765.

Borkowski, J. G., Carr, M., & Pressley, M. (1987). "Spontaneous" strategy use: Perspectives from metacognitive theory. *Intelligence, 11*, 61–75.

Costa, J. (1997). *Estudo sobre capacidades metacognitivas nas aulas de física através da formulação de preguntas* [A study of metacognitive abilities in physics classrooms through question asking] (Unpublished masters thesis). Universidade de Coimbra, Coimbra.

Fantuzzo, J. W., Riggio, R. E., Connelly, S., & Dimeff, L. A. (1989). Effects of reciprocal peer tutoring on academic achievement and psychological adjustment: A component analysis. *Journal of Educational Psychology, 81*, 173–177.

Frase, L. T., & Schwartz, B. J. (1975). Effect of question production and answering on prose recall. *Journal of Educational Psychology, 67*, 628–635.

Fulton, K. (2012). Upside down and inside out: Flip your classroom to improve student learning. *Learning & Leading with Technology, 39*, 12–17.

Garner, R. (1990). When children and adults do not use learning strategies: Toward a theory of settings. *Review of Educational Research, 60*, 517–529.

Graesser, A. C., & Olde, B. A. (2003). How does one know whether a person understands a device? The quality of the questions the person asks when the device breaks down. *Journal of Educational Psychology, 95*, 524–536.

Hattie, J. (2008). *Visible learning: A synthesis of over 800 meta-analyses relating to achievement.* New York, NY: Routledge.

Hmelo-Silver, C. E., Duncan, R. G., & Chinn, C. A. (2007). Scaffolding and achievement in problem-based and inquiry learning: A response to Kirschner, Sweller, and Clark (2006). *Educational Psychologist, 42*, 99–107.

Ikuta, J., & Maruno, S. (2005). Change of children' questioning in elementary school class through questioning generating centered instruction [Shitsumon zukuri wo chushin to shita shidou ni yoru jido no jyugyo chu no shitsumon seisei katudou no henka]. *Japan Journal of Educational Technology, 29*, 577–586.

King, A. (1992). Facilitating elaborative learning through guided student-generated questioning. *Educational Psychologist, 27*, 111–126.

King, A. (1995). Designing the instructional process to enhance critical thinking across the curriculum inquiring minds really do want to know: Using questioning to teach critical thinking. *Teaching of Psychology, 22*, 13–17.

Manalo, E., & Uesaka, Y. (2012). Elucidating the mechanism of spontaneous diagram use in explanations: How cognitive processing of text and diagrammatic representations is influenced by individual and task-related factors. *Lecture Notes in Artificial Intelligence, 7352*, 35–50.

Michita, Y. (2011). Effect of question-asking training in a college lecture class on learners' attitudes and ability to ask questions [Jyugyo ni oite samazama na sitsumon keiken wo surukotoga sitsumon taido to sitsumon ryoku ni oyobosu kouka]. *Japanese Journal of Educational Psychology, 59*, 193–205.

Miyake, N., & Norman, D. A. (1979). To ask a question, one must know enough to know what is not known. *Journal of Verbal Learning and Verbal Behavior, 18*, 357–364.

Murayama, K. (2003). Test format and learning strategy use [Test keisiki ga gakushu houryaku ni ataeru eikyo]. *Japanese Journal of Educational Psychology, 51*, 1–12.

Otero, J., & Graesser, A. (2001). PREG: Elements of a model of question asking. *Cognition and Instruction, 19*, 143–175.

Pedrosa-de-Jesus, H., & Watts, M. (2014). Managing affect in learners' questions in undergraduate science. *Studies in Higher Education, 39*, 102–116.

Sato, J. (1998). Effects of learners' perceptions of utility and costs and learning strategy preference [Gakushu horyaku no yukousei no ninchi cost no ninchi konomi ga gakushu horyaku siyou ni oyobosu eikou]. *Japanese Journal of Educational Psychology, 40*, 367–376.

Schraw, G., & Dennison, R. S. (1994). Assessing metacognitive awareness. *Contemporary Educational Psychology, 19*, 460–475.

Tanaka, H. (1999). *Farewell to lecture style education: Introduction to the question card method* [Sayonara Furui Kogi]. Hokkaido: Hokkaido University Press.

Uesaka, Y., & Manalo, E. (2012). Task-related factors that influence the spontaneous use of diagrams in math word problems. *Applied Cognitive Psychology, 26*, 251–260.

Uesaka, Y., Manalo, E., & Ichikawa, S. (2007). What kinds of perceptions and daily learning behaviors promote students' use of diagrams in mathematics problem solving? *Learning and Instruction, 17*, 322–335.

Yeşil, R., & Korkmaz, Ö. (2010). A comparison of different teaching applications based on questioning in terms of their effects upon pre-service teachers' good questioning skills. *Procedia – Social and Behavioral Sciences, 2*, 1075–1082.

CHAPTER 10

Student-Centred Inquiry and the Awareness of One's Own Lack of Knowledge

Building Unknowns about Objects

José Otero and Cleci T. Werner da Rosa

Introduction

Posing problems and generating questions are an essential element of scientific activity. In their classic work *The evolution of Physics*, Einstein and Infeld (1938), highlighted the importance of problem formulation in relation to the problem of determining the velocity of light,

> The formulation of a problem is often more essential than its solution, which may be merely a matter of mathematical or experimental skill. To raise new questions, new possibilities, to regard old questions from a new angle, requires creative imagination and marks real advance in science. (p. 95)

Regarding science education, unknowns that need to be unveiled, obstacles that block understanding, or anomalies in need for explanation play important roles in several learning and instructional activities. The awareness of one's own lack of knowledge or one's own incomprehension is a central element in inquiry-based approaches to teaching and learning (Loyens & Rikers, 2011; Minner, Levy, & Century, 2010). For instance, problem-based learning involves problems as a central component around which the instructional activities are organized (Hmelo-Silver, 2004). These problems, similar to those that may be found in real life, may be provided by the teacher or, alternatively, generated by students themselves (Chin & Chia, 2004; Chin & Kayalvizhi, 2002; Gallas, 1995; Hmelo-Silver, 2004). Therefore, students should be able to identify obstacles to understanding that may be amenable to scientific study, something that is not always easily achieved. Chin and Kayalvhizi (2002) reported the types of questions that 11 and 12 year-old students ask when requested to pose problems for investigation in the classroom. When these problems were individually generated, about 88% of them were non-researchable. These included basic-information questions that could be answered by looking up in a book, complex problems involving knowledge beyond the understanding of students at this level, and philosophical and religious problems such as, "When is judgement day?"

Awareness of one's own lack of knowledge and incomprehension is also centrally involved in questioning, a skill closely related to critical thinking (Pedrosa-de-Jesus, Moreira, Lopes, & Watts, 2014). As a first step, question generation involves the detection of anomalies such as knowledge gaps or comprehension obstacles (Graesser & McMahen, 1993). Being aware of these obstacles when trying to understand technical material, and trying to remove them through questioning, significantly improves comprehension: students process information more actively, activate relevant prior knowledge, and focus their attention on important segments of information (Rosenshine, Meister, & Chapman, 1996). Moreover, students prefer investigating their own questions compared with answering questions posed by others (Chin & Kayalvizhi, 2005).

In addition, students' questions are also useful for teachers. Questions reveal students' understanding and difficulties (Watts, Gould, & Alsop, 1997; Hadzigeorgiou, 1999; Maskill & Pedrosa-de-Jesus, 1997) and also students' interests (Baram-Tsabari, Sethi, Bry, & Yarden, 2006; Baram-Tsabari & Yarden, 2005). Therefore instruction may be tailored so that it responds to students' needs.

Given the roles described above, examining the features of the consciously unknown or of what is not understood, and the processes involved in achieving the awareness of lack of knowledge or lack of understanding seems worthwhile. Perhaps justifiably, research on inquiry-based learning has devoted considerable more attention to the processes involved in the acquisition of knowledge and skills through problem solving, than to processes involved in the first stage of question generation or problem posing. In this chapter we intend to examine features of the consciously unknown, or of the knowledge gaps that science students are aware of, when they deal with some of the objects included in their science curriculum.

Failures in knowing and understanding have already been analysed in studies on misconceptions, i.e., students' replacement of scientific concepts by alternative conceptions intended to describe and explain natural phenomena (Driver & Easley, 1978; Wandersee, Mintzes, & Novak, 1994). However the very nature of misconceptions implies that students are unaware of their failure to provide appropriate explanations of the natural world in terms of these ideas. For instance, students holding alternative conceptions about force and motion (Watts, 1983), who believe that velocity implies the existence of a net force, are not really aware of their failure in understanding the relation between force and acceleration. Our focus is on the unknowns that students are aware of in a given learning situation.

Awareness of unknowns or of misunderstandings is indeed implied in the generation of information seeking questions, as pointed out above. Therefore, taxonomies of information-seeking questions could be used to indirectly categorize conscious lack of knowledge or conscious lack of understanding. However, these taxonomies are not always based on the obstacles that questioners are aware of. For example, Graesser Person and Huber's (1992) taxonomy, involving 18 types of questions, is not based on the obstacles that trigger questions but on semantic, conceptual and pragmatic criteria. Moreover, studies that did analyse the causes of questions frequently deal with relatively complex tasks, that only allow for a relatively coarse-grained analysis of the obstacles resulting in questioning. For instance, Chin and Chia (2004) examined students' inspirations for problems and questions that were individually generated or generated in collaborative groups while involved in problem-based learning. Students requested explanations of previously observed phenomena (26.0% of individual questions), or the validation of common beliefs (10.4%). The majority of individual questions, 54.2%, were caused by need of basic information. But what type of basic information do students request? Or, what precisely are their explanatory needs? A response to these questions certainly involves reducing degrees of freedom regarding the variables involved in noticing knowledge or understanding gaps. Pedrosa-de-Jesus et al. (2014) argue for the importance of context in critical questioning. An analysis of the unknowns and of the understanding obstacles that students may be aware of, and that could lead to inquiry, involves adequately controlling context, besides input, individual, and task variables in the situation where inquiry is taking place.

A convenient starting point to characterize the awareness of what is unknown or not understood, and the variables influencing this awareness could be the analysis of a relatively simple situation: the identification of unknowns about an object. Students may be asked to report what they do not know about an object such as a leaf or a battery, normally included in science curricula, in order to include this information in a textbook or an encyclopedia. In this situation, what do students know that they do not know, and what variables influence the awareness of these unknowns? In the next section we focus on what students declare not to know about objects such as those mentioned above, and the structure of these knowledge gaps. Then we examine the effects of domain knowledge, one of the variables that influence this structure. Finally we synthesize some instructional implications of these analyses.

The Structure of Unknowns about Objects

A fundamental question facing anyone trying to characterize the knowledge gaps about an object is how to conceptualize these gaps. A basic assumption of sociological and historical studies on the unknown is that conscious ignorance increases as knowledge increases (Einsiedel & Thorne, 1999; Gross, 2007; Stocking & Hollstein, 1993). The idea is summarized in the metaphor of the island of knowledge surrounded by an ocean of unconscious ignorance or 'meta-ignorance', i.e., what is not known not to be known (Otero & Ishiwa, 2014; Smithson, 2008). Conscious ignorance occurs on the border between the island and the ocean of meta-ignorance, and it becomes greater as the knowledge, i.e., the perimeter of the island, increases. In accordance with this assumption about the constructive character of conscious ignorance, what is consciously not known about an object can be expected to build upon what is known about this object. Different knowledge about several objects should result in different conscious unknowns about them.

Based on this rationale, Vaz-Rebelo, Fernandes, Morgado, Monteiro, and Otero (2016) attempted a categorization of the constitutive elements of unknowns about objects by comparing with the constituent elements of knowledge about these objects. In that study, Vaz-Rebelo et al. asked 7th grade and 12th grade students to make explicit through questioning what they did not know about two classes of objects included in their science curriculum: natural objects, such as 'leukocyte' or 'glacier', and artefacts, such as an ultrasound scanner or a battery. The structure of what may be unknown about an object was based on the identification of what may be known about this object as formalised in knowledge sources such as dictionaries, or in lexical databases such as Wordnet (Fellbaum, 1998). The definition scheme 'genus + differentiae', based on Aristotle's work, is still widely used to define object concepts in dictionaries. This definition consists of a superordinate of the object concept "… followed by a relative clause that describes how this instance differs from all other instances" (Miller, 1990, p. 245). Wordnet identifies three kinds of features that differentiate objects within a category: parts, attributes and functions. Vaz-Rebelo et al. (2016) classified the possible unknowns associated with an object into the same categories as the elements that lexicographers associate with the meaning of nouns denoting objects: the superordinate category of a certain object may be unknown ('Is this a mineral?'), its parts or constitution ('What is it made of?'), its attributes ('What size is it?'), or its functions ('What is it for?').

However, these categories taken from typical dictionary definitions do not exhaust all that is known about an object. Encyclopaedias or textbooks include additional information about coordinate or subordinate entities associated with an object through various relationships such as cause or consequence. For example, the entry for 'electric battery' in Wikipedia includes basic definitional information: '[A] device [*superordinate category*] consisting of one or more electrochemical cells [*parts*] that convert stored chemical energy into electrical energy [*function*]'. But there is also plenty of information about related entities such as the battery industry: 'According to a 2005 estimate, the worldwide battery industry generates US $48 billion in sales each year'. This suggested a new kind of unknown associated with an object, based on knowledge beyond the elements of the Aristotelian definition, consisting in temporal, spatial, causal or other relations between the target object and other entities. The unknowns associated with this kind of knowledge were termed *Extrinsic* unknowns, expressed through questions such as 'What is the country producing most batteries in the world?' or 'What is the white stuff that leaks from a battery when it is old?'

According to this, Vaz-Rebelo et al. (2016) categorized unknowns about objects into a few basic categories. In the first place, there were unknowns about the superordinate of a target object, X, that would be expressed by questions such as 'Is X a Y?' Second, there may be unknowns directly associated with knowledge about the intrinsic properties of objects, such as parts, attributes or functions. These were termed *Intrinsic* unknowns. Third, there may be unknowns about other relations, such as comparison or contingency relations, involving he target object. These were termed *Extrinsic* unknowns.

The unknowns generated in the Vaz-Rebelo et al.'s (2016) study were inferred from the questions asked, as in other studies (Ishiwa, Sanjosé, & Otero, 2013; Kemler-Nelson, Egan, & Holt, 2004). However, the unknown underlying a particular question is sometimes difficult to identify. This is found especially in the case of the ambiguous 'What is X?' questions that were very frequently asked in the study of Vaz-Rebelo et al. (2016). One possibility is that the question addresses the superordinate of a target object, but other possibilities exist also. A question such as 'What is a scalpel?' cannot be associated to a precise unknown. It could be conceivably answered by the superordinate 'A knife', or by providing information about the function of a scalpel 'Something that surgeons use to cut'. Therefore a category of unspecified *What* unknowns was used also, corresponding to those expressed through imprecise 'What is X?' questions. Explicit questions about superordinates were also included in this category, although they were very few. Finally, a category *Other* included unknowns not classifiable into the previous categories, such as unknowns about the linguistic representation of an object ('What is the origin of the word "leucocyte"?').

Table 10.1 synthesizes the types of unknowns with some examples of the questions from which they are inferred. Unknowns about functions were not included in the *Intrinsic* category, where they belong, but counted in a category of their own given the special role that they played in the experiment.

According to this framework, how are students' knowledge gaps about objects distributed among the above categories? A basic result of the Vaz-Rebelo et al.'s (2016) study was the dependence of this distribution on the ontological category of the target object. At the two grade levels considered in the experiment, the students reported significantly more unknowns about the function of artefacts, including what an entity does and how it does it, than about the functions of natural objects. The result is consistent with the importance of functional features in the knowledge of artefacts, as shown by research on the categorisation of objects by both adults and children (Barton & Komatsu, 1989; Keil, 1989). It also concurs with studies such as the one by Kemler-Nelson et al. (2004), mentioned above. Significantly, fewer follow-up questions were asked by the children participating in this study when an initial 'What is X?' question was answered by providing the function of an artefact than when the answer gave its name. The authors concluded than when children ask a 'What is X?' question about an artefact, they are primarily concerned with knowing its function rather than its name.

According to the above, functions appear to play a central role in the structure of unknowns about artefacts generated by students from primary level to college level. More generally, the findings of these studies show that unknowns are not randomly found in the infinite pool of meta-ignorance. They are dependent on variables such as the ontological category of the target objects, and the knowledge associated with this category. Therefore, in the next section we consider in a more general way the effect of knowledge on the awareness of unknowns: how does domain knowledge influence the unknowns students are aware of?

TABLE 10.1 Scheme for categorising unknowns about objects, and examples of the corresponding questions

Unknown	Corresponding questions
What	Is X a Y? What is X?
Intrinsic	What are the parts of X? What is X made of?
Functions	What does X do? What can be done with X?
Extrinsic	What is the relation between X and Y? How does X influence Y?
Other	Why this name? In which year did we study this?

Awareness of Unknowns about Objects and Domain Knowledge

Knowledge provides the foundation for the awareness of lack of knowledge, according to a basic assumption mentioned above. The influence of knowledge on the awareness of lack of knowledge has already been shown in some studies on question asking (Flammer, 1981; Miyake & Norman, 1979; Van der Meij, 1990). Several of these studies have found a positive relationship between knowledge and the quality of the unknowns, or of the misunderstandings expressed through questioning.

Scardamalia and Bereiter (1992) studied 'text based' questions, i.e., those "prompted by a text and generally about the text" (p. 178), and 'knowledge-based' questions, i.e., those that "spring[s] from a deep interest of the child or arise[s] from an effort to make sense of the world" (p. 178). In this study, primary school students asked questions on the topics of fossil fuels and endangered species, about which they had different knowledge. They found that students adjusted the questions asked to their level of knowledge about the subjects. The students, having little knowledge about fossil fuels, asked questions that reflected a basic ignorance, such as 'What are fossil fuels?' Also they asked questions addressed to relatively simple features such as the composition of fossil fuels: 'What are fossil fuels made of?' However, these basic unknowns were less frequent when students asked about the issue of endangered species, which was better known for the students. Unknowns in this case were more elaborated and they were expressed through what Scardamalia and Bereiter (1992) called 'wonderment questions'. These are questions that reflect speculation and elaborations based on knowledge on the subject, such as, 'How do scientists count a species to know that is in danger [of extinction]?'

Other studies on questioning converge on these findings. Van der Meij (1990) compared the questions raised by 11 year-old students who had different level of knowledge about words like 'tardy'. He found that students with poor knowledge of words produced questions reflecting "a somewhat unspecified search for information about a target word" (p. 506). Again, little knowledge corresponded to more imprecise knowledge gaps. In the same vein, Torres, Duke, Ishiwa Sanchez, Portoles, and Sanjosé (2012) analysed the questions asked by secondary school students on surprising devices or phenomena, such as the Cartesian diver or the change in colour of a solution that is stirred. Among other results they found that older, more knowledgeable students asked more questions caused by gaps in a scientific model of the situation than the younger, less knowledgeable students.

The studies of Graesser and Olde (2003) and Graesser, Lu, Olde, Copper-Pye, and Whitten (2005) about failures in mechanical devices such as locks, also illustrate the influence of knowledge in accurately recognizing what is unknown. College students who participated in the experiments had to ask questions in order to identify the source of malfunction of a lock. Students with more technical knowledge were able to ask questions about the components and processes that could explain the malfunction. In other words, they were able to identify crucial knowledge gaps, unlike students with less knowledge. The latter asked more global and imprecise questions or focused on unknown components or processes that would not explain the lock's malfunction. Their conscious unknowns were of a lesser quality

One of the results of the study by Vaz-Rebelo et al. (2016), mentioned above, concerned the effect of domain knowledge on the object unknowns made explicit through questioning. Not surprisingly, the 'What' unknowns, consisting of unspecified ignorance expressed through the ambiguous 'What is X?' questions, were more frequently associated with the less knowledgeable, primary school students, than with the secondary school students. Also, within any of the grade levels, they were more frequently associated with the less well-known objects of the sample than with the better-known objects. In sum, knowledge was found again to be of basic importance in identifying well defined unknowns.

Otero and Gallástegui (2016) directly studied the role of knowledge in asking questions about unfamiliar objects. Seventh grade students had to ask questions on a sample of familiar objects, such as bicycle or battery, or less familiar objects, such as a missile or electronic capacitor, typically studied in science classes. The questions asked were categorized depending on their generality. A question was considered general when it could be sensibly asked about any object belonging to the superordinate category of the target object ('Vehicle' and 'Electrical device', for the examples above). Otherwise, the question was considered specific. For instance, 'When was it [bicycle] invented?' was considered a general question because it may be asked about any object belonging to the 'Vehicle' category. However, the question 'How is power transmitted from pedals?' was considered specific as it can only be sensibly asked about bicycles and not about a vehicle such as a sailboat. The applicability of the question to the target object only, is a reflection of its specificity. The results showed that the students asked questions that could sensibly be asked about superordinate categories of the target object more frequently on the unfamiliar objects than on the familiar objects. Not knowing much about an object, such as a capacitor, led to questions such as 'What is it used for?' applicable to any electric device or, indeed, to any device. More knowledge about batteries allowed asking specific questions such as 'How does it transform chemical energy into electric energy?' that could not be asked about any electrical device but only on batteries. This substantiates the relation described above: less knowledge of a questioner is associated with less accurate unknowns.

Finally, the findings of a study by Roth and Roychoudhury (1993) illustrate this relation in an instructional setting. The study was aimed at investigating the development of science students' process skills in open-inquiry laboratories of the 8th grade and the 11th grade. Among other results, they found that both the 8th grade students and the 11th grade students doing experiments in an unfamiliar domain started asking unfocused questions on vague, general variables such as 'type of plants' or 'light bulbs', that were measured qualitatively only: 'What different types of animal and plant life live in different amounts of light?', 'Do light bulbs act like resistors?'. Over the course of the project the questions, and unknowns, became more focused involving more specific variables: 'What is the relationship between the amount of light and leaf growth in one week? What is the relationship between the voltage across and the current through a light bulb?' Knowledge and accuracy of conscious unknowns were related again.

Instructional Implications

Monitoring one's own lack of knowledge and understanding is a basic component of the metacognitive strategies involved in learning (Hacker, Dunlosky, & Graesser, 1998; Schunk & Zimmerman, 2003) and crucially important for academic achievement (Wang, Haertel, & Walberg, 1993). Metacognitive strategies have been shown to be particularly relevant in science learning (Schraw, Crippen, & Hartley, 2006; Veenman, 2012; Zohar & Barzilai, 2013), when understanding science texts (Koch, 2001; Leopold & Leutner, 2015; Otero & Campanario, 1990) or when doing laboratory work (Metz, 2004; Rosa, 2014). The metacognitive awareness of unknowns, obstacles to understanding, anomalies, or problems is also an essential constituent of inquiry-based approaches to learning, as shown in the introduction. The awareness of one's own lack of understanding involves complex processes, as demonstrated in numerous studies on comprehension monitoring (Baker, 1989) calibration of comprehension (Lin & Zabrucky, 1998), or 'meta-comprehension' (Thiede, Griffin, Wiley, & Redford, 2009). Being aware of one's own lack of knowledge, even in the relatively simple case of unknowns about an object, is not a trivial task as the studies described in the previous sections attest.

One central conclusion following from the analyses above is that students' conscious unknowns should not be conceived as an unstructured void, or undifferentiated gaps in their knowledge, but as constructions endowed with certain structure. The awareness of different components of this structure varies depending on the ontological category of the target object, probably among several other factors. For instance, students from primary to tertiary education are especially aware of unknowns about the functions of artefacts, compared with unknowns about other intrinsic features, such as their parts. To be sure, the result should be situated within the context and simple tasks that were examined in the studies above: to freely ask about an unknown artefact available to the children in the Kemler-Nelson et al.'s (2004) experiment, or to declare what a student does not know about an object as a suggestion to write an encyclopedia in the Vaz-Rebelo et al.'s (2016) experiment. Keeping this in mind, the instructional implication of the results point to sensitivity of these students to problems related to what an artefact is for or how it performs a function, rather than to their intrinsic features or relations with other entities. Instruction decisions or curricular decisions based on science students' own problems and interests (Gallas, 1995) may take this into account.

A second main conclusion of the studies reviewed above concerns the effect of knowledge in students building their unknowns. Knowledge plays a decisive role in students' awareness of their own lack of knowledge. Elaborated unknowns should not be expected when students have little knowledge about an object or a process studied in a science class. A teacher involved in inquiry-based learning should expect that low levels of students' knowledge would result in difficulties to generate appropriate problems for inquiry. In the early stages of learning about a certain topic, low knowledge levels result in poorly defined unknowns expressed through vague and imprecise questions. As this study progresses, the students should be able to identify better defined obstacles and to ask deeper questions.

References

Baker, L. (1989). Metacognition, comprehension monitoring, and the adult reader. *Educational Psychology Review, 1*(1), 3–38.

Baram-Tsabari, A., Sethi, R. J., Bry, L., & Yarden, A. (2006). Using questions sent to an ask-a-scientist site to identify children's interests in science. *Science Education, 90*(6), 1050–1072. doi:10.1002/sce.20163

Baram-Tsabari, A., & Yarden, A. (2005). Characterizing children's spontaneous interests in science and technology. *International Journal of Science Education, 27*(7), 803–826. doi:10.1080/09500690500038389

Barton, M. E., & Komatsu, L. K. (1989). Defining features of natural kinds and artefacts. *Journal of Psycholinguistic Research, 18,* 433–447.

Chin, C., & Chia, L. G. (2004). Problem-based learning: Using students' questions to drive knowledge construction. *Science Education, 88*(5), 707–727.

Chin, C., & Kayalvizhi, G. (2002). Posing problems for open investigations: What questions do pupils ask? *Research in Science & Technological Education, 20*(2), 269–287. doi:10.1080/0263514022000030499

Driver, R., & Easley, J. (1978). Pupils and paradigms: A review of literature related to concept development in adolescent science students. *Studies in Science Education, 5,* 61–84.

Einsiedel, E. F., & Thorne, B. (1999). Public responses to uncertainty. In S. M. Friedman, S. Dunwoody, & C. L. Rogers (Eds.), *Communicating uncertainty: Media coverage of new and controversial science* (pp. 43–58). Mahwah, NJ: Lawrence Erlbaum Associates.

Einstein, A., & Infeld, L. (1938). *The evolution of physics.* Cambridge: Cambridge University Press.

Fellbaum, C. (1998). *Wordnet: An electronic lexical database.* Cambridge, MA: MIT Press.

Flammer, A. (1981). Towards a theory of question asking. *Psychological Research, 43,* 407–420.

Gallas, K. (1995). *Talking their way into science: Hearing children's questions and theories, responding with curricula.* New York, NY: Teachers College Press.

Graesser, A. C., Lu, S., Olde, B., Cooper-Pye, E., & Whitten, S. N. (2005). Question asking and eye tracking during cognitive disequilibrium: Comprehending illustrated texts on devices when the devices break down. *Memory & Cognition, 33,* 1235–1247.

Graesser, A. C., & McMahen, C. L. (1993). Anomalous information triggers questions when adults solve quantitative problems and comprehend stories. *Journal of Educational Psychology, 85,* 136–151.

Graesser, A. C., & Olde, B. A. (2003). How does one know whether a person understands a device? The quality of the questions the person asks when the device breaks down. *Journal of Educational Psychology, 95,* 524–536.

Graesser, A. C., Person, N. K., & Huber, J. D. (1992). Mechanisms that generate questions. In T. Lauer, E. Peacock, & A. C. Graesser (Eds.), *Questions and information systems* (pp. 167–187). Hillsdale, NJ: Lawrence Erlbaum Associates.

Gross, M. (2007). The unknown in process: Dynamic connections of ignorance, nonknowledge and related concepts. *Current Sociology, 55,* 742–759.

Hacker, D., Dunlosky, J., & Graesser, A. (2009). *Handbook of metacognition in education.* New York, NY: Routledge.

Hadzigeorgiou, Y. (1999). On problem situations and science learning. *School Science Review, 81*(294), 43–48.

Hmelo-Silver, C. E. (2004). Problem-based learning: What and how do students learn? *Educational Psychology Review, 16*(3), 235–266.

Ishiwa, K., Sanjosé, V., & Otero, J. (2013). Questioning and reading goals: Information-seeking questions asked on scientific texts read under different task conditions. *British Journal of Educational Psychology, 83*, 502–520.

Keil, F. C. (1989). *Concepts, kinds, and cognitive development*. Cambridge, MA: MIT Press.

Kemler-Nelson, D. G., Egan, L. C., & Holt, M. B. (2004). When children ask, 'what is it?' What do they want to know about artefacts? *Psychological Science, 15*, 384–389.

Koch, A. (2001). Training in metacognition and comprehension of physics texts. *Science Education, 85*(6), 758–768.

Leopold, C., & Leutner, D. (2015). Improving students' science text comprehension through metacognitive self-regulation when applying learning strategies. *Metacognition and Learning, 10*(3), 313–346.

Lin, L., & Zabrucky, K. (1998). Calibration of comprehension: Research and implications for education and instruction. *Contemporary Educational Psychology, 23*, 345–391.

Loyens, S. M., & Rikers, R. M. J. P. (2011). Instruction based on inquiry. *Handbook of Research on Learning and Instruction*, 361–381.

Maskill, R., & de Jesus, H. P. (1997). Pupils' questions, alternative frameworks and the design of science teaching. *International Journal of Science Education, 19*(7), 781–799.

Metz, K. (2004). Children's understanding of scientific inquiry: Their conceptualization of uncertainty in investigations of their own design. *Cognition and Instruction, 22*, 219–290.

Miller, G. A. (1990). Nouns in wordnet: A lexical inheritance system. *International Journal of Lexicography, 3*, 245–264.

Minner, D. D., Levy, A. J., & Century, J. (2010). Inquiry-based science instruction: What is it and does it matter? Results from a research synthesis years 1984 to 2002. *Journal of Research in Science Teaching, 47*, 474–496.

Miyake, N., & Norman, D. A. (1979). To ask a question one must know enough to know what is not known. *Journal of Verbal Learning and Verbal Behavior, 18*, 357–364.

Otero, J., & Campanario, J. M. (1990). Comprehension evaluation and regulation in learning from science texts. *Journal of Research in Science Teaching, 27*(5), 447–460.

Otero, J., & Gallástegui, J. R. (2016). Knowledge gaps on objects about which little is known: Lack of knowledge leads to questioning on basic levels of an ontological branch. *Learning and Individual Differences, 45*, 193–198. doi:10.1016/j.lindif.2015.11.009

Otero, J., & Ishiwa, K. (2014). Cognitive processing of conscious ignorance. In D. N. Rapp & J. L. G. Braasch (Eds.), *Processing inaccurate information: Theoretical and applied perspectives from cognitive science and the educational sciences*. Cambridge, MA: MIT Press.

Pedrosa-de-Jesus, H., Moreira, A., Lopes, B., & Watts, D. M. (2014). So much more than just a list: Exploring the nature of critical questioning in undergraduate sciences. *Research in Science & Technological Education, 32*(2), 115–134.

Rosa, C. T. W. (2014). *Metacognição no ensino de Física: Da concepção à aplicação.* Passo Fundo: Editora Universidade de Passo Fundo.

Rosenshine, B., Meister, C., & Chapman, S. (1996). Teaching students to generate questions: A review of the intervention studies. *Review of Educational Research, 66*(2), 181–221.

Roth, W. M., & Roychoudhury, A. (1993). The development of science process skills in authentic contexts. *Journal of Research in Science Teaching, 30,* 127–152.

Scardamalia, M., & Bereiter, C. (1992). Text-based and knowledge based questioning by children. *Cognition and Instruction, 9*(3), 177–199.

Schraw, G., Crippen, K. J., & Hartley, K. (2006). Promoting self-regulation in science education: Metacognition as part of a broader perspective on learning. *Research in Science Education, 36*(1–2), 111–139.

Stocking, S. H., & Holstein, L. S. (1993). Constructing and reconstructing scientific ignorance. *Knowledge: Creation, Diffusion, Utilization, 15,* 186–210.

Thiede, K. W., Griffin, T. D., Wiley, J., & Redford, J. S. (2009). Metacognitive monitoring during and after reading. In D. J. Hacker, J. Dunlosky, & A. C. Graesser (Eds.), *Handbook of metacognition in education* (pp. 85–106). New York, NY: Routledge.

Torres, T., Duque, J., Ishiwa, K., Sánchez, G., Solaz-Portolés, J. J., & Sanjosé, V. (2012). Preguntas de los estudiantes de Educación Secundaria ante dispositivos experimentales. *Enseñanza de las Ciencias, 30*(1), 49–60.

Van der Meij, H. (1990). Question asking: To know that you do not know is not enough. *Journal of Educational Psychology, 82,* 505–512.

Vaz-Rebelo, P., Fernandes, P., Morgado, J., Monteiro, A., & Otero, J. (2016). Students' conscious unknowns about artefacts and natural objects. *Educational Psychology, 36*(1), 176–190.

Veenman, M. V. (2012). Metacognition in science education: Definitions, constituents, and their intricate relation with cognition. In A. Zohar & Y. J. Dori (Eds.), *Metacognition in science education* (pp. 21–36). Dordrecht: Springer. Retrieved from http://www.springer.com/us/book/9789400721319

Wandersee, J. H., Mintzes, J. J., & Novak, J. D. (1994). Research on alternative conceptions in science. In D. L. Gabel (Ed.), *Handbook of research in science teaching and learning* (pp. 17–210). New York, NY: Palgrave Macmillan.

Wang, M. C., Haertel, G. D., & Walberg, H. J. (1993). Toward a knowledge base for school learning. *Review of Educational Research, 63*(3), 249–294. doi:10.3102/00346543063003249

Watts, D. M. (1983). A study of schoolchildren's alternative frameworks of the concept of force. *European Journal of Science Education, 5*(2), 217–230.

Watts, D. M., Gould, G., & Alsop, S. (1997). Questions of understanding: Categorising pupils' questions in science. *School Science Review, 79*(286), 57–63.

Zohar, A., & Barzilai, S. (2013). A review of research on metacognition in science education: Current and future directions. *Studies in Science Education, 49*(2), 121–169.

CHAPTER 11

Can 'Feed-Forward' Work?
University Students' Perceptions of Their Preflective Practice

Richard Malthouse and Jodi Roffey-Barentsen

Introduction

This chapter builds on the notion that studying for a degree in higher education requires an element of autonomous or independent learning. It is not uncommon, however, for some students to experience feelings of self-doubt, lack of confidence, even anxiety, during their time studying at a university. Arguably, constructive feedback on students' assessment tasks, which highlights strengths and identifies specific areas for improvement, can be an effective tool to alleviate some of those negative feelings. Furthermore, 'feed-forward', which offers students an insight into the learning outcomes, assessment criteria, and general expectations of them while on the programme of study, may remove some elements of the 'unknown' in relation to these expectations, thus reducing levels of nervousness or anxiety. As demonstrated in a study by Roffey-Barentsen (2015), students felt they would benefit from detailed information prior to the commencement of the programme, as this would help them manage their expectations. The concept of feed-forward is not dissimilar to the ideas of Ausubel (1960), who introduced the use of advance organisers, which offer relevant subsuming concepts in advance, as a strategy to enhance learning. We argue that for feed-forward to be most effective, students need to develop their *preflective* skills, that is, their thoughts and considerations prior to an action in preparation for a specific assessment task. In order to do so, they need to engage in reflective self-questioning. To provide a clearer idea of those preflective skills we conducted a survey, which sought the perceptions of students registered at a London university, with regard to their cognitive approaches to a new task. The outcomes of this research form the main focus and discussion of this chapter.

A Brief Summary of the Relevant Literature

Self-Regulated Learning

Students who attend university are expected to engage in self-directed learning (SDL) (Zimmerman & Shank, 1989a). SDL is concerned with the desire to achieve specific goals and is composed of three processes: metacognitive, motivational and behavioural (Low & Jin, 2012; Zimmerman, 1986). A significant factor that may determine an individual's ability to become self-directed is that of self-efficacy. This relates to an individual's perception of him or herself in relation to achievement and ability (Bandura, 2006). Zimmerman (1990, p. 5) highlights the need to 'distinguish between self-regulating processes, such as self-efficacy and strategies designed to optimise these processes such as intermittent goal setting'. He further observes that 'self-learning strategies refer to actions and processes directed at acquisition of information or skills that involves agency, purpose, and instrumentality perceptions by learners' (ibid.). Features associated with SDL are planning, monitoring, control and evaluation (Zimmerman & Shunk, 2001). These were attributed to Zimmerman's (1998, 2000, 2008) three cyclic-reflective stages:

1. Pre-actional
2. Actional
3. Post-actional.

The 'pre-actional stage' relates to setting future goals or learning outcomes. Associated actions could be setting goals and general planning. The 'actional stage' is concerned with the actual process of learning and involves monitoring one's self during this process. The 'post-actional' stage refers to reflective practices where the process is considered and evaluated. As Zimmerman (1990, p. 5) observes, '... self-regulated learners are distinguished by their (a) awareness of strategic relations between regulatory processes or responses and learning outcomes and (b) use of these strategies to achieve these academic goals'. It is a combination of behavioural strategies, methodical and organised use of motivational strategies and effective metacognitive strategies that are key to the success of the self-regulated learner (ibid.).

Student Concerns and Pressures

Literature draws attention to what Galatzer-Levy, Burton, and Bonanno (2012, p. 543) describe as the 'stressful nature of college life both in terms of the prevalence of daily stressors and in terms of what appears to be an unusually high occurrence of potentially traumatic life events'. These include the loss of previous social support networks combined with a change of environment, increased personal responsibility, the need to manage accommodation and financial concerns and the issues with new peer relationships (Vaez & LaFlamme, 2008; Voelker, 2003). These factors, combined with the associated academic pressures, can add a significant amount of pressure on students. Arguably, this pressure may distract or divert the student from academic tasks and prevent them from engaging in those tasks. Literature suggests that students possess coping strategies to deal with these concerns and stresses. For example, Fredrickson (1998, 2001) refers to the broaden-and-build theory, which posits that when an individual experiences positive emotion, this in turn engenders a willingness to embark on activities that enable that person to grow in thought and action. As a result, their personal resources are built upon, ranging from physical and intellectual resources to social and psychological resources (The Royal Society, 2004). Fredrickson (2002, p. 120) adds that, 'The bottom line message is that we should work to cultivate positive emotions in ourselves and in those around us not just as an end state, but also as a means to achieving psychological growth and improved psychological and physical health over time'. She advocates that, conversely, negative thoughts will lead to negative feelings and behaviours.

With this in mind, one role (or responsibility) of the university lecturer could be that of engendering a positive attitude by reducing the anxiety associated with study. This applies in particular to students in their first year of study, many of whom feel ill-prepared to perform academically at Level 4, as demonstrated by recent research that noted students who had newly entered a higher education programme agreed that it had been a 'daunting', 'scary', 'overwhelming' or 'terrifying' experience (Roffey-Barentsen, 2015).

What is the Purpose of Feedback?

As Taras (2003, p. 550) notes, feedback 'is not a freestanding piece of information, but forms part of a learning context where all the protagonists need to be engaged in the process'. Brown (2007) views feedback as a means of communicating vital comment enabling the students to engage in a self-reflecting process. Further, Rust (2002), stated the need for feedback to be prompt and that is should start with a positive, encouraging observation. Race (1995) agreed that feedback should be prompt and advocated that it should also ensure all aspects of the assessment are included. Those critical of assessment practice include Webster et al. (2000), who observed wider variations and interpretations in relation to criteria. Further, Higgins et al. note that 'the feedback comments convey a message based on an implicit understanding of particular academic terms, which in turn reflect a much more complex academic discourse, which in turn may be only partially understood by students' (Higgins et al., 2001, p. 272). In relation to these 'academic terms', Randall and Mirador (2003) viewed the tutor's feedback to be aimed not at the student but internal and external examiners and those within the university. On the other hand, Rust et al. (2003, p. 151), found 'students ... identified exemplars and further explanation as useful in making the assessment criteria more comprehensible'. Furthermore, Chanok (2000) regarded students who did not recognise the value of feedback; either did not understand comments offered or simply did not heed them.

However, characteristic of Brown (2007), Chanok (2000), Higgins et al. (2001), Race (1995), Randel and Mirador's (2002), Rust (2002) and Webster et al.'s (2000) observations are that feedback is generally provided at the end of a process. This need not necessarily be the case. We propose a system of feeding-forward into a piece of work, rather than simply 'feeding back' (Higgins et al., 2001, p. 274). We view feedback as something that is offered at the start of learning rather than at the end and we share Orsmond et al.'s (2000) observation that feedback is inseparable to the learning process. Sadler (1983, p. 74), a proponent of feedforward identified that: 'students should be given an opportunity and incentive to rework and resubmit papers, with continuous rather than single-shot access to evaluative feedback during the reworking'. Rust (2002), too, recognised the importance of feedforward and stated that students should benefit from suggestions of how to improve on their next assignment.

We go further than this and believe that feedforward should consider not just feedback upon an assignment or piece of work but rather it should encompass other dispositions of a student. In which case we suggest that feedforward should include guidance on all aspect of the preparatory tasks a student is likely to engage in, including:

1. Student expectations
2. Lecturer expectations
3. Use of academic services (e.g., the library)
4. Supporting mechanisms
5. Writing academically
6. Time management
7. The grade criteria
8. Marking conventions
9. Study skills
10. Deadlines
11. Exemplars
12. Opportunities for formative comment
13. Engaging in individual reflective practice
14. Engaging in group reflective practice.

This list above represents elements that can be included within feedforward. The benefits are that they can allay students' anxiety, fears, doubts and uncertainties. As a result, we suggest that students' concerns and worries will be reduced and Fredrikson's (1998, 2001) broaden-and-build theory may pave the way for a successful university experience.

PReflection

Here we bring together two strands of our own work over time. The first employs a particularly Deweyesque approach to reflective practice because central to John Dewey's philosophy is the concept of questioning in both his theory of 'inquiry' and his focus on practical problem-solving. Moreover, for Dewey, questioning *is* reflective thinking. He noted that reflective thinking is better than other forms of thinking (such as streams of consciousness, day dreams or beliefs) (1971, p. 4) because it forms an ordered chain of thoughts. The purpose of questioning, he said, is to bring about an answer to a problem in which the problem itself is dissolved, no longer exists.

The second strand explores further the notion of Situated Reflective Practice (SRP) (Malthouse, 2012; Roffey-Barentsen & Malthouse, 2013; Malthouse & Roffey-Barentsen, 2014; Malthouse, Roffey-Barentsen, & Watts, 2014, 2015). Situated Reflective Practice builds on ideas from Schön (1987), Kolb (1984) and Gibbs (1988), and adds to this body of knowledge in a way that enables people to make sense of their world by observing the extended or external influences. Essentially, it is the fact that the influences *can* be external that distinguishes this from traditional reflective practice. Questioning itself draws upon a considerable body of work on the nature of questions and question-asking (Pedrosa-de-Jesus, Almeida, Teixeira-Dias, & Watts, 2006; Pedrosa-de-Jesus, Watts, & da Silva Lopes, 2009). The overlap with SRP provides valuable insights into personal and professional reflective practice. The purpose of the work we discuss here is to draw upon a phenomenological perspective to examine our respondents' particular situations and to see these as 'profound centres of human experience' (Cresswell, 2004, p. 23). One form of reflective questioning rose to prominence in the 1980s and 1990s under the label 'self-questioning'. This work predominated in studies of textual analysis, comprehension of texts and narrative, and the production of writing. In this sense, self-questioning is regarded as a cognitive, rather than a meta-cognitive, strategy that can help students focus attention, organise new material and finally integrate the new information with existing knowledge (Doerr & Tripp, 1999; Glaubman & Ofir, 1997; King, 1989, 1992; Wong, 1985).

The intention is that novices ask the right questions of themselves, learn how to think like an expert and, eventually, organise their knowledge like an expert. PReflection is an extension of our studies and the associated literature to date, however, in this case we introduce a temporal change. Traditionally, reflective practice takes place towards the end of a phenomenon, whereas PReflection takes place at the start. It is anticipated that self-questioning will be an important aspect of this study because it can be argued that it is only the students themselves who actually know how they are functioning. Further, the introduction of Situated Reflective Practice will enable the students to recognise what they can change and what they cannot. As a result, coping strategies can be designed and implemented.

PReflection is the processes of thought prior to engaging with an academic task. The objectives of our study have been to identify the nature of thought prior to an action; to differentiate the nature of that thought to a deliberate or casual contemplation, and to identify students' perceptions in relation to preparation for a specific task. Our broad hypothesis was that students employ various cognitive strategies prior to a task such as writing an essay or assignment, preparing for an exam or presentation. The purpose of the research was to identify those strategies with a view to supporting the students with these processes. The anticipated benefits included an enhancement in the students' learning experience and better achievement/success rates for the students involved. This research project took the form of a survey and relied on a generally accepted technique of an on-line questionnaire.

The study focused on the survey responses of 175 students registered at a London university. It is anticipated that this work will enable students' understanding of themselves by use of self-questioning and support them with their planning processes. The most important point of a student's learning journey is not the last step at the graduation ceremony, but the steps taken at each assessment from when they first enter a university programme to their final piece of work (such as a dissertation or even a post-graduate work or a thesis). It is at those stages, by informing them of alternative strategies, that we can enhance the students' learning experience and achievements. The new knowledge takes the form of insights into the students' perceptions of themselves and their approach to study, as a result we will be able to design appropriate learning interventions. This in turn will assist with retaining students.

The Research Methods and Analysis of Data

It was anticipated that by teasing out the different cognitive strategies students employ, teachers can offer these for consideration as alternative strategies to other students. We all approach tasks in a way we have always done it and feel comfortable with. In a Meno's paradox fashion, you don't know what you don't know. Therefore, for teachers to offer alternative strategies might widen the range of tools student can utilise in planning their work. Ultimately, our aim is to have a positive impact on successful teaching and learning, resulting in enhanced student achievement. This heightened rate of success may impact upon the economic and social opportunities available to the students, thus touching upon areas of equality. The participating university benefits from a diverse student population, with a number of students entering university via an untraditional route. Offering strategies and opportunities to succeed may contribute to address issues of inequality for those non-traditional students.

The research was conducted in the form of an online survey. All registered students at a London university were invited to complete this survey, which consisted of 20 questions. As mentioned, the survey was online, making use of Bristol Online Surveys (BOS), a tool for creating online surveys used by over 300 organisations in the UK and internationally, including 130 universities (BOS website, 2015). The survey was available for one month. The questionnaires were anonymous; it was assumed that those participating offered their consent by actually undertaking the survey. The university's Research Ethics Committee granted ethical approval for the research. The data collected was analysed quantitatively; responses were coded, summarised and tabulated.

Questions and Responses Contained in the Survey

The survey was divided into three parts:
1. Myself
2. My forms of 'PReflection'
3. My Learning Habits.

1. *Myself*
All respondents (175) to the survey were registered at a London university. The majority were female (72.6%), with two thirds (67%) aged over 25 years old. As shown in Figure 11.1, most respondents were registered on undergraduate programmes.

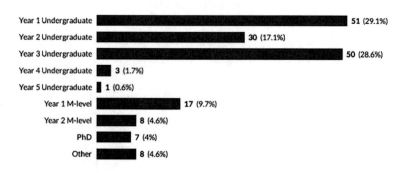

FIGURE 11.1 Respondents and their programmes

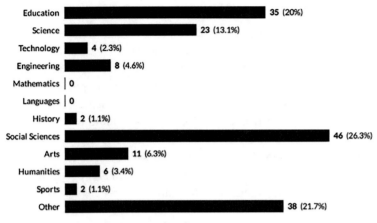

FIGURE 11.2 Respondents' areas of study

As indicated in Figure 11.2, the main areas of study were Education and Social Sciences, however, over 20% of respondents were registered on 'Other' programmes.

When asked whether respondents would describe themselves as a naturally reflective person, 97% agreed. This high percentage surprised us – however, there are some areas for caution: did only reflective students complete the survey? In other words, did those who do not reflect decline to participate in the research? Further, without offering a definition, can we be certain that we all mean the same by being 'reflective'? It is not always clear how systematic reflection is different from other types of thought (Rodgers, 2002, p. 842); therefore, it cannot be assumed that all participants used the same or even similar interpretation. Most respondents (77%), however, did agree that when they really think hard about something, like an essay, their thinking is different from normal everyday thinking. This type of thinking may be PReflective.

The next part of the survey was relevant to the 'feed-forward' question. The data suggested that just over 90% of the respondents preferred to start thinking about a learning task well in advance of the submission deadline, with only 9% claiming they did not prefer this (Figure 11.3).

The above is a surprising outcome, as anecdotal stories from some of our students suggest that they leave starting their tasks, such as writing an assignment, too late, which may then result in panic and last-minute, or even late

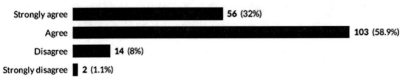

FIGURE 11.3 Thinking ahead about a learning task

submissions (or, in the worst scenario, academic misconduct, in the form of plagiarism or the buying of assignments).

Students at the participating university generally have access to the learning outcomes, content and assessment criteria, of each of their modules of study, at the beginning of the academic year. It was therefore pleasing to note that the majority of respondents, 80%, agreed that they usually have a good understanding of the task with some fairly clear ideas about how to complete it, before they embark upon it (Figure 11.4). In relation to the 'feed-forward' question, it therefore appears that offering students module/assessment information early, allows them to gain a good insight into what is expected of them. This clarity, in its turn, may contribute to reduce the feelings of stress and anxiety mentioned earlier.

2 My Forms of PReflection

The next set of questions focused upon the types of thinking respondents claimed to have undertaken before starting a task. Despite the suggested clarity above, approximately 80% of the respondents described their pre-thinking as 'muddled', as they first approached a task. However, this thinking did become steadily clearer as they engaged with the task in more detail. When asked about relying on their hunches and intuition with regard to a task, the responses were split, as 55% agreed but 45% disagreed (Figure 11.5).

Respondents did, however, agree on a preference to analyse tasks systematically, break them down to their component parts and think about each one of those components in more depth (Figure 11.6).

Respondents further agreed that their PReflection really depends on the exact nature of the task, and that they change their way of thinking depending on that nature (Figure 11.7).

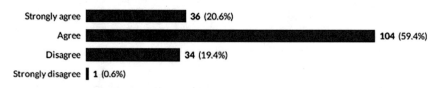

FIGURE 11.4   Providing information early

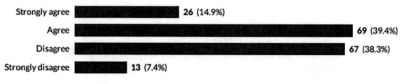

FIGURE 11.5   Clear thinking about tasks

CAN 'FEED-FORWARD' WORK?   139

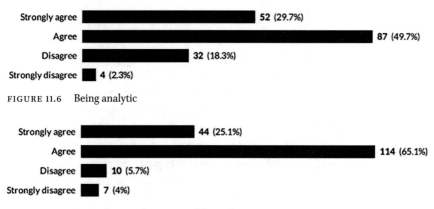

FIGURE 11.6   Being analytic

FIGURE 11.7   Dependent on the nature of the task

Most of the respondents (over 80%) agreed that their early thinking is unspoken, as they try to let the task 'sit in my head' for a while before they get started. This suggests that students try to think about how to address a task by themselves, without sharing their thoughts with peers and others. This solemn approach was confirmed, as 34% of the respondents who agreed that they only start to think about tasks once they have talked it over with other people and heard their views.

3   My Learning Habits

The third part of the survey focussed on the respondents' learning habits.

It confirms that most respondents (65%) start to think about a task before they actually address the task. However, 35% do not engage in this process and leave the thinking until they start working on the task properly, which is presumably when a submission date looms. For these students, it seems, that 'feed-forward' could be less beneficial. With regard to gathering information before embarking upon a task, with a view start thinking about how to answer it, over 80% of respondents agreed that they like to do this from a range of sources (Figure 11.8).

The next question focussed on the importance of verbal instructions, compared to written ones published in a handbook or module guide, which are mostly available from the beginning of an academic year and could therefore be

FIGURE 11.8   Used a range of sources

an element of a 'feed-forward' process. Nearly 60% of respondents agreed that they preferred spoken instructions rather than relying on the written ones. It cannot be assumed, however, that these students do not cogitate over the written instructions. It is interesting to note that students do appear to value verbal instructions, maybe to illuminate what is expected of them in terms of an academic task, however, as demonstrated above, they do not appreciate discussing their approach to addressing a task with their peers or others. Finally, 73% of the respondents agreed that they need to fully understand a task before they can start thinking about it, which leaves a maybe worryingly 27% who will consider addressing a task without fully understanding what is required of them, thus potentially spending time on studying irrelevant areas (for that task).

With the above in mind, the final part of this chapter discusses a model that may support the development of preflective skills (see Figure 11.9).

The PReflection Model
1   Recognition

The first step is for the student to recognise his or her own preflective thoughts and associated behaviours when approaching a new task. Some of these may have become habits or tendencies that they, so far, have been unaware of. The student may realise that one initially tends to feel uncertain, muddled or confused about a task; he or she may rely heavily on your hunches and intuition about what needs to be done, or feel unable to start the task until you fully understand what is required. For others it may be second nature to immediately analyse a task systematically, breaking it down to its component parts and to think about each of those components individually. Letting the task 'sit in your head' for a while before getting started is another frequently occurring habit, while gathering as much information from a range of sources before starting to think about how to answer a task, is another.

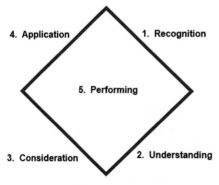

FIGURE 11.9   The PReflective model

2   Understanding

The second step requires you to understand why you do what you do. Akin to critical thinking, this process involves the ability to question and reason, but this time with yourself. It requires you to be honest with yourself, which may, on occasion, be a bit unpleasant or even painful. For instance, if your initial response to a task is that of confusion, you may have to look into that and possibly discover that you use the 'confusion' as a strategy to appear helpless, which then results in what is sometimes referred to as 'spoon-feeding' by a teacher or more confident peer. Thoughts can be limiting, preventing you to progress. It would, therefore be most helpful to you to understand why these thoughts occur.

3   Consideration

Thirdly, now you understand why you think and behave the way you do, you can start thinking of and considering alternative approaches. As well as doing this individually, you may consider sharing your thoughts. Working in groups provides an environment where you can listen to each other and hear how others approach a task. Maybe it does not always have to start with a state of 'confusion', as in the example above.

4   Application

After considering a range of approaches, as discussed with peers in your groups, the next step is to apply one or some of them, depending on what you think may work for you. For instance, the once confused person might like to try gathering information in relation to the task, or may take a more analytical approach. It is important that it is you who has decided to try the new approach and not a teacher or any other party.

5   Performing

The final step of the model is that of performing, or trying out the alternative strategy, when embarking upon a task. On some occasions, the alternative approach may be more effective, on others it may not be. However, trying out alternatives will offer you a choice of approach and a deeper understanding and awareness of yourself. If what you do is not working for you or if you feel your efforts are not constructive, it may be appropriate to re-engage with the model.

To summarise the project, we are suggesting that the respondents, who were all students, perceive themselves to be reflective. Further, they recognise that the type of thinking they engage in before embarking upon a new task is different in nature from everyday thinking, which we refer to as preflection. They like to start the thinking process well in advance of a deadline, and the majority generally has clear ideas of what is expected of them. Feed forward strategies, which, according to the survey, need to include verbal instructions, are therefore of the utmost importance in the support of independent learning and potentially in the reduction of anxiety and stress in the relation to 'the unknown'. In our view, students with well-developed preflective skills will be able access and benefit from the feed forward strategies offered the most.

References

Ausubel, D. (1960). The use of advance organizers in the learning and retention of meaningful verbal material. *Journal of Educational Psychology, 51*(5), 267–272.

Bandura, A. (2006). Guide for constructing self-efficacy scales. In F. Pajeres & T. Urdan (Eds.), *Self-efficacy beliefs of adolescents* (Vol. 5, pp. 307–337). Hershey, PA: Information Age Publishing.

Bristol Online Surveys. (2016). *Homepage*. Retrieved March 2, 2016, from https://www.onlinesurveys.ac.uk/about/

Brown, J. (2007). Feedback: The student experience. *Research in Post-Compulsory Education, 12*(1), 33–51.

Brunel University. (2016). *About campus*. Retrieved March 2, 2016, from http://www.brunel.ac.uk/about/campus

Chanock, K. (2000). Comments on essays: Do students understand what tutors write? *Teaching in Higher Education, 5*(1), 95–105.

Cresswell, T. (2004). *Place, a short introduction*. Maiden, MA: Blackwell Publishing.

Dewey, J. (1971). *How we think: A restatement of the relation of reflective thinking to the educative process*. Chicago, IL: Henry Regnery.

Fredrickson, B. L. (2001). The role of positive emotions in positive psychology. *American Psychologist, 56*, 218–266.

Fredrickson, B. L. (2002). Positive emotions. In S. R. Syder & S. J. Lopes (Eds.), *Handbook of positive psychology*. Oxford: Oxford University Press.

Galatzer-Levy, I. R., Burton, C. L, & Bonanno, G. A. (2012). Coping flexibility, potentially traumatic life events, and resilience: A prospective study of college student adjustment. *Journal of Social and Clinical Psychology, 31*(6), 542–567.

Gibbs, G. (1988). *Learning by doing: A guide to teaching and learning methods*. Oxford: Oxford Polytechnic.

Glaubman, R., Ofir, L., & Glaubman, H. (1997). Effects of self-directed learning, story comprehension, and self-questioning in Kindergarten. *Journal of Educational Research, 90*(6), 361–374.

Higgins, R., Hartley, P., & Skelton, A. (2001). Getting the message across: The problem of communicating assessment feedback. *Teaching in Higher Education, 6*(2), 269–274.

Kolb, D. (1984). *Experiential learning: Experiences as the source of learning and development*. Upper Saddle River, NJ: Prentice Hall.

Low, R., & Jin, P. (2012). Self-regulated learning. In L. N. Seed (Ed.), *Encyclopaedia of the sciences of learning* (pp. 3015–3018). New York, NY: Springer.

Malthouse, R. (2012). *Reflecting blues: Perceptions of policing students in relation to reflective practice and associated skills.* Saarbrucken: Lambert Academic Publishing.

Malthouse, R., & Roffey-Barentsen, J. (2014). Teachers' reflective practice: I'm a scientist. In D. M. Watts (Ed.), *Debates in science education.* Routledge.

Malthouse, R., Roffey-Barentsen, J., & Watts, D. M. (2014). Reflectivity, reflexivity and situated reflective practice. *Professional Development in Education, 40*(4), 597–609.

Malthouse, R., Roffey-Barentsen, J., & Watts, D. M. (2015). Reflective questions, self-questioning and managing professionally situated practice. *Research in Education, 94*(1), 71–87.

Orsmond, P., Merry, S., & Reiling, K. (2000). The use of student derived marking criteria in peer and self-assessment. *Assessment and Evaluation in Higher Education, 25*(1), 21–38.

Pedrosa-de-Jesus, M. H., Almeida, P., Teixeira-Dias, J. J., & Watts, M. (2006). Students' questions – building a bridge between Kolb's learning styles and approaches to learning. *Education + Training, 48*(2–3), 97–111.

Pedrosa-de-Jesus, M. H., Watts, D. M., & da Silva Lopes, B. (2009). Teaching approaches in higher education: The role of classroom questioning. In J. Fanghanel, N. Rege Colet, & D. Bernstein (Eds.), *London scholarship of teaching and learning 7th international conference (2008) proceedings.* London: University London.

Race, P. (1995). What has assessment done for us – and to us? In P. Knight (Ed.), *Assessment for learning in higher education* (1st ed.). London: Kogan Page.

Randall, M., & Mirador, J. (2003). How well am I doing? Using a corpus-based analysis to investigate tutor and institutional messages in comment sheets. *Assessment and Evaluation in Higher Education, 28*(5), 515–526.

Rodgers, C. (2002). Defining reflection: Another look at John Dewey and reflective thinking. *Teachers College Record, 104*(4), 842–866.

Roffey-Barentsen, J. (2015). Smoothing the ride: An exploration of students' experiences and perceptions of the transition from a level 3 qualification to a higher education programme (Level 4) in a further education institution. *Research in Teacher Education, 2*(5), 12–16.

Roffey-Barentsen, J., & Malthouse, R. (2009). *Reflective practice in the lifelong learning sector.* Exeter: Learning Matters.

Roffey-Barentsen, J., & Malthouse, R. (2013). *Reflective practice in education and training* (2nd ed.). London: Sage Publications.

Royal Society. (2004). The broaden-and-build theory of positive emotions. *Philosophical Transactions of the Royal Society B: Biological Sciences, 359*(1449), 1367–1377.

Rust, C. (2002). The impact of assessment on student learning: How can the research literature practically help to inform the development of departmental assessment strategies and learner-centred assessment practices? *Active Learning in Higher Education, 3*(2), 145–158.

Rust, C., Price, M., & O'Donovan, B. (2003). Improving students' learning by developing their understanding of assessment criteria and processes. *Assessment and Evaluation in Higher Education, 28*(2), 147–164.

Sadler, D. R. (1983). Evaluation and the improvement of academic learning. *Journal of Higher Education, 54*, 60–79.

Schön, D. (1987). *Educating the reflective practitioner*. San Francisco, CA: Jossey-Bass.

Taras, M. (2003). To feedback or not to feedback in student self-assessment. *Assessment and Evaluation in Higher Education, 28*(5), 549–565.

University of East London. (2015). *Homepage*. Retrieved March 2, 2016, from https://www.uel.ac.uk/

Vaez, M., & LaFlamme, L. (2008). Experience stress, psychological symptoms, self-rated health and academic achievement: A longitudinal study of Swedish university students. *Social Behavior and Personality, 36*, 183–196.

Voelker, R. (2003). Mounting student depression taxing campus mental health services. *Journal of the American Medical Association, 289*, 2055–2056.

Webster, F., Pepper, D., & Jenkins, A. (2000). Assessing the undergraduate dissertation. *Assessment and Evaluation in Higher Education, 25*(1), 72–80.

Wong, B. Y. L. (1985). Self-questioning instructional research: A review. *Review of Educational Research, 55*, 227–268.

Zimmerman, B. J. (1986). Development of self-regulated learning: Which are the key sub processes? *Contemporary Educational Psychology, 16*, 307–313.

Zimmerman, B. J. (1989a). Models of self-regulated learning and academic achievement. In B. J. Zimmerman & D. H. Shunk (Eds.), *Self-regulated learning and academic achievement: Theory, research and practice* (pp. 1–25). New York, NY: Springer.

Zimmerman, B. J. (1998). Developing self-fulfilling cycles of academic regulation: An analysis of exemplary instructional models. In D. H. Shunk & B. J. Zimmerman (Eds.), *Self-regulated learning and academic achievement: Theory, research and practice* (pp. 1–25). New York, NY: Springer.

Zimmerman, B. J. (2000). Attaining self-regulation: A social cognitive perspective. In M. Boekarts, P. R. Pintrich, & M. Ziedner (Eds.), *Handbook of self-regulation* (pp. 13–39). San Diego, CA: Academic Press.

Zimmerman, B. J. (2008). Investigating self-regulation and motivation: Historical background, methodological developments and future prospects. *American Educational Research Journal, 45*(1), 166–183.

Zimmerman, B. J., & Shunk, D. (2001). Theorise of self-regulated learning and academic achievement: An overview and analysis. In B. J. Zimmerman & D. H. Shunk (Eds.), *Self-regulated learning and academic achievement theoretical perspectives* (pp. 1–37). Mahawa, NJ: Lawrence Erlbaum Associates.

CHAPTER 12

Research, Design, Approaches and Methods

Helena Pedrosa-de-Jesus, Mike Watts and Betina da Silva Lopes

Introduction

This chapter describes the research endeavours surrounding processes of teaching and learning that have been undertaken from 2000 to 2015 at the University of Aveiro, Portugal. This research has involved close and continuous collaboration between academics and educational researchers. While it is a chapter that stands by itself, it can also be read as an introduction to each of the Chapters 13 to 17 to follow, which focus on specific outputs and outcomes of the project. This chapter is composed by four major sections: (i) research context and brief overview; (ii) paradigmatic models that sustained the investigations; (iii) the global research approach and specific research styles and (iv) the data gathering and data analysis strategies we used. We are very aware of the challenges associated with research into real-time learning and teaching and, rather than generate a sense of foreboding in those who wish to attempt something similar, we write 'in the positive' so that, despite the challenges, we illustrate affirmative ways to work within naturalistic settings. The research outputs, as well as the experience *per se*, make us definitely say: go for it!

Research Context and Brief Overview

The 'Aveiro research project' is relatively unique in researching teaching and learning processes at university level: very few involve the construction of knowledge and maturation of research expertise in one particular context over a period of fifteen years, being supported by three public research grants, namely:

1. A study of student generated questions in undergraduate sciences (POCTI/36473/CED/2000).
2. A study of university teaching, learning and assessment using students-generated questions (PPCDT/CED/59336/2004).
3. A study of academic development in universities through innovative approaches in teaching, assessment and feedback (PTDC/CPE-CED/117516/2010).

The first grant supported the first stage of the research endeavour, developed between 2000 and 2005. During this period innovative teaching and learning strategies were designed and implemented, principally in the context of

TABLE 12.1 Research around undergraduate science at the University of Aveiro (2000–2015)

Study	Research focus	Research aims
1	The role of questions on the learning of chemistry in Higher Education (Neri de Souza, 2006) Further reading: http://hdl.handle.net/10773/4996	Understand the learning difficulties of undergraduate chemistry students Design and implement didactical strategies that promote students questioning
2	Students Questions and learning styles: a study with science students in Higher Education (Almeida, 2007) Further reading: http://hdl.handle.net/10773/1461	Identify and describe the relationship(s) between learning styles and students' questions Develop didactical strategies that optimize the teaching and learning processes
3	Students questions and the assessment in Chemistry (Moreira, 2006) Further reading: http://ria.ua.pt/handle/10773/3370	Align teaching, learning and assessment processes using students questions Design problem cases in undergraduate chemistry that can be used for formative and summative purposes
4	Researching the learning, teaching and assessment at universities in undergraduate biology context using students' questions Further reading: Pedrosa-de-Jesus, Silva Lopes & Watts (2009a, b)	Characterize teaching, learning and assessment processes in a new context, namely Higher Education of Biology Design and implement two didactical strategies based on students' questions "Question Box" and "Questions in Biology" Online Discussion Forum (ODF). Analyse the characteristics of oral and written questions of students

(cont.)

TABLE 12.1 Research around undergraduate science at the University of Aveiro (2000–2015) (*cont.*)

Study	Research focus	Research aims
5	The role of questioning for the alignment between teaching, learning and assessment (Moreira, 2012) Further reading: http://ria.ua.pt/handle/10773/10233	Align teaching, learning and assessment processes using students questions Design problem cases in undergraduate biology (Genetics, Microbiology) that can be used for formative and summative purposes
6	Teaching Approaches and Questioning Practices in Higher Education (Silva Lopes, 2013) Further reading: http://hdl.handle.net/10773/11930	Design, implement and disseminate pedagogical strategies promotors of university teachers reflection about teaching and learning Create pedagogical opportunities for undergraduate students questioning Identify, describe and understand the relationship between concepts of Teaching and Learning and Questioning practices at university level Explore the possible impact of teachers' questioning on learners' outputs.
7	A study of academic development in universities through innovative approaches in teaching, assessment and feedback Further reading: http://edaun.web.ua.pt/	Design of innovative e-based teaching, learning, assessment and feedback strategies that contribute to a constructive alignment between learning and teaching Construct knowledge about academic development by researching the implementation of didactical innovation in naturalistic research environments

undergraduate chemistry, involving one university teacher and his students throughout three sequential studies (see Table 12.1) The research findings here, as well as the field knowledge obtained, gave the educational research team encouragement and motivation to embrace a second science disciplinary area, namely biology, and to include a greater number of university teachers, leading to a second application for public funding with the proposal entitled *A study of university teaching, learning and assessment using students-generated questions*.

Within the second research grant, and from 2007 to 2011, the original project design and philosophy was 'replicated' at the Department of Biology of the University of Aveiro, with the direct collaboration of five academics who specialised in domains of Genetics, Microbiology and Evolution, and who were involved in lecturing both undergraduate and master students (see Table 12.1, namely studies 4, 5 and 6).

Finally, during the year 2010, the need to assess the global impact of what had been investigated and intervened along the previous twelve years led to the third funding application. The grant obtained was applied in the development of the final study, entitled *A study of academic development in universities through innovative approaches in teaching, assessment and feedback* (see Table 12.1, study 7), aimed at reflecting how far the global research-intervention strategy had contributed to a conceptual and empirical shift from the traditional 'teacher, experiences, lectures' to a 'students, experiences, activities' focused model (Nicholas, 2008).

Considering a holistic perspective of this 15-year research endeavour, we stand alongside Cohen, Manion, and Morrison (2003) when they say:

> Though styles of research can be located within a particular research paradigm, this does not necessitate the researcher selecting a single paradigm, nor does it advocate a paradigmatic-driven research. (p. 182)

The project philosophy, then, can be associated with two major paradigms: interpretative-naturalistic and socio-critical. Our broad research aims can be categorised as conceptual or basic in nature (Coutinho, 2011), since we aspired to describe and understand the characteristics of several phenomena related to the quality of teaching and learning at university level. These have included: Misconceptions in science learning (Study 1), Learning Styles (Study 2), Alignment between teaching, and assessment strategies according to learning goals (Study 3 & 4), Critical thinking (Study 5), Preferential Teaching Approaches (Study 6) and Academic Development (Study 7).

Within these seven 'component' studies, we have explored the relation between the formulation and answering of questions, since questions, as we have discussed in previous studies (both in this book and elsewhere), are seen to be crucial for enhancing the quality of teaching and learning at this level. From the very start, we were aware of the complexity and the multiplicity of our focus of attention, even though we believed it was possible to grasp the 'essence' (Poisson, 1991), the 'heart' (Morin, 2008) of concepts and behaviours in these zones of teaching and learning. We also believe that the outputs we obtained are useful – not least for the problematisation and interpretation of such phenomena for other contexts, other universities. So, despite the embedding of these studies in a specific context (Portuguese chemistry and biology education at higher level) and in a specific time (2000–2015), we look for broader generalisation within the context of the Bologna Reform implementation in Portugal and beyond.

Instead of perceiving the naturalistic teaching and learning setting as a handicap, we believe strongly that it is a positive dimension to research. We have collected the majority of data in real-life settings (namely lectures, tutorials or laboratorial classes) or within/through 'real' complementary pedagogical strategies (such as online repositories of resources – Moodle, e-mails between teachers and students, 'chat' spaces and online discussion forums). Interviews with university teachers were focused principally on their pedagogic decisions, motivations, feelings about lectures or during lectures, or their face-to-face interactions with other teachers and students. Interviews with students were also concerned primarily with learning and any difficulties related to the lectures they attended and/or the tasks they had to perform throughout a specific academic semester. The essence of university teaching-learning dynamics was not changed radically, but underwent a series of small, incremental shifts in a relatively smooth and realistic way. We deliberately avoided 'high profile' or individualistic 'showmanship' strategies and interventions, not least because these risked the exhaustion of the collaborating academics and are difficult to replicate by others. In this sense, the slogan 'less is more' became central to our considerations. It is also important to highlight that none of the seven studies that comprise the Aveiro Project was aimed at establishing positivistic relationships between variables (Bodgan & Biklen, 1994), identifying causes and consequences. The overall aim was unremittingly qualitative, ways of creating opportunities to identify aspects that provide evidence for possible interrelationships, and then using those as a basis of sustained reflection about teaching and learning, generating helpful tools to manage this in a more efficient and 'joyful' approach.

The ultimate aim has been to help in overcoming real problems, and has led us to adopt the socio-critical nature of our research. It is our conviction that research in education can be of an applied nature, in the sense that it should be concerned with obtaining outputs and outcomes that have potential to solve problems and challenges in education. Educational research can be – and has been, in our case – used as an instrument for informed interventions and transformation. While some educational research is strongly ideologically oriented within a socio-critical approach, this has not been our mode of operation. Our research has focussed on individuals and how they and we can contribute to maximise positive learning-teaching experiences at a personal level – their individual interactions with others in the classroom and work environments. In this sense we assume that the research endeavour 'flowed' between two poles: (i) where data collected during sessions was the prime responsibility of the researcher only, and so was 'researcher dependent', and (ii) the second pole of 'participative researcher', where the emergence of data was deliberately generated in co-management with the teachers, for example through the design and implementation of a new strategy with the support of the educational researchers.

Research Approach and Research Styles

The task of producing sound, innovative, and informative research is formidable. As noted earlier, and given our aim of investigating naturalistic teaching and learning environments, our primary instinct has been to use qualitative approaches to research. Our conviction is that this brings high context validity (Silva Lopes, Pedrosa-de-Jesus, & Watts, 2016) in the sense that other teachers and researchers will recognise the characteristics, the constraints and potentials, quite easily. Sometimes termed the ecological validity of a study, it means that the methods, materials and setting of the study work are as close as possible to the real-world that is being examined. Bronfenbrenner's (1977, 1979) classic definition of ecological validity refers to the extent to which the environment experienced by the subjects in a scientific investigation has the properties it is supposed or assumed to have by the experimenter' (Bronfenbrenner, 1977, p. 16). In our studies, the experimental environment has been the real-world. For us the proximity between researchers and the object of investigation (teachers and students) was crucial, face-to-face interactions were deliberately sought, but never imposed. We assumed right from the start that the outputs of our research would be the product of interaction between the researchers and the subjects under study (Bisquerra, 1996; Goetz & Le Compte, 1998). While we are conversant with the Hawthorne Effect, that there will be behaviour changes due simply to the act of research on respondents, we worked to minimise this through increasing familiarity: the teachers and students were fully informed of the research and seemed to accept the researchers quickly as part of their regular teaching and learning 'landscape'.

The close interaction between the researchers and the participants in the study also justified the emerging shape of the global research design. The research strategy and the complementarity between the seven studies were not fully defined right from the start, a property that is described in detail by authors such as Gray (2004), Quivy and Campenhoudt (2008) as well as Robson (2002). In our case, the sense of emergence enabled the choice of design methodology that contributed to sustained and critical reflections about the success, or failure of the education reforms that were being explored.

Data collection and analysis procedures evolved over the course of the research project in response to what was experienced and learned in the earlier phases of the study. In particular, if the research questions and goals changed in response to new information and insights, then the research design needed to change accordingly. The methodological approach of the Aveiro Project, then, is composed primarily by the fusion of three main research styles, namely case study, ethnographical studies and action-research.

Case Studies

Case Studies focus on the detailed description of well-defined identities, such as an institution, a programme, a curricular unit or a person (Coutinho, 2011; Ponte, 2004). As Willig (2008) asserts, case studies are not necessarily characterised by the methods used to collect and analyse data, but rather 'its focus on a particular unit of analysis: a case' (p. 74). The research is deliberately particularistic, since it focuses on specific situations that are to be considered unique (Yin, 2003). In our case, naturalist case studies sought to describe issues from the ground-up, embedded in the particular context of the science laboratory, lecture hall or tutorial room. Case studies were used, for example, in Study 2 (Almeida, Pedrosa-de-Jesus, & Watts 2011); Study 4 (Pedrosa-de-Jesus & Silva Lopes, 2009a; Silva Lopes, 2013); and Study 7 (Pedrosa-de-Jesus, Guerra, & Watts, 2017).

Each case study included detailed chronological and contextual descriptions in order to allow the capture of the entire research scenario (Coutinho, 2011; Ponte, 2004). In this sense the data gathered by several strategies was privileged in order to constitute strong 'instances in action', investigations that allow the reader to understand each case and the properties under study. For example, within this book Chapter 14 draws on the description of the differentiated innovation path of two teachers, while Chapter 14 is focused on presenting a critical reflection of three innovative strategies all implemented one teacher in one singular curricular unit.

Studies with Ethnographical Features

Ethnography has found a growing use in educational research and literally means 'a portrait of a people'. Ethnographies are descriptions of a particular culture – the customs, beliefs, and behavior – based on information collected through fieldwork (Harris & Johnson, 2000). The main technique is participant observation. As in our case, the researchers became as much a part of the two existing 'cultural groups' as possible, namely the group of undergraduate students and the group of university creating complementary identities to their educational researcher role (Amado, 2009; Costa, 2003; Gray, 2004), in which they had to observe and take extensive notes on relevant aspects of the teaching and learning life.

This participation continued for a fairly long period. Within every new research context, our over-riding concern has been to make contact with, and describe – portray – the teaching and learning situation, to capture the particular teacher-student or student-student interactions. In the majority of our seven studies this 'naturalistic ethnographic approach' slowly evolved to become a 'critical ethnographic approach' (Amado, 2009; Cohen, Manion, & Morrison, 2003), where the intention has gone beyond description towards a greater understanding, to question and to make changes. Needless to say, we have been very aware that our presence changed the professional experience of the teachers, as well as the learning experience of the students.

The ethnographic dimensions of the Aveiro Project are also present by the fact that the knowledge produced has its origins in the fieldwork (Goetz & Le Compte, 1998). In this case the several real teaching-learning contexts that happened at the departments of Biology and Chemistry.

Action-Research Studies

The definitions of 'action-research' studies are quite disparate/divergent (Coutinho, 2011), and even non-consensual (Amado, 2009). However, according to Gray (2004) there are three key-components associated to action-research projects and which are present in our research endeavour, namely: (i) research intention orientated to change; (ii) close relationship between researchers and research subjects, in this case the academics and their undergraduates, allowing all involved to obtain benefits from this co-researcher model (Macaro & Mutton, 2002); and finally (iii) the reflexivity spiral between the seven studies, which involved strategical planning, followed by implementation of the research strategy and its assessment by critical reflection of the outputs and the design of new and/or complementary follow up studies.

Data Gathering Strategies

Considering the qualitative research approach, the data gathering method implied long periods of field work with all the involved academics and with at least one educational researcher during two or more academic years. In all the seven studies, which comprise the fifteen year research endeavour, primary data was gathered through multiple processes namely observation of teaching and learning sessions (lectures, tutorials and lab classes) and enquiry to academics and students by means of questionnaires, inventories and interviews. All the documents that were produced by students and teachers throughout the process were also integrated in the corpus of data whenever it was considered relevant for the research goals.

Observation of Lectures and Complementary Teaching-Learning Environments

Observation of lectures and similar teaching moments moved between a continuum of non-participant observation and participant observation (Amado, 2009), resulting in an almost everyday contact between academics and elements of the educational research team throughout each academic year. In many situations it were the teachers, by requiring help or asking for comments to the educational researchers, who have decided, even not intentionally, the switch from a non-participant mode to a participant mode of observations. All observations were supported by observation sheets elaborated for the specific purposes (Almeida, 2007; Moreira, 2012; Silva Lopes, 2013). The majority of teaching and learning interactions were also audio-recorded, in first place to minimize the risk of losing data, and in some cases to help collect, and then transcribe, specific didactical episodes (studies 4, 5, 6 and 7).

Other moments of participant observations correspond to work meetings or (in)formal 'chats' after or before classes. The movement between participant and non-participant observation requires great effort and flexibility as well reflexivity from the qualitative researcher, justifying the maintenance of research diaries along these extensive periods of field work, being useful in making and maintaining consciousness of the several identities, roles that were embraced by each educational researcher during the project: "researchers should acknowledge and disclose their own selves in the research, they should hold themselves up to the light" (Cohen, Manion, & Morrison, 2003, p. 141).

Inquiry by Questionnaires, Inventories and Interviews

Throughout the investigation several inventories and questionnaires were applied, some of them representing central data gathering strategies, resulting from the translation of validated instruments developed by other research groups, such as in study 2 (Kolb's Learning inventory) or study 6 (Trigwell and co-workers Approaches to Teaching Inventory – ATI), or representing complementary instruments designed by the educational research team itself in order to obtain specific information in need (for example in study 2 and 3). In study 6 the repeated application of the same Inventory (ATI) to the academics was also used as a strategy to promote teachers reflection on their pedagogical activity, as it can be read in Chapter 14.

Considering interviews, the most privileged types that were used with students and teachers were the semi-structured interviews. All interviews were audio-recorded and verbatim transcribed. Teachers' interviews were content validated by the interviewees which allowed using this type of data gathering method also as a strategy to promote teachers' reflection. Finally, in study 6

Identification	Name XXXX
Questions	1 - I wonder if the evolutionary perspective is really the best way to explain the origin of new species (24/02/2010) 2 – Is evolution infinite? Or can we consider it as a cycle that has begun in the past and will end in the future? (10/03/2010) 3 - In the mating season males do everything to conquer the female, why are not females doing so, with males being responsible for natural selection? 4 – By definition, co-evolution implies at least two species which evolve at the same time and that interfere with each other (one species conditions the other, if one extinguishes the other also does) .
I choose question _4_ because ...	... it refers to the influence that the human species has over other species. People who study animal and plant diversity are more and more concerned with issue, since humans seem to be the main cause of the most recently species extinctions. In my view, question four is a good choice that deserves a response.

FIGURE 12.1   Example of a semi-annual compilation of students' written question within a specific curricular unit and his personal selection of those he considered to be most relevant for his/her learning path

RESEARCH, DESIGN, APPROACHES AND METHODS   155

TABLE 12.2   Questions coding throughout the 'Aveiro project'

Study	Context	What was being categorized?	Description of the adopted coding system
1 & 2	Undergraduate Chemistry	Students' oral and written questions formulated during lectures, group work and lab sessions	Almeida, 2007; Neri de Souza, 2006
3 & 4		Students written questions during formative and summative assignments	Moreira, 2009, 2012
5 & 6	Undergraduate Biology	Teachers' oral questions	Pedrosa-de-Jesus & Silva Lopes, 2009a
		Nature (dialogic vs. non dialogic reaction) of the teacher to students' questions and answers	Pedrosa-de-Jesus & Silva Lopes, 2011; Silva Lopes, 2013

an innovative approach was implemented, namely by asking the academics to reflect out aloud on transcribed interaction episodes between themselves and the students. In methodological terms the applied interviews were quite similar to the 'task-based-interviews' described by Koichu and Harel (2007) or 'think aloud interviews' (Amado, 2009). A detailed description of this data gathering strategy can be read in Pedrosa-de-Jesus and Silva Lopes (2012).

Data Analysis Strategies

Considering that our research approach was mainly of a qualitative nature, the data gathered were also mainly qualitative, being subjected to content analysis with the support of N'Vivo© and WebQDA©. In some cases descriptive statistical analysis was also used, for instance considering students' and teachers' questions, and we have already noted one such research and intervention instrument like this. We were particularly interested in teacher or student questions that promote or evidence high order reasoning which led us to develop specific instruments dedicated to the collection of those questions (see as an example Figure 12.1) and also to develop or adapt specific categorization/coding systems (Table 12.2).

The process here is important. The student relates her understanding of evolution in humans as a species, and illustrates a high level of response to the tasks the class was set – this format allowed us to collect a range of such data.

Concluding Remarks

Fifteen years of qualitative naturalistic research is difficult to compress into just a few short pages. In this chapter we have described the broad path of the project conducted around teaching and learning in undergraduate science at two Departments (Biology and Chemistry) of the University of Aveiro. The research, design, approaches and methods of seven 'component' studies have been explored in detail in alignment with two major outcome goals:

1. To promote understanding within the following chapters, where some of the main research outputs are presented as well as its theoretical and empirical (pedagogical) implications;
2. To 'tease' other scholars into experimenting and extending similar research strategies at their own universities despite its associated challenges since it may allow them to:
    1. Create opportunities to deepen their knowledge/understanding of particular phenomena/problems that are associated to teaching and learning contexts at higher education
    2. Promote peer interaction based on a co-researcher approach
    3. Sustain teacher reflection and enhance the willingness/motivation towards pedagogical innovation.

The following chapters in the book develop some of the major themes drawn both from the project as a whole and from the seven studies outlined here.

References

Almeida, P. (2007). *Questões dos alunos e estilos de aprendizagem – um estudo com um público de ciências no ensino universitário* (Unpublished PhD thesis). University of Aveiro, Aveiro.

Almeida, P., Pedrosa-de-Jesus, M. H., & Watts, M. (2011). Kolb's learning styles and approaches to learning through the use of students' critical questions. In S. Rayner & E. Cools (Eds.), *International perspectives on style differences in human performance: Leading edge research, theory and practice*. London: Routledge.

Amado, J. (2000). A técnica de análise de conteúdo. *Revista de Educação e Formação em Enfermagem, 5,* 53–63.

Amado, J. (2009). *Relatório da Unidade Curricular – Introdução à Investigação Qualitativa em Educação* (Unpublished dissertation). University of Coimbra, Coimbra.

Bisquerra, R. (1996). *Métodos de Investigação Educativa-Guia prático* (2ª edição). Barcelona: Educaiones CEAC.

Bodgan, R., & Biklen, S. (1994). *Qualitative research in education: An introduction to theory and methods.* Porto: Porto Editora.

Bronfenbrenner, U. (1977). Toward an experimental ecological of human development. *American Psychologist, 32*, 513–531.

Bronfenbrenner, U. (1979). *The ecology of human development: Experiments by nature and design.* Cambridge, MA: Harvard University Press.

Cohen, J. H., Manion, L., & Morrison, K. (2003). *Research methods and education* (2nd ed.). New York, NY: Routledge Falmer.

Costa, A. F. (2003). A pesquisa de terreno em sociologia. In A. S. Silva & J. M. Pinto (orgs), *Metodologia das Ciências Sociais* (12ª ed.). Porto: Edições Afrontamento.

Coutinho, C. P. (2011). *Metodologia de Investigação em Ciências Sociais e Humanas: teoria e prática* (2ª edição). Coimbra: Almedina.

Dillon, J. T. (1982). The effect of questions in education and other enterprises. *Curriculum Studies, 14*(2), 127–152.

Estrela, A. (1994). *Teoria e prática de observação de classes – uma estratégia de formação de professores* (4ª edição). Porto: Porto Editora.

Figueiredo, A. D. (2005). Learning contexts: A blueprint for research. *Interactive Educational Multimedia, 11*, 127–139.

Goetz, J., & Le Compte, M. (1998). *Ethnography and qualitative design in educational research.* Orlando: Orlando Academic Press.

Gray, D. E. (2004). *Doing research in the real world.* London: Sage Publications.

Harris, M., & Johnson, O. (2000). *Cultural anthropology* (5th ed.). Needham Heights, MA: Allyn & Bacon.

Koichu, B., & Harel, G. (2007). Triadic interaction in clinical task-based interviews with mathematics teachers. *Educational Studies in Mathematics, 66*, 349–371.

Kolb, D. A. (1976). *The learning style inventory: Technical manual.* Boston, MA: McBer & Co Pusblishing.

Lincoln, Y. S., & Guba, E. G. (2000). *Naturalistic inquiry* (8th ed.). Thousand Oaks, CA: Sage Publications.

Lopes, B., Pedrosa-de-Jesus, M. H., & Watts, M. (2016). The old questions are the best: Striving against invalidity in qualitative research. In M. Tight & J. Huisman (Eds.), *Theory and method in higher education research* (Vol. 2, pp. 1–22). Bradford: Emerald Group Publishing.

Macaro, E., & Mutton, T. (2002). Developing language teachers through a co-researcher model. *Language Learning Journal, 25*(1), 27–39.

Martin, E., Trigwell, K., Prosser, M., & Ramsden, P. (2003). Variation in the experience of leadership of teaching in higher education. *Studies in Higher Education, 28*(3), 247–259.

Moreira, A. (2006). *As questões dos alunos na avaliação em Química* (Unpublished master dissertation). University of Aveiro, Aveiro.

Moreira, A. (2012). *O questionamento no alinhamento do ensino, da aprendizagem e da avaliação* (Unpublished PhD thesis). University of Aveiro, Aveiro.

Morin, E. (2008). *Introduction to complex thinking* (5th ed.). Lisbon: Instituto Piaget.

Neri de Sousa, F. (2006). *Perguntas na aprendizagem de Química no ensino superior* (Unpublished PhD thesis). University of Aveiro, Aveiro.

Nicholas, S. P. (2008). The development of basic education in Shanghai, China and its challenges ahead. In T. H. Seren & W. L. Megan (Eds.), *Education in China*. New York, NY: Nova Science Publisher.

Pedrosa-de-Jesus, M. H. (1987). *A descriptive study of some science teacher questioning practices* (Unpublished master dissertation). University of East Anglia, Norwich.

Pedrosa-de-Jesus, M. H. (1997). *An investigation of pupils questions in science teaching* (Unpublished PhD thesis). University of East Anglia, Norwich.

Pedrosa-de-Jesus, M. H., & da Silva Lopes, B. (2009a, August 31–September 4). *Classroom questioning and teaching approaches: A study with biology undergraduates*. Paper presented at the ESERA Conference, Istambul.

Pedrosa-de-Jesus, M. H., & da Silva Lopes, B. (2009b, June 17–19). *The interplay of preferential teaching approaches and classsroom questioning in higher education: Two case studies*. Paper presented at the 14th ELSIN Conference, Learning in Higher education – How Styles Matters, Switzerland.

Pedrosa-de-Jesus, M. H., & da Silva Lopes, B. (2011). The relationship between teaching and learning conceptions, preferred teaching approaches and questioning practices. *Research Papers in Education, 26*(2), 223–243.

Pedrosa-de-Jesus, M. H., & da Silva Lopes, B. (2012). Exploring the relationship between teaching and learning conceptions and questioning practices, towards academic development. *Higher Education Research Network Journal (HERN-J), 5,* 37–52.

Pedrosa-de-Jesus, M. H., & Guerra, C. (2018). Teachers' written formative feedback on students' critical thinking: A case study. *MIE Journal of Education* (in press).

Pedrosa-de-Jesus, M. H., Guerra, C., & Watts, M. (2017). University teachers' self-reflection on their academic growth. *Professional Development in Education, 43*(3), 454–473. doi:10.1080/19415257.2016.1194877

Pedrosa-de-Jesus, M. H., Moreira, A., da Silva Lopes, B., Guerra, C., Pedrosa, J., Cunha, A., Almeida, A., & Watts, M. (2015, June 11–13). *A study of academic development in universities through innovative approaches in teaching, assessment and feedback*. Paper presented at Third International Seminar on Research on Questioning, Department of Education, University of Aveiro, Aveiro.

Poisson, Y. (1991). *La Recherche qualitative en education*. Québec: Presses de l'Université du Québec.

Ponte, J. P. (2004). O estudo de caso na investigação em educação matemática. *Quadrante, 3*(1), 3–17.

Postareff, L., Kaajavuoi, N., Lindblom-Ylänne, S., & Trigwell, K. (2008). Consonance and dissonance in descriptions of teaching of university teachers. *Studies in Higher Education, 33*(1), 49–61.

Postareff, L., Lindblom-Ylänne, S., & Nevgi, A. (2008). A follow-up study of the effect of pedagogical training on teaching in higher education. *Higher Education, 56*, 29–43.

Quivy, R., & Campenhoudt, L. V. (2008). *Manual de Investigação em Ciencias Sociais* (5ª edição). Lisboa: Gradiva.

Robson, C. (2002). *Real world research* (2nd ed.). Oxford: Blackwell Publishing.

Rosenshine, B., Meister, C., & Chapman, S. (1996). Teaching students to generate questions: A review of intervention studies. *Review of Educational Research, 66*(2), 181–222.

Silva Lopes, B. (2013). *Teaching approaches and questioning practices in higher education* (Unpublished PhD thesis). University of Aveiro, Aveiro.

Trigwell, K., Prosser, M., & Ginns, P. (2005). Phenomenographic pedagogy and a revised approach to teaching inventory. *Higher Education Research and Development, 24*(4), 349–360.

Veiga, A., & Amaral, A. (2009). Survey on the implementation of the Bologna process in higher education in Portugal. *Higher Education, 57*, 57–69.

Willig, C. (2008). *Introducing qualitative research in psychology: Adventures in theory and method*. London: Open University Press.

Yin, R. (2003). *Case study research: Design and methods*. Thousand Oaks, CA: Sage Publications.

CHAPTER 13

Approaches to Student Inquiry-Led Learning

Helena Pedrosa-de-Jesus, Aurora Coelho Moreira and Mike Watts

Introduction

In this chapter we begin with discuss a core theme of the book: students' classroom, and out-of-classroom, questioning. We use this as the basis for a broader consideration of inquiry-led learning, and position this as a component of student-centred learning. Yoshi Oyama and Emmanuel Manalo in Chapter 9, and Jose Otero in Chapter 10, discuss their own projects within the realm of questions and questioning. In Chapters 7 and 8, first Carol Evans and then Aisha AlSaadi and Sarmin Hossain discuss their work on learning styles. In this chapter we tread a path that trades on both these bodies of work, and look to answer: Are there such things as 'styles of question-asking'? We follow this with an attempt at: Are there such things as styles of inquiry-led learning? And, if so: How best might we manage student-centred learning along these lines?

Questioning

Our interest in students' questioning has persisted over many years, for example, from Watts (1985) and Pedrosa-de-Jesus (1991), to Watts, Gould, and Alsop (1997) and Pedrosa-de-Jesus et al. (2005) and much beyond. Over this long period we have, at various times, discussed the qualities of an 'ideal student questioner', as a person who:

1. Is an active, self-directed, constructive, learner. While there are many kinds of questions in life and in study, this is a learner who asks questions that forge relational patterns, make connections, interpret and associate issues in specific ways to help 'meaningful' or 'transformative' learning. This implies that the student is adding to a high level of structure, internal logic and consistency in his or her knowledge
2. Is a critical questioner, asking questions that use the skills of analysis, critique and synthesis, and which generally lead to an increase in learner autonomy Being able to challenge orthodoxy, discover something new (to the learner), to articulate and question this with a secure degree of independence of thought, is normally thought to be valuable 'high level' learning

3. Works closely with peers, combining challenge with collusion to generate quality output from different constellations of co-learners. He or she has a feel for the 'power' of questions and can ask questions from a basis of 'managed feelings'
4. Has the ability to engineer, shape and manipulate questions and to appreciate the domain from which a response might be made. Asking questions is one part of inquiry-based learning, of problem solving and our 'ideal questioner' asks questions related to 'actionable knowledge', where he or she can confidently draw together data, information, experience and insight to first articulate and then work towards solutions to investigable, experimental and problem-based situations.

So, when a student asks a question during a lecture, in a class session or a tutorial, (s)he is undertaking a range of intellectual tasks: constructing, connecting and clarifying information into his or her knowledge system; giving the teacher and peers a window into thinking; providing evidence of conceptual change; authentically miming the practice of science, a discipline based on asking questions and seeking answers (Chin, Brown, & Bruce, 2002; Cuccio-Schirripa & Steiner, 2000; Harper & Etkina, 2003). The long-term benefits of students generating questions have been widely heralded, and are seen to include improved problem solving skills; higher ordered and creative thinking; improved reading comprehension and content retention; the ability to identify anomalies in his or her own understanding of the topic; take steps towards a lifetime of self-directed learning (AAAS, 1989, 1993; Dori & Herscovitz, 1999; Chin et al., 2002; Harper & Etkina, 2003; Iwasyk, 2000; Loy et al., 2004; Pedrosa-de-Jesus et al., 2003). And, as we have argued elsewhere (Teixeira-Dias et al., 2005), question-asking is central to a learner's 'enculturation' into the patterns of language and thought, discussion and criticism, that are characteristic of an academic discipline such as, for example, chemistry.

One aspect of work in this area (Pedrosa-de-Jesus, Almeida, Teixeira-Dias, & Watts, 2006) has focused upon differentiating between modes of questioning – adapted in part from Kolb's (1984) 'cone of experiential learning'. Kolb explains this experiential learning model of development where the lower levels of development form the base of the cone and the point as their climax, which indicates increased integration of learning towards the higher levels. Such a process of progression is characterised by an increasing composite structure and relativity in managing the world and one's own experiences (Mainemelis, Boyatzis, & Kolb, 2002). Taking this, we have used an 'acquisition questioning' mode to indicate a basic 'lower level' need for information, knowledge 'gap-filling', and essential clarification. Beyond this, 'specialisation questioning' entails 'mid-level' probing of the discipline under scrutiny, so that the questions relate to quite specific issues within the subject matter being studied. We refer to the third, higher-level mode as 'integrative questioning' wherein these questions explore across and between disciplines, are inter- and multi-disciplinary. We have pictured these three modes as pyramidal (Almeida, Pedrosa-de-Jesus, & Watts, 2008) the broad 'acquisition' base representing the most ordinary and numerous of questions and questioners, the less-common 'specialist' mid-section, and then the more rarefied attempts by students to be wide-thinking and 'integrative' across knowledge systems and contexts. Our early data monitored the number and type of questions asked in a variety of circumstances and it was clear that students most regularly asked numerous acquisition questions, least regularly asked integrative ones. We understood this as a need to 'clear the ground', establish an explicable and unambiguous knowledge platform before learners felt comfortable and confident enough to ask more detailed or more sweeping questions.

However, it also became clear that the context of teaching and learning was very influential. Understandably, the physical setting, a large raked lecture theatre, a substantial audience of peers, can be intimidating for most questioners, certainly for basic, perhaps 'should-be-known' issues being asked aloud. Small-group and tutorial settings, on the other hand, allow students to ask these questions more easily and comfortably. Teachers, too, could lead with – and demand – more integrative questioning, requiring, for instance, a discussion of evolution within wider social contexts. In this case, students duly responded and the 'integrative question' count rose accordingly. Where teachers made time and space for 'quality questions' in their planning over successive sessions, then learners picked up the 'baton' and responded appropriately (Pedrosa-de-Jesus, Leite, & Watts, 2016). Similarly, if students were formally assessed on the attributes of the questions they asked as part of their graded assignments (we discuss this later in Chapter 16) then, again, the questions changed character. Moreover, outside the need to meet formalised criteria, where students had greater time and opportunity to think and reflect, as within the realms of an online discussion forum, then the intricacy of the questions being asked increased noticeably. In this latter case, we referred to the data we collected as a 'reverse Kolb' effect, in that the number of students asking integrative questions exceeded the specialist and the acquisitional questions, turning the 'question-mode pyramid' on its head.

A fourth mode of questioning has focused on empirical work, those questions that can lead to investigation, experiment and resolution. 'Investigable' questions (Chin & Kayalvizhi, 2002; Graesser & McMahen, 1993) require a particular form of construction. They entail identifying an issue and, from our experience, the source of students' questions can be a simple 'data gap' or discrepancy in their knowledge, or a need to extend their knowledge in a particular direction. According to Chin and Kayalvizhi (2002) and Arnold (2009), a good investigative question requires students to: Generate and collect data for a selected pathway; represent, analyse and interpret their findings using the data collected; draw a conclusion using their results; and justify their findings to the question based on the data they have collected. Chin and Kayalvizhi (2002) further suggests that in order to fully engage students and sustain their interest, these questions should be conceptually challenging, meaningful and relevant to their personal experiences whilst remaining broad enough to enable critical and creative thinking. Such challenging questions can spring from odd events, passing thoughts or conversations, a technological problem, some difficult results, a curious occurrence, a chance observation, a fascination with some particular area of science, a claim on a science press-release, a TV advert, a pet's habits, a family discussion, their sporting life, obsessions or hobbies. That is, the processes of 'disequilibrium detection', of problem finding (Watts & Pedrosa-de-Jesus, 2011), come from students' interactions with life – and often from the clash between experience of 'life issues' and the overlay of scientific knowledge derived from school and other informative sources (Watts & Alsop, 1995). That said, Walsh and Sattes (2005) make the point that formulating investigative questions is a skill that needs to be explicitly taught.

Inquiry-Led Learning
We choose to use the expression 'inquiry-led learning' in order to emphasise the formal basis within teaching and learning in higher education in which our examples occur. Ours is one of a clutch of similar expressions such as inquiry-based instruction (IBI), autonomous learning, independent learning, inquiry learning, self-directed learning, self-regulated learning or inquiry-based learning (IBL) and so on. Here, though, we want to discuss both the directions taken by the teacher as well as the autonomy afforded to the students. In this vein, we examine how teachers facilitate students to activate, control, and regulate their learning as a part of an overall instructional approach.

So, for instance, the 'Micro-talk strategy' (Pedrosa-de-Jesus, Guerra, & Watts, 2017) was first intended as a strategy to stimulate and engage students' knowledge and interest in current research in microbiology, in the first instance about the topic of bacteria with antibiotics' resistance. Each micro-talk consisted of a twelve-minute presentation by academic researchers from the Department of Biology, followed by five minutes for discussion with students. In the following academic year, rather than 'live' presentations of their research work, the Microtalks were filmed, thus making them available on Moodle so that students could review them and submit questions and/or queries either to the module teacher or directly to the original researcher, the micro-talk presenter. The module teacher saw this research-inquiry-led strategy as an opportunity for students to access several topics in microbiology, all closely related to the contents of the curricular unit, and discussed the strengths of this approach in a post-session evaluation interview:

> First, it brings authentic research inquiry to the classrooms, which is related to my own research interests. Second, it shows some diversity of topics in microbiology in a concrete way. Third, it shows that research is an activity that people can do. Can be a profession, does it not? Because students have the opportunity to see real researchers and can question them, can discuss issues directly with them.

This teacher went on to say that this way of working certainly allowed students to expand their knowledge of microbiological research:

> I noticed that, especially in smaller groups of students, there was strong interest because they asked several questions – not least about whether the Microtalks could happen more often. That shows that there was both interest and motivation ... they [students] felt that there were areas of work that were more interesting for them.

He 'seeded' some of the students' discussions with a few of questions of his own, intending in part to be provocative of issues:

> My perception was that the sessions went very well and were very productive. Students asked questions ... there were not actually that many... but those did serve as a starting point to explore themes. Some questions connected and triggered discussions about other topics. Just for that alone, it has been very useful ... In the second part [of the session], I presented some of my own questions. I have a sense that some of these led to the outbreak of even more students' questions ... about the adequacy of the concepts involved, how they could be applied [in another contexts], as well as some concept definitions. All in all, it was good.

Specific laboratory tasks lie at the more 'practical end' of curriculum design and planning, and examples here (Pedrosa-de-Jesus, Teixeira-Dias, & Watts, 2003) have been as follows:
1. *Phenolphthalein* – plan and execute experiments for observing the colour changes of phenolphthalein in the pH range approximately from pH -1 to

pH 12. Among the phenolphthalein structures provided in the laboratory manual, identify those involved in each observed colour change. Write the corresponding acid-base reactions. What is the structural feature, the presence of which provides colour? And what is the one that makes a particular phenolphthalein structure uncoloured?
2. *Separation of substances* – plan and execute experiments for separating copper sulphate and salicylic acid from a provided ethanol-water solution where both of those substances are in solution. Base your experimental strategy on test-tube experiments carried out to answer the following questions: is copper sulphate soluble in water? And in ethanol? Is salicylic acid soluble in water? And in ethanol? Explain your findings in your lab book.
3. *Corrosion of iron* – plan and execute experiments for studying the corrosion of iron. In particular, the planned experiments should provide clear answers to the following questions: what is (are) the effect(s) of strong electrolytes in the corrosion process? How might one confirm that cathodic protection prevents corrosion?

While these are not 'recipe practicals', and leave considerable scope for student autonomy, they are fairly clearly circumscribed. A more open-ended approach was the introduction 'mini-projects', where students were given six weeks to choose, negotiate and develop a small project on a topic within chemistry of interest to themselves. The majority of these mini-projects became library-based exercises, with a great deal of discussions within the group and with the teacher, although some were based upon laboratory experiments (Pedrosa-de-Jesus, Teixeira-Dias, & Watts, 2003). The following are examples of those topics chosen by one class of 26 students: 'Blood gases and deep-sea diving', 'Self-replicating molecules', 'Catalytic converters', 'Hydrogen as a fuel', 'CO_2 and the greenhouse effect', 'Catalysts based on zeolites', 'Magnetic resonance imaging in medicine', 'Chemistry and the forensic science'. Work was conducted in groups of 2, 3 or 4, in their own time (outside formal sessions). During this period, each group had various tutorials with teachers, in which only the students had the initiative to question their topic and the teacher would only provide appropriate orientation and guidance for the students to identify and solve their questions. Each 'project team' then made presentations of their work to the other students and to members of staff in the department. These presentations took place on an evening over a period of three hours – with each presentation being subjected to numerous questions from both peers and tutors. In some instances the presentations were organised around a series of the team's own questions. In the second year of this project the general process was repeated, though this time other seminar-tutorial groups were invited to participate from a wider selection of topics, with a total of 13 projects being presented involving 42 students.

A third example here is a description of cooperative teamwork in a group of three students who developed a project on 'Thermochemistry of fitness'. As we observed this particular group, it became clear to us that some of their questions performed several important functions in the structure of their work in, for example, organising ideas, delimiting the scale of the theme, identifying and discussing on the many strands and sources of information available to them, and in their reflections on the whole theme. These organisational questions became useful tools in the self-management and organisation of group inquiry. These examples illustrate how opportunities were created in each class meeting for students to:

a   Engage in purposeful dialogue with each other about content, even where this was just a few minutes side-by-side discourse to identify key concepts, explain to each other, or think of additional examples from their experience
b   Share perceptions of the important elements of the task, setting goals and targets
c   Express interest in the subject matter by assuring choices in selecting essay or project topics
d   Work in groups, not exclusively on their own
e   Adopt and expanding diverse roles and engage in broader activities such as giving each other feedback about ideas and otherwise practicing evaluation elements, and
f   Build into the curriculum decision points at which students can set some of the goals they should be accomplishing.

Student-Centred Learning

A substantial body of research suggests that when students value a learning activity in terms of utility, interest, attainment and future goals, they become increasingly likely to engage actively in that topic, to persist with it over time, to achieve highly, to show relatively sophisticated self-regulation, and to understand what they are trying to learn (Jang, 2008). In our experience, as students make the transition from high school to university, and from early years in graduate study to the final years,, their workload becomes greater, academic demands increase, grading becomes more stringent, and instruction can become less personalised. Not surprisingly, students' academic motivation can steadily decline and – especially older students – report that the learning activities they encounter lack direct or personal relevance to their lives as well as being unexciting, unappealing, overly complex and difficult, and/or more time-consuming. Such studies examining undergraduate students' preferences and expectations of teaching include those by Sander et al. (2000) and Kember and Wong (2000). Sander et al.'s quantitative study sought students' perspectives of which form of delivery (i.e. lectures, interactive sessions, group work, etc) students expected and preferred. In general their study showed that students preferred more interactive, student-centred teaching to transmission-type lectures. This is increasingly in line with what is called 'active learning' in higher education (for example, Reddish, 2003). Kember and Wong give a more detailed picture showing that preference for interaction or transmission really depends upon students' views about the act of learning, and of the nature of the structure of knowledge in physics and chemistry. Early work by van Rossum et al. (1985) relates teaching style to learning preference via the notions of directedness versus openness in teaching methods.

In our view, designing inquiry-based-learning with and for university students has developed their problem-solving skills, logical reasoning and reflective thinking. Also, it has involved working as a member of a team, questioning, being creative and shaping the skills for continued intellectual development. For Light and Cox (2001), this is one of the most important learning experiences that a university can offer because it enables the exploration of theoretical ideas and conceptual change. This trades on the benefits of peer interactions to co-construct contextual understandings (Chin, Brown, & Bruce, 2002) and assist students to clarify and focus their questions (Chin & Osbourne, 2008; Lowrie, 2002).

Bandura (1997), in his social cognitive theory, proposes that individuals' self-efficacy is the major determinant of goal-setting, choice of activity, willingness to expend effort, and persistence. Choosing to engage in an activity and choosing a mode of engagement are conceptualised as being affected by three key factors: the person's disposition, the social community, and the physical learning environment (Pedrosa-de-Jesus, da Silva Lopes, Moreira, & Watts, 2012). For example, teachers' organisation of student group-feedback in the teaching room (factors within the learning environment and in the community of learners) can influence students' self-confidence (a personal disposition) and can lead students to choose more complex tasks and strategies that promote acquisition of critical thinking skills (Pedrosa-de-Jesus et al., 2012). One student we interviewed, Ana, said:

> I felt an improvement throughout the year ... Practice helped us a lot, we have been training in solving those situations [problem-based cases] ... I think that if we continue with this method we will be able to attain a higher level in formulating questions and answering them so that we really understand things.

Furtak et al. (2012) used a similar approach in a meta-analysis of experimental and quasi-experimental studies of inquiry-based instruction to clarify what dimensions are and are not included or emphasised in purportedly different models of IBI.

References

Almeida, P., Pedrosa-de-Jesus, M. H., & Watts, D. M. (2008). Developing a mini-project: Students' questions and learning styles. *Psychology of Education Review, 32*(1), 6–17.

American Association for the Advancement of Science (AAAS). (1989, 1993). *Science for all Americans*. Retrieved from http://www.project2061.org/publications/articles/articles/cellbioed.htm

Arnold, P. (2008, July 6–13). *What about the P in the PPDAC cycle? An initial look at posing questions for statistical investigation*. Proceedings of the 11th International Congress of Mathematics Education, Monterrey. Retrieved from http://tsg.icme11.org/tsg/show/15

Bandura, A. (1997). *Self-efficacy: The exercise of control*. New York, NY: W H Freeman.

Chin, C., Brown, D. E., & Bruce, B. C. (2002). Student generated questions: A meaningful aspect of learning in science. *International Journal of Science Education, 24*(5), 521–549.

Chin, C., & Kayalvizhi, G. (2002). Posing questions for open investigations: What questions do pupils ask? *Research in Science & Technological Education, 20*(2), 269–287.

Chin, C., & Osborne, J. (2008). Student's questions: A potential resource for teaching and learning science. *Studies in Science Education, 44*(1), 1–39.

Cuccio-Schirripa, S., & Steiner, H. (2000). Enhancement and analysis of science question level for middle school students. *Journal of Research in Science Teaching, 37*(2), 210–224.

Dori, Y. J., & Herscovitz, O. (1999). Question-posing capability as an alternative evaluation method: Analysis of an environmental case study. *Journal of Research in Science Teaching, 36*(4), 411–430.

Furtak, E. M., Seidel, T., Iverson, H., & Briggs, D. C. (2012). Experimental and quasi-experimental studies of inquiry-based science teaching: A meta-analysis. *Review of Educational Research, 82*, 300–329. Retrieved from http://dx.doi.org/10.3102/0034654312457206

Graesser, A. C., & McMahen, C. L. (1993). Anomalous information triggers questions when adults solve problems and comprehend stories. *Journal of Educational Psychology, 95*, 524–536.

Harper, K., Etkina, E., & Lin, Y. (2003). Encouraging and analysing student questions in a large physics course: Meaningful patterns for instructors. *Journal of Research in Science Teaching, 40*(8), 776–791.

Iwasyk, M. (2000). Kids questioning kids: "Experts sharing". In J. Minstrell & E. H. van Zee (Eds.), *Inquiring into inquiry learning and teaching in science* (pp. 130–138). Washington, DC: American Association for the Advancement of Science.

Jang, H. (2008). Supporting students' motivation, engagement, and learning during an uninteresting activity. *Journal of Educational Psychology, 100*(4), 798–811.

Kember, D., & Wong, A. (2000). Implications for evaluation from a study of students' perceptions of good and poor teaching. *Higher Education, 40*(1), 69–97.

Kolb, D. A. (1984). *Experiential learning*. Englewood Cliffs, NJ: Prentice Hall.

Light, G., & Cox, R. (2001). *Learning and teaching in higher education: The reflective professional* (1st ed.). London: Paul Chapman Publishing.

Lowrie, T. (2002). Young children posing problems: The influence of teacher intervention on the type of problems children pose. *Mathematics Education Research Journal, 14*(2), 87–98.

Loy, G. L., Gelula, M. H., & Vontver, L. A. (2004). Teaching students to question. *American Journal of Obstetrics and Gynecology, 191*(5), 1752–1756.

Mainemelis, C., Boyatzis, R., & Kolb, D. A. (2002). Learning styles and adaptative flexibility: Testing the experiential theory of development. *Management Learning, 33*, 5–53.

McGill, I., & Brockbank, A. (2004). *The action learning handbook*. London: Routledge Falmer.

Pedrosa-de-Jesus, M. H. (1991). *An investigation of pupils' questions in science teaching* (Unpublished PhD thesis). University of East Anglia, Norwich.

Pedrosa-de-Jesus, M. H., Almeida, P., Teixeira-Dias, J. J., & Watts, D. M. (2006). Students' questions – building a bridge between Kolb's learning styles and approaches to learning. *Education + Training, 48*(2–3), 97–111.

Pedrosa-de-Jesus, M. H., Guerra, C., & Watts, D. M. (2017). University teachers' self-reflection on their academic growth. *Professional Development in Education, 43*(3), 454–473. doi:10.1080/19415257.2016.1194877

Pedrosa-de-Jesus, M. H., Leite, S., & Watts, D. M. (2016). 'Question moments': A rolling programme of question opportunities in classroom science. *Research in Science Education, 46*(3), 329–341. doi:10.1007/s11165-014-9453-7

Pedrosa-de-Jesus, M. H., Lopes, B., Moreira, A., & Watts, D. M. (2012). Contexts for questioning: Two zones of teaching and learning in undergraduate science. *Higher Education, 64*(4), 557–571. doi:10.1007/s10734-012-9512-9

Pedrosa-de-Jesus, M. H., Souza, F. N., Teixeira-Dias, J. J. C., & Watts, D. M. (2005). Students' questions as organisers for small group learning in chemistry. In S. A. Glazar & D. Krnel (Eds.), *Proceedings of the 7th European Conference on Research in Chemical Education – ECRICE* (pp. 183–196). Slovenia: University of Ljubljana.

Pedrosa-de-Jesus, M. H., Teixeira-Dias, J. J. C., & Watts, D. M. (2003). Questions of chemistry. *International Journal of Science Education, 25*(8), 1015–1034.

Reddish, E. F. (2003). *Teaching physics with the physics suite*. Hoboken, NJ: John Wiley & Sons.

Roth, W.-M., McRobbie, C. J., Lucas, K. B., & Boutonne, S. (1997). Why do students fail to learn from demonstrations? A social practice perspective of learning in physics. *Journal of Research in Science Teaching, 34*(5), 509–533.

Sander, P., Stevenson, K., King, M., & Coats, D. (2000). University students' expectations of teaching. *Studies in Higher Education, 25*, 309–323.

Teixeira-Dias, J. J. C., Pedrosa-de-Jesus, M. H., Neri de Souza, F., & Watts, D. M. (2005). Teaching for quality learning in chemistry. *International Journal of Science Education, 27*(9), 1123–1137.

Van Rossum, E., Deijkers, R., & Hamers, R. (1985). Students learning conceptions and their interpretations of significant educational concepts. *Higher Education, 14*, 617–641.

Walsh, J., & Sattes, B. (2005). *Quality questioning: Research-based practice to engage every learner*. Thousand Oaks, CA: Corwin Press.

Watts, D. M. (1985). *Children's alternative frameworks in science* (Unpublished PhD thesis). University of Surrey, Guildford.

Watts, D. M., Gould, G., & Alsop, S. J. (1997). Questions of understanding: Categorising pupils' questions in science. *School Science Review, 79*(286), 57–63.

Watts, D. M., & Pedrosa-de-Jesus, M. H. (2005). The cause and affect of asking questions: Reflective case studies from undergraduate sciences. *Canadian Journal of Science, Mathematics and Technology Education (CJSMTE/RCESMT), 5*(4), 437–452.

Watts, D. M., & Pedrosa-de-Jesus, M. H. (2011). Questions and science (Chapter 7). In R. Toplis (Ed.), *How science works: Exploring effective pedagogy and practice* (pp. 85–102). London: Routledge.

CHAPTER 14

Academics' Conceptions about Teaching and Its Implication towards Pedagogical Innovation

Betina da Silva Lopes

Introduction

That academics shape their teaching practices according to what it means to teach at university level is presently considered a 'common' wisdom. But the simplicity of this reasoning hides lose ends that still needs to be unravelled. How many teaching conceptions does a teacher have? Does a teaching conceptions change across time? If yes, how? This chapter aims to give new insights towards this complex thematic being sustained on a brief overview considering research around academics teaching conceptions and on the discussion of some empirical findings obtained through a longitudinal study involving two university teachers. Finally, based on the explored argumentation, some brief recommendations, potentially helpful towards the operationalization of pedagogical innovation at universities, are presented.

Research around Academics' Teaching Conceptions – Brief Overview

In the last decades, particularly since 1980, research considering the investigation of academics' conceptualisations of teaching and their teaching practices has grown substantially (Kane, Sandretto, & Heath, 2002; Kember, 1997; Norton et al., 2005). One key-aspect that emerges from these studies is that university teachers have distinct interpretations of what means learning, of what means teaching and therefore how to implement optimized' practices of teaching (Entwistle & Walker, 2000; Prosser, Martin, Trigwell, Ramsden, & Luevkenhausen, 2005).

Two broad theoretical models have been used as major references for many investigations and reflections around this thematic, namely the constructs *Orientations to teaching* and *Teaching Approaches,* which will be described with more detail in the following section.[1] Key issue for the present discussion is that the corresponding models assume a different transition between teaching conceptions, namely substitution versus integration (Figure 14.1). Trying

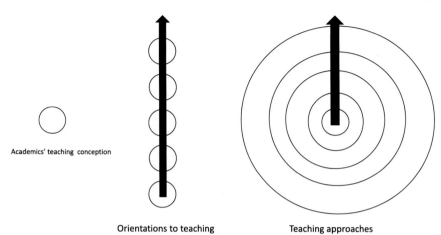

FIGURE 14.1 The process of changing teaching conceptions – two different models

to unravel this divergence is of crucial relevance considering the efficiency of strategies that aim academic development and/or pedagogical innovation.

Orientations to Teaching

The concept of Orientation to Teaching was initially developed by David Kember (Kember, 1997) and Lyn Gow (Kember & Gow, 1994; Gow & Kember, 1993). According to these authors two broad teaching conceptions can be identified, one intimately linked to 'knowledge transmission' and another associated to 'learning facilitation', differing between them on the following dimensions: (i) role of the teacher, (ii) role of the student, (iii) meaning of teaching, (iv) basis of teaching contents and (v) source of knowledge from the discipline that is lectured (Figure 14.2). Follow up work (Kember, 1997, 1998; Kember & Kwan,

	Knowledge Transmission	**Learning Facilitation**
Role of the teacher	Presenter of information	Agent of change
Role of the student	'Container'	Active agent supported by the teacher
Meaning of Teaching	Knowledge Transmission	Development of peoples and concepts
Basis of the contents	Defined by the curriculum	Constructed by the students
Source of the knowledge	Owned by the teacher	Constructed by the group

FIGURE 14.2 Main differences between two broad teaching conceptions according to David and co-authors model[2]

FIGURE 14.3 David Kember and co-workers' "five-teaching-conceptions-two-orientations-to-teaching" model (based on Kember, 1997, p. 260)

2000; Kember, Kwan, & Ledesma, 2001) allowed the conceptualization of a broader model which includes an ordered set of five different teaching conceptions being those organized in two main *Orientations to Teaching* (Figure 14.3). According to this model progression from one teaching conception is possible, but not easy, particularly between conceptions of different orientations, and may imply losing some elements of previous beliefs (Kember, 1997).

Based on this theoretical model an inventory was designed aimed at distinguishing academics according to their orientations to teaching through their responses on 46 items related to teaching and learning at universities (Kember & Kwan, 2000; Kember, Leung, & Ma, 2007; Lam & Kember, 2006).

Teaching Approaches

A phenomenographic analysis of individual interview transcripts with 24 university teachers from two Australian universities lecturing Physics and Chemistry at undergraduate level allowed the identification of six different teaching conceptions (Figure 14.5). In a follow up work (Trigwell & Prosser, 1996a, 1996b; Prosser & Trigwell, 1997) the data of the 24 interview transcripts was re-analysed. Obtained findings lead to the characterization of five distinct, but in some cases inter-related, teaching approaches (from A to E) according to the intention that

Transmission and acquisition	A) teaching as transmitting concepts of the syllabus
	B) teaching as transmitting the teachers knowledge
	C) teaching as helping students acquire concepts of the syllabus
Development and change	E) teaching as helping students develop conceptions
	F) Teaching as helping students change conceptions

FIGURE 14.4 Main teaching conceptions of university teachers' according to Prosser and Trigwell (1997). Based on Prosser, Trigwell, and Taylor (1994, pp. 200–204). Original labels A, C, D, E and F for teaching conceptions was maintained, in order to facilitate cross interpretations of the reader between this particular chapter and the original studies

Teachers' Approach	Teachers' intention	Teachers' strategy
Approach A Teacher focused strategy with the intention of transmitting information to the students	The teacher aims to transmit with the hope that students receive information about the discipline. Students are expected to add the information to their present store of knowledge. There is little or no focus on relationships between pieces of information.	The teacher engages in little or no interaction at all with students. Students have little or no responsibility at all for the teaching-learning situation. If questions are asked by the student, the teacher may answer that specific question, but makes little or no adjustments to his/her planned strategy.
Approach B Teacher focused strategy with the intention that students acquire the concepts of the discipline	The teacher's aim is to help students acquire the concept of the discipline and their underlying relationship.	The teacher believes that the students need to be active in their learning and so engages in an interaction with students. The teacher maintains responsibility for the teaching-learning situation. For example the teacher asks questions, and encourages students to ask questions, which are mainly answered by the teacher. However, by answering the questions, the teacher may depart from his/her pre-planned structure.
Approach C Teacher/student interaction strategy with the intention that students acquire the concepts of the discipline		
Approach D Student-focused strategy aimed at developing their conceptions	The teacher aims to help students to develop further their knowledge within a world view or conception, assuming that students' world view or conception is consistent with that of the discipline. Students construct their own knowledge.	The teacher believes that it is what the student does, and not what the teacher does, that determines what the student learns. The teacher structures teaching and learning situations in which the students are encouraged to accept responsibility for their own learning. For example, detailed lecture notes are not supplied to students. Students are encouraged to write their own notes. Small groups and "buzz groups" are implemented to encourage students to interact with each other.
Approach E Student-focused strategy aimed at Students changing their conceptions	The teacher's aim is that students confront and qualitatively change their world view or conception, in relation to the phenomena that they are studying. By doing this, the teacher doesn't assume that students' world view is consistent with the discipline they are studying, and so they may need to reconstruct their world view or conception.	

FIGURE 14.5 Teaching approaches of academics (based on Trigwell, Prosser, & Taylor, 1994)

sustains the teachers' decision for adopting a particular (teaching) strategy. Teaching Approaches A and B share the same teachers' strategy, while Teaching Approaches B and C share the same teachers' intention. Finally Teaching Approaches D and E have the same strategy, differing slightly on the teachers' intention. The five teaching approaches can be grouped in two major *Preferential Teaching Approaches* namely: ITTF – Information Transmission Teacher Focused (Teaching Approaches A + B + C) and CCSF – Conceptual Change Student Focused (Teaching Approaches D + E) since Teaching Approaches A, B and C do not have any intention or any strategy in common with the Teaching Approaches D and E. (Figure 14.4). However it is important to notice that, according to the mentors of this model teaching conceptions are "(…) hierarchically related in the sense that teachers whose approach is towards the E end of the range are aware of the full ranges of approaches and how it may apply to their teaching, while those who approach their teaching closer to the A end of the range do not seem to be aware of the full range" (Prosser & Trigwell, 1997, p. 26).

The need in broaden the research, as well as the desire to apply the model within real lecture contexts, lead to the development of an inventory with 22 items that allows the identification of the *Preferential Teaching Approach* (PTA) of an university teacher (Trigwell & Prosser, 1999; Trigwell & Prosser, 2004; Prosser & Trigwell, 2006; Trigwell, Prosser, & Ginns, 2005). In the *Approaches to Teaching Inventory*, in short ATI, Teachers are asked to position themselves based on the information of each item signaling their opinion on a Likert scale from 1 to 5. The PTA is indicated by the higher mean value for each scale (CCSF vs. ITTF). Since its dissemination the inventory has been applied in diverse investigations aiming at relating teaching conceptions with other personal characteristics of university teachers and/or other contextual factors that integrate the teaching-learning environment at universities (for example, Eley, 2006; Silva Lopes, Pedrosa-de-Jesus, & Watts, 2016).

New Contributions on Academics Teaching Conceptions – Evidences from a Portuguese Longitudinal Case Study

The longitudinal case study that is presented is integrated in the broader research endeavour reported in this book as being the "Aveiro – Project". Global aim of this research endeavour as well as transversal methodological approaches were already described in Chapter 12.

This specific study reported in this chapter intended to describe and relate the individualized teaching practices of the participating academics with their personal questioning practices. Within this backdrop two university teachers were observed and supported in their daily teaching activities related with

	School year I				School year II	
	Application 1 (beginning of the semester)		Application 2 (end of the semester)		Application 3 (beginning of the semester)	
	ITTF	CCSF	ITTF	CCSF	ITTF	CCSF
Barbara	4.2	3.4	4.0	3.7	3.8	3.3
Charles	3.2	4.0	3.0	4.0	3.0	3.3

FIGURE 14.6 PTA identification through the ATI responses of two academics

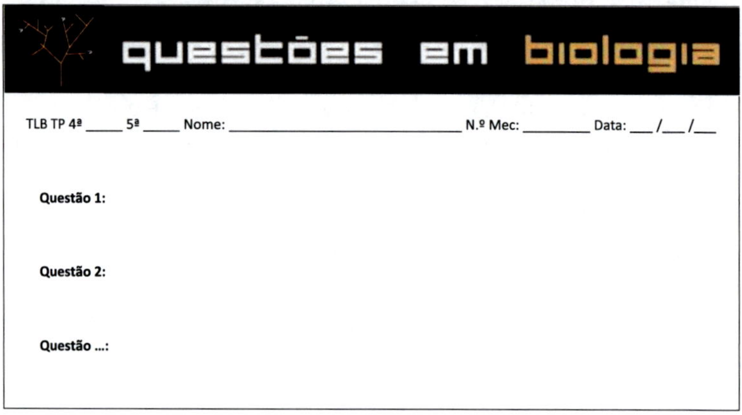
questões em biologia

TLB TP 4ª _____ 5ª _____ Nome: ______________________________ N.º Mec: ________ Data: ___/___/___

Questão 1:

Questão 2:

Questão ...:

FIGURE 14.7 The question sheet strategy: Global description and an illustrative example

lecturing undergraduate students during two schoolyears (2009/2010 and 2010/2011). During each year it was possible to observe both teachers lecturing Biology topics to the same class although with a slight time lag: Teacher Barbara[3] taught Microbiology during *the first semester*, while teacher Charles[4] taught topics around *Evolution* during the second semester.

The operationalization of the defined research intention, namely investigating how teachers use questions and how this is related to their teaching conceptions, implied two methodological decisions: (i) the adoption of a theoretical framework considering the relationship between teaching conceptions and teaching practices in order to sustain the analysis of the collected data; and (ii) the creation of a facilitative environments towards questioning during lectures in order to be able to collect teacher and students questions, which were selected as the primary data that would be used to codify teacher and students questioning practices and students' questioning competences.

Considering the first issue it was decided to adopt the theoretical framework of PTA, since the theoretical model entails the dimension *teachers' intention*, considered to be a key-element that bridges 'espoused teaching theories' with 'teaching theories in action' and because of the associated instruments, namely the ATI. This inventory, since its development, has been widely used and subjected to scientific scrutiny (Trigwell & Prosser, 2004).[5] Moreover, the inventory is composed of (only) 22 items being shorter than its equivalent instrument aimed at identifying Orientations to Teaching. Since it was planned to apply the instruments several times and in different contexts it was considered to be wiser to use a short and concise inventory that could easily be answered, repeatedly, by busy university teachers without being too 'plagay'. The inventory (Figure 14.6) was applied three times, and according to the obtained results the two teachers have 'opposite' PTAs. While Teacher Charles was identified as having and CCSF approach, Barbara's responses indicates that she has an ITTF approach. Interesting is that both cases maintained their PTA, throughout the four semesters. The implications of these results considering teaching conceptions and its relation with pedagogical innovation will be the focus of the discussion.

On what concerns to the promotion of teacher-student and student-student interaction through questioning during lectures the educational researcher at the beginning of the study suggested the implementation of several pedagogical strategies, being one of them the *Question sheet* (Figure 14.7). It is important to notice that the researcher presented the same teaching strategies to both teachers. How they were adopted, and eventually adopted will be explored further on. During the second year it was intended to give more freedom to the teachers. Therefore it was decided not to impose the previous implemented strategies. The teachers had the chance to adopt new strategies, to adapt the previous ones or to implement them again, according to their personal preference. Again this aspect will be discussed in the findings having in mind their PTA and the corresponding teaching conceptions.

Finally, data collection was mainly focused on obtaining evidences related to academics teaching conceptions and teaching practices, particularly those involving questioning. Therefore, besides applying repeatedly the ATI, the educational researcher observed all lectures that were taught by each teacher and realized eight individual semi-structured interviews (one at the beginning and one at the end of each school semester, for each teacher). Relevant insights collected during informal chats before or after the lectures that were observed, and which were registered on the researchers' diary were also used (for more information please read Chapter 12).

Barbara's Pedagogical Innovation Path

Barbara welcomed the suggestion of implementing the *question sheet* very well "since it could help students to be aware of the importance in studying and taking notes during lectures" (interview 2). Along the semester Barbara brought to each lecture a print out of the students' question collected at the end of the previous lecture. She used to read out load those questions, picking up particular students' from the audience to answer.

When she was challenged during the second time to implement an innovative strategy, Barbara asked for some time to think about it. One week later she decided to apply the *same strategy*, changing only the name to "Questions in Microbiology". Despite the fact that she was responsible for two classes at this particular school year, she decided to implement it only with the class were students seem to have a better performance "the students of this class seem to be more mature and they probably are more able to formulate interesting questions" (interview 3).

After the second lecture, she expressed her worries about 'time management': "If they start to make too many questions I will not have time to answer them all" (observational note, quoting Barbara), considering even to drop this strategy. Within this confidence, the educational researcher remembered that she was not obligated to 'get stuck' at the original strategy, that she was free to adapt it before considering to lose it completely: "not all questions had to be answered during lectures, some of them could be explored through the online learning platform". Barbara did not drop the strategy, but did not use the online platform either. During the next lectures she started to select some questions of the complete list commonly stating that these questions were good questions and "could even be integrated in the final exam" (observational note, quoting Barbara during one lecture).

At the middle of the semester Barbara again shared with the educational researcher her worries that some questions continued to be of low quality and that she would like to empathize this aspect with the students, that 'good questions need preparation at home ... they need work and effort' (observational note, quoting Barbara during one informal briefing). Considering this both prepared one 'joint' lecture that was dedicated to analyse and comment specific student question using the ASI categorization system (Pedrosa-de-Jesus et al., 2006) as a reference.[6]

Near to the end of the semester, it was interesting to observe that Barbara started to bring the printed compilation of student question to the lectures of the class were she had decided not to implement the strategy. She even introduced a final revision for the exam in this class sustaining the exploration of contents based on those questions and using them as a prompter for the students to share their doubts also

Barbara, according to the three inventory results can be described as a teacher having an Information-Transmission-Teacher-Focused (ITTF) approach, which signals that she is mainly a teacher that intends to "help students acquire the contents of the discipline and the relationship between those contents" anticipating that she "(...) asks, and encourages students to ask questions, which are in the main answered by the teacher. But in answering the questions the teacher may depart from his/her pre-planned structure" (confront with the global PTA description of Figure 14.5).

Data gathered from lecture observation and complemented with the interviews, confirms this profile indicated by the ATI results. However despite maintaining her PTA, continuing to be focused on her and the transmission of information, smooth changes on her teaching practices were observed which helped her to 'fulfil' better her role as a teacher and to operationalize her teaching conceptions. Interviews allowed perceiving that those included a mixture of teaching as transmitting concepts of the syllabus, teaching as transmitting the teachers knowledge and teaching as helping students acquire concepts of the syllabus:

> For me the goal of teaching Microbiology is to teach them some basic concepts to make them able to understand Microbiology. With this first year students I have to transmit the basic concepts so they can know and understand them, only then they will be able to comprehend the laboratorial techniques ... They need to know what microorganisms are, what they do and how they grow ... Their impact on our daily life ... at industry ... in health and in restaurants. (interview 1)

Charles's Pedagogical Innovation Path

Like his colleague, Charles, was also very enthusiastic about the suggestion in implementing the Question sheet. However, right from the start he was quite assertive about its operationalization: "Yes, we can do this, but we probably have to manage a strategy that makes them participate' throughout the semester ... *we have* to include this into their evaluation" (interview 1).[7]

Considering this aspect the strategy was adapted right from the beginning. Several meetings were dedicated to establish the evaluation criteria.[8] Perhaps the most crucial adaption was that each student at the end of the semester received a compilation of his/her own question he/she had been delivering at the end of each lecture. The pedagogical intention beneath it was to create an opportunity to confront the student with his/her personal learning processes. Students were asked to read their questions and to choose at least one question that they considered to be the one with a greater impact (positive or negative) on their learning outputs related to the topics of Evolution and to justify their selection.

During the second year the teacher decided right away to drop the question sheet and to experiment another one, namely asking the students for a "critical essay about a scientific paper related to Evolution". Again, Charles invested some of his time in developing a feedback strategy and defining the evaluation criteria, which were explained to the students during one of the first lectures.

Finally, focusing our attention on Charles PTA, the ATI results identify him as having a conceptual-change-student-focused approach. Considering this output, it is expected that Charles is a teachers that tries to structure teaching learning situations in order to encourage students to accept their responsibility for their own learning. Again this indirect result, since it is based on Charles reflection about himself, being expressed on a particular answer at the ATI, is aligned with direct observation of lectures and complementary daily activity. Right from the beginning Charles tried to create opportunities for peer interaction, in order to help students "to deal with their knowledge, make them use and expand that knowledge by discussing it with me and with their colleagues"[10] However, despite his focus on students' development and change, he also assumes that teaching implies knowledge transmission:

> I see this [developing students] as a whole. There are some evolutionary mechanisms that the students have to know and understand. For instance, the mechanisms of speciation, if the process is sympatric or allopatric. The students have to understand these concepts in order to apply them in a scientific discussion. But these concepts are not very difficult. Probably the concepts just need to be red on a book. So if I explain the concept during lectures, probably with some graphics ... they probably will understand it and we can move to the next step ... apply them on a broader discussion. This is what is really interesting. (interview 1)

Final Comments

Understanding the connection between teaching conceptions, teaching intentions and teaching practices is crucial to the design and implementation of successful strategies envisaging quality teaching and, consequently, learning at higher education. At the beginning of this chapter it was highlighted that the academic community has not yet reached to consensus considering the nature of teaching conceptions and the nature of their changes. For some researchers, teachers' conceptions have a hierarchical organization, meaning that the teaching conceptions that are focused on students' development are more complex and integrate previous elements of the less complex teaching conceptions, which tend to be more focused on the transmission of information. On contrary, other investigators, such as assume that teachers *change* their teaching conception, losing some previous elements.

The 'Aveiro Project' and in particular this two case study, allowed the gathering of data that points to an integrative nature of academics conception. This may be at seen at best with Charles, whose PTA approach is at the more complex pole, and therefore there are more chances to collect evidences of the different teaching conceptions (having more of them, pushed up the possibility of identifying those). However even with Barbara it was possible to see that she sees teaching not only as transmitting information, but also as interacting with students, even though she made have some punctual operationalization difficulties of this last conception.

The integrative nature of teaching conceptions might be the answer for reported mismatches between espoused teaching theory and teaching theory in action (Kane, Sandretto, & Heath, 2002). For instance Professor Charles during undergraduate lectures revealed to have a CCSF approach. However in the context of master classes he confesses adopted a very transmissive approach, despite his conviction. When questioned about this, he mentioned that the students' pressure to transmit knowledge was quite intense so he decided to adapt his practice to this contextual factor. Key point here is that it is a conscious mismatch. In this case it is important to support the teacher to overcome external difficulties, help them to negotiate with students. But there might also be teachers with unconscious mismatches. Here strategies that support the teacher to focus on reflecting on his/her personal teaching motivations and actions would perhaps be most appropriate.

Finally, considering pedagogical innovation, the integrative nature of teaching conceptions may also explain why some teachers have more flexibility in adopting or adapting a teaching strategy, already reported by Coffey and Gibbs (2002), and why a particular political-institutional orientation/instruction rarely will have the same outputs (is this even desirable?) in lecture contexts. Teachers think different about teaching, therefore they will appropriate differently the strategy and will take different decisions throughout the way. Considering this the core aim within the process of 'transforming the pedagogy of universities' should be the creation of opportunities for teachers to reflect on their daily activity and to assist them, if asked, in the implementation of their own ideas. It is the teachers' obligation, but also right, to identify the problems of their lectures, and to implement solutions they consider to be adequate instead of 'copy-paste' top-down bologna instructions.

Notes

1 A third research domain can be identified namely the study of *Lecturing Styles*. However this research domain is of broader and highly heterogeneous nature (Quinlan, 1999) which is mainly evident by the enormous diversity of instruments (questionnaires and inventories) aimed at characterizing the teaching strategies that academics use during their lectures. This can be related to the absence of an

integrative theoretical model, as well as to the fact that the majority of studies have a more applied and very contextualized approach, since they are designed mainly as reflection instruments that are intended to assist teachers on their reflection about teaching and eventually prompting their acknowledgement about possible mismatches between their lecturing styles and the students learning style. For more information read, for example, Leung, Lue, and Lee (2003); Kassab, Al-Shboul, Abu-Hijleh, and Hamdy (2006).

2 Scheme elaborated based on Gow and Kember (1993). Frontiers between conceptions integrating the same orientation to teaching are deliberately diffuse, evidencing close connection between them, which is not the case between teaching conceptions of different orientations to teaching.
3 Fictional name.
4 In this study the authors analyse the use of the instrument in ten independent investigations from 15 different countries and over 650 responses.
5 More information about this categorization system in Chapter 13.
6 This position was later explained further on at the second interview: "the motivation of first year students has 'structural problems', which may be related to an 'overload' of stimulus that the integration at universities entail ... everything is new for them ... to focus them the teachers has to motivate them to interact with each other and with the teacher ... and I try to do this during lectures ... but the integration of what we ask to do them into the assessment criteria is the most efficient strategy. If it doesn't count for the final grade, they will not do it".
7 More about this process can be read in Chapter 15.
8 Interview excerpt that was coded as being expression of a teaching conceptions E and F, according to Prosser and Trigwell's categorization. Please consult Figure 14.4.

References

Biggs, J. (1989). Approaches to the enhancement of tertiary teaching. *Higher Education Research and Development, 8,* 7–26.
Coffey, M., & Gibbs, M. (2002). Measuring teachers repertoire of teaching methods. *Assessment & Evaluation in Higher Education, 27,* 383–390.
Dall'Alba, G. (1991). *Foreshadowing conceptions of teaching.* Paper presented at the 6th Annual Conference of the Higher Education Research and Developmente Society of Autralasia, Brisbane.
Devlin, M. (2006). Challenging accepted wisdom about the place of conception of teaching improvement. *International Journal of Teaching and Learning in Higher Education, 18*(2), 112–119.

Eley, M. E. (2006). Teachers' conception of teaching and the making of specific descisions in planning to teach. *Higher Education, 51*, 191–214.

Ford, N., & Chen, S. (2001). Matching/mismatching revisited: An empirical study of learning and teaching styles. *British Journal of Educational Technology, 32*, 5–22.

Gow, L., & Kember, D. (1993). Conceptions of teaching and their relationship to students learning. *British Journal of Educational Psychology, 63*, 20–33.

Gow, L., Kember, D., & Sivan, A. (1992). Lecturers' views of their teaching practices: Implication for staff development needs. *Higher Education Research and Development, 11*, 135–149.

Kane, R., Sandretto, S., & Heath, C. (2002). Telling half the story: A critical review of research on teaching beliefs and practices of university academics. *Review of Educational Research, 72*, 177–228.

Kassab, S., Al-Shboul, Q., Abu-Hijleh, M., & Hamdy, H. (2006). Teaching styles of tutors in a problem based curriculum: Students' and tutors perception. *Medical Teacher, 28*(5), 460–464.

Kember, D. (1997). A reconceptualization of the research into university academics' conception of teaching. *Learning and Instruction, 7*(3), 255–275.

Kember, D. (1998). *Teaching beliefs and their impact on students' approach to learning*. Melbourne: Australian Council for Educational Research.

Kember, D., & Gow, L. (1989). A model of student approaches to learning encompassing ways to influence and change approaches. *Instructional Science, 18*, 263–288.

Kember, D., & Gow, L. (1994). Orientations to teaching and their effect on the quality of student learning. *Higher Education, 65*, 58–74.

Kember, D., & Kwan, K. P. (2000). Lecturers approaches to teaching and their relationship to conceptions of good teaching. *Instructional Science, 28*, 469–490.

Kember, D., Kwan, K. P., & Ledesma, J. (2001). Conceptions of good teaching and how they influence the way adults and school leavers are taught. *International Journal of Lifelong Education, 20*(5), 393–404.

Kember, D., Leung, Y. J. P., & Ma, R. S. F. (2007). Characterizing learning environments capable of nurturing generic capabilities in higher education. *Research in Higher Education, 48*(5), 609–632.

Lam, B. H., & Kember, D. (2006). The relationship between conceptions of teaching and approaches to teaching. *Teachers and Teaching: Theory and Practice, 12*(6), 693–713.

Leung, K., Lue, B., & Lee, M. (2003). Development of a teaching style inventory for tutor evaluation. *Medical Education, 37*, 410–416.

Lindblom-Ylänne, S., Trigwell, K., Nevgi, A., & Ashwin, P. (2006). How approaches to teaching are affected by discipline and teaching context. *Studies in Higher Education, 31*(3), 285–298.

Lopes, B., Moreira, A. C., & Pedrosa-de-Jesus, M. H. (2012). Questions in biology: Designing an online discussion forum for promoting active learning about evolution.

In F. Gonçalves, R. Pereira, W. Leal Filho, & U. M. Azeiteiro (Eds.), *Contributions to the UN decade of education for sustainable development*. Frankfurt: Peter Lang.

Lopes, B., Pedrosa-de-Jesus, M. H., & Watts, D. M. (2016). The old questions are the best: Striving against invalidity in qualitative research. In M. Tight & J. Huisman (Eds.), *Theory and method in higher education research* (Vol. 2, pp. 1–22). Bradford: Emerald Group Publishing.

Mälkki, K., & Lindblom-Ylänne, S. (2012). From reflection to action? Barriers and bridges between higher education teachers' thoughts and actions. *Studies in Higher Education, 37*(1), 33–50.

Marton, F., Dall'Alba, G., & Beaty, E. (1993). Conceptions of learning. *International Journal of Educational Research, 46*, 115–127.

Meyer, J. H. F., & Malcolm, G. E. (2006). The approaches to teaching inventory: A critique of its development and applicability. *British Journal of Educational Psychology, 76*, 633–649.

Norton, L., Richardson, J., Hartley, T. E., Newstead, S., & Mayes, J. (2005). Teachers' beliefs and intention concerning teaching in higher education. *Higher Education, 50*, 537–571.

Pajares, M. F. (1992). Teachers' beliefs and educational research: Cleaning up a messy construct. *Review of Educational Research, 62*, 307–332.

Pedrosa-de-Jesus, M. H., & da Silva Lopes, B. (2011). The relationship between teaching and learning conceptions, preferred teaching approaches and questioning practices. *Research Papers in Education, 26*(2), 223–243.

Pedrosa-de-Jesus, M. H., da Silva Lopes, B., Moreira, A., & Watts, D. M. (2012). Contexts for questioning: Two zones of teaching and learning in undergraduate science. *Higher Education, 64*(4), 557–571.

Pedrosa-de-Jesus, M. H., da Silva Lopes, B., & Watts, D. M. (2013). *Striving against invalidity in qualitative research: Discussing a reflective framework*. Proceedings of the 18th annual conference of the education, learning, styles, individual differences network (ELSIN), Billund, Dinamarca.

Postareff, L., Kaajavuoi, N., Lindblom-Ylänne, S., & Trigwell, K. (2008). Consonance and dissonance in descriptions of teaching of university teachers. *Studies in Higher Education, 33*(1), 49–61.

Prosser, M., Martin, E., Trigwell, K., Ramsden, P., & Luevkenhausen, G. (2005). Academics experiences of understanding their subject matter and the relationship of this to their experiences of teaching and learning. *Instructional Science, 33*, 137–157.

Prosser, M., & Trigwell, K. (1997). Relations between perceptions of the teaching environment and approaches to teaching. *British Journal of Educational Psychology, 67*, 25–35.

Prosser, M., & Trigwell, K. (1999). *Understanding learning and teaching: The experience in higher education*. Buckingham: Open University Press.

Prosser, M., & Trigwell, K. (2001). *Understanding learning and teaching.* Philadelphia, PA: The Society for Research into Higher Education.

Prosser, M., & Trigwell, K. (2006). Confirmatory factor analysis of the approaches to teaching inventory. *British Journal of Educational Psychology, 76,* 405–419.

Prosser, M., Trigwell, K., & Taylor, P. (1994). A phenomenographic study of academics' conception of science learning and teaching. *Learning and Instruction, 4,* 217–231.

Quinlan, K. M. (1999). Commonalities and controversy in context: A study of academic historians educational beliefs. *Teaching and Teacher Education, 15,* 447–463.

Quinn, L. (2012). Understanding resistance: An analysis of discourse in academic staff development. *Studies in Higher Education, 37,* 66–83.

Ramsden, P., Prosser, M., Trigwell, K., & Martin, E. (2007). University teachers' experiences of academic leadership and their approaches to teaching. *Learning and Instructional Design, 17,* 140–155.

Samuelowicz, K., & Bain, J. D. (2001). Revisiting academic belief about teaching and learning. *Higher Education, 41,* 299–325.

Singer, E. R. (1996). Espoused teaching paradigms of college faculty. *Research in Higher Education, 37*(6), 659–679.

Trigwell, K., & Prosser, M. (1991). Relating approaches to study and quality of learning outcomes at the course level. *British Journal of Educational Psychology, 61,* 265–275.

Trigwell, K., & Prosser, M. (1993). Approaches adopted by teachers of first year university science courses. *Research and Development in Higher Education, 14,* 223–228.

Trigwell, K., & Prosser, M. (1996a). Changing approaches to teaching: A relational perspective. *Studies in Higher Education, 21,* 275–284.

Trigwell, K., & Prosser, M. (1996b). Congruence between intention and strategy in university science teachers' approaches to teaching. *Higher Education, 32,* 77–87.

Trigwell, K., & Prosser, M. (2004). Development and use of the approaches to teaching Inventory. *Educational Psychology Review, 16,* 409–424.

Trigwell, K., Prosser, M., & Ginns, P. (2005). Phenomenographic pedagogy and a revised approach to teaching inventory. *Higher Education Research and Development, 24*(4), 349–360.

Trigwell, K., Prosser, M., & Taylor, P. (1994). Qualitative differences in approaches to teaching first year university science. *Higher Education, 27,* 75–84.

Van Driel, J. H., Verloop, N., & Van Werven, H. I. (1997). Teachers' craft knowledge and curriculum innovation in higher engineering education. *Higher Education, 34,* 105–122.

CHAPTER 15

Models of Teachers' SoTL

Helena Pedrosa-de-Jesus, Cecilia Guerra and Mike Watts

Introduction

This chapter focuses on academic growth of four university teachers across the academic years 2006/2014, using naturalistic contexts of collaborative research. Our own role has been that of supportive co-researchers, facilitating and enhancing discussion about scholarship of teaching and learning (SoTL) (Boyer, 1990; Cleaver, Lintern, & McLinden, 2014; Hutchings, Huber, & Ciccone, 2011). We adopt the view that SoTL is an essential part of every university teacher's academic practice (D'Andrea & Gosling, 2005). The four university teachers critically reflected about their teaching, within a supportive educational community and, more importantly for us, to explore students' learning processes. The goals were to: (i) work alongside these four university teachers in designing and adopting novel practices to meet new demands on their time and teaching; (ii) evaluate innovative teaching and learning strategies in action, and (iii) stimulate university teachers' academic reflection on issues of teaching and learning at this level. In our case, this had taken place within a positive change environment that has largely enabled academic growth to take place for these four university teachers.

Scholarship of Teaching and Learning

The Teaching and Learning International Survey (OECD, 2009, p. 49) describes professional pedagogical training and development as those 'activities that develop an individual's skills, knowledge, expertise and other characteristics as a teacher'. In this vein, a report to the European Commission on 'Improving the Quality of Teaching and Learning in Europe's Higher Education Institutions' (European Commission, 2013, p. 13) states that: 'A good teacher, like a good graduate, is also an active learner, questioner and critical thinker'. The same report recommends that: 'All staff teaching in higher education institutions in 2020should have received certified pedagogical training' (p. 64).

Academic growth can be seen as the process that promotes university teacher's knowledge related to teaching, learning, assessment and feedback practices. There are arguments that university teacher development proceeds first by teachers changing their teaching orientation (Gilmore, Maher, Feldon, & Timmerman, 2014) before they can change practice. That is, they must first re-orientate their 'conceptual map for instructional decision making' – commonly from teacher-centred to student-centred – as a prerequisite to changing within the context of the classroom or lecture hall. Our reading of the literature, however, is that there are a vast array of disparate characterisations of teachers and little documented evidence that re-orientation necessarily precedes re-directed practice.

The importance of the Scholarship of Teaching and Learning (SoTL) in integrating the main dimensions of a university teacher's academic work – teaching and research – has been highlighted by many (for example, Cleaver, Lintern, & McLinden, 2014; D'Andrea & Gosling, 2005). Krebber (2015) has defined SoTL as 'formal or informal, critically reflective inquiry into teaching and learning, underpinned by virtues and standards of excellence, directed at promoting the important interests of students' (p. 111). Our interest in supporting and furthering SoTL is linked to two trends, as indicated by Krebber (2015, p. 101), where universities feel increased pressure to: Demonstrate accountability, to both the public and governments, for the quality of teaching they provide (and thus for how tax payers' money is being spent), and Produce highly skilled graduates, i.e., 'knowledge workers', who will eventually contribute to local and national communities and, by extension, support the country's economic competitiveness in a global market.

This form of SoTL lies at the very centre of D'Andrea and Gosling's model of academic development (2005), and these authors are adamant that all university teachers should develop this kind of research on their practices.

However, it still remains a tendency to give priority to disciplinary research, quite commonly an activity divorced from the teaching practices (Trigwell & Shale, 2004). Hutchings, Huber, and Ciccone (2011) argue that the role of SoTL should emphasise principles of learning through inquiry (into and about practices and results), collaboration, reflection and action in the service of ongoing improvement of university teachers' academic knowledge. According to McKinney (2006, p. 39), 'teaching scholarship' involves not only a systematic study of teaching and learning, but also 'the public sharing and review of such work through live or virtual presentations, performances or publications'. That is, these new perspectives need not remain tacit or local. Teachers at this level must present their work to others and share insights with other colleagues about the different ways in which academics respond to growth opportunities in terms of their teaching practice. And, not only to present and publish their ideas and outcomes as widely as possible, but also seek both internal and external funding to develop these further. As Krebber (2015) points out, it is to be encouraged through critical dialogue and debate and in community with others.

In our view, SoTL is a worthy goal, enabling university teachers to be suitably critically reflective about their teaching, within a supportive educational community and, importantly, to explore students' learning processes (Hutchings & Shulman, 1999; Shulman, 1987; Weston & McAlpine, 2001). Our over-riding impetus behind teaching, learning, assessment and feedback innovations has been a drive towards increasing teachers' critical questioning and critical reflection (Pedrosa-de-Jesus, Moreira, Lopes, & Watts, 2014; Pedrosa-de-Jesus, Lopes, Moreira, & Watts, 2012). Reflective practice implies a level of structured questioning and of systematic review by the teacher that should be carefully considered and often documented (Clarke, & Reid, 2013; Clarke & Hollingsworth, 2002; Kreber, 2002; Kreber & Cranton, 2000). In our view, then, an inevitable product of teachers' reflection on their teaching practices in this way would be new understandings and altered perspectives of these practices (Clarke & Hollingsworth, 2002; van Schalkwyk, Cilliers, Adendorff, Cattell, & Herman, 2013).

We follow Barnett (1997), beginning with the skills required for critical questioning, progressing then through an awareness of the standards of reasoning within disciplines. His 'being critical' is an approach to life to which a university educated person should aspire, involving dispositions and abilities to think criticality in order to act/intervene: 'Critical persons are more than just critical thinkers. They are able critically to engage with the world and with themselves as well as with knowledge' (1997, p. 1). Being critical involves cognitive knowledge, skills and the dispositions to apply those skills in a specific context. This view of critical thinking involves attitudes/dispositions and skills (Barnett, 1997; Ennis, 1996, 1997, 1998), is 'thinking without a critical edge' (Barnett, 1997, p. 17). From this perspective, being critical is part of a dialogue where individuals and group members seek to share in the 'unpacking' of aspects of their individual or shared knowledge and experience, and work through descriptions, analyses, evaluations and critiques of these experiences and the contexts in which they take place. That is, criticality can be developed and enacted in the context of specific subject domains and, as an ultimate goal, could be transferable across disciplines and domains.

A good starting point for us here is Biggs's (1999) 'constructive alignment' between a programme's learning outcomes, teaching strategies and methods of assessment. According to Biggs (1999), a constructive alignment between teaching strategies, learning outcomes and assessment methods is essential to promoting students' critical thinking.

A Report to the European Commission on Improving the Quality of Teaching and Learning in Europe's Higher Education Institutions (European Commission, 2013, p. 13) states that: 'A good teacher, like a good graduate, is also an active learner, questioner and critical thinker'. The same report also recommends that: 'All staff teaching in higher education institutions in 2020 should have received certified pedagogical training' (p. 64). So, in our version of Biggs's (1999) constructive alignment, we have added elements of feedback and academic self-reflection (Guerra, Pedrosa-de-Jesus, Correia, Cunha, Almeida, & Watts, 2015) (Figure 15.1).

We add two further elements to the Biggs's (1999) original diagram, that of academic self-reflection and feedback. This feedback can take the form of discussions with colleagues at programme level on what exactly the course aims to achieve, 'feed-forward' to students on what they are expected to do to meet the learning outcomes, peer discussions on strategies for teaching and learning, dialogue with students on various classroom approaches, formative and summative feedback on assessment, etc. In this way we have traded heavily on university teachers' academic self-reflections, what we sometimes refer to as their 'situated critical reflection' (Malthouse, Roffey-Barentsen, & Watts, 2014). Teachers' critical reflections were collected through semi-structured interviews at the end of each academic year (2012/2014). The first part of each interview was aimed at capturing their perceptions about the impact of the research collaboration on teaching and learning experimentation. The latter parts considered teachers' opinions regarding the impact of this collaboration in teachers' academic development and students' learning, respectively. The responses made in the teachers' interviews were transcribed and coded, and we developed a finer-grained analysis of the data to designate their comments.

Since the data gathered were mainly qualitative and descriptive, the principal methodology adopted has been content analysis (Bardin, 2000). We used an analytic framework, entitled a *Maintenance/Adaptation/Innovation academic practice (MAI model)* for analysing university teachers' academic growth (Guerra, Pedrosa-de-Jesus, Correia, Cunha, Almeida, & Watts, 2015) (Figure 15.2).

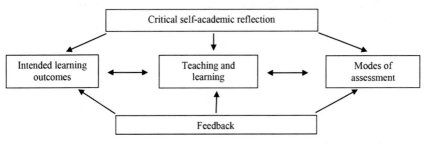

FIGURE 15.1   The role of feedback and academic self-reflection on academic growth

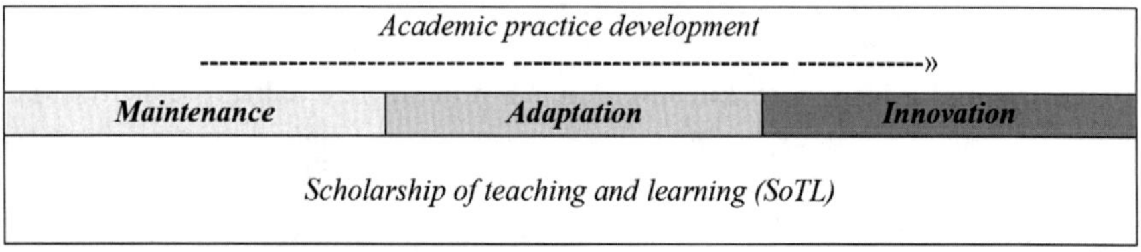

Academic practice development »»		
Maintenance	Adaptation	Innovation
Scholarship of teaching and learning (SoTL)		

FIGURE 15.2 Maintenance/adaptation/innovation academic practice (MAI model)

This model is organised in three main dimensions: Maintenance practice entails sustaining a teaching, learning, assessment and feedback strategy, without researchers' collaboration, with the purpose of delivering benefit(s) for student's learning; Adaptation practice entails adapting a previous teaching, learning, assessment and feedback strategy, one which was developed with this research team (between 2007 and 2010), with the purpose of delivering benefit(s) for student's learning; and Innovation practice entails designing a new teaching, learning, assessment and feedback strategy with the purpose of delivering benefit(s) for student's learning.

Research Approach

This research approach is based on a critical social paradigm, assuming principles of action-research methodology (Cohen, Manion, & Morrison, 2007; Schmuck, 2006). Our research preference has been for a transitional 'instructional coaching approach' (Burkins & Ritchie, 2007; Kennedy, 2005; Knight, 2004; Schrum, English, & Galizio, 2012). Such an approach entails co-researcher investigations (Macaro & Mutton, 2002), which allows each participant to benefit from the enterprise. In this case we collaborated with the four university teachers over two academic years (2012/2014) and, as researchers, had the opportunity to study natural teaching-learning settings. Research data were collected through a 'participant observation' of one researcher during twenty nine 'Instructional coaching meetings' with the four university teachers and the research group, along with online interactions, mainly throughout email (Figure 15.3).

		Number of meetings	
		2012/2013	2013/2014
Group coaching seminars		4	1
Individual coaching sessions	Formal and informal meetings	13	11
Total		17	12

FIGURE 15.3 The instructional coaching meetings

The coaching meetings were organised in two forms: 'Group coaching seminars', which involved the whole research group, that is, six educational researchers, four university teachers and one external consultant; and 'Individual coaching sessions', involving individual formal and informal meeting (before and after classes) with the teachers. The four university teachers had considerable support in enacting, reflecting upon, analysing and evaluating new approaches to teaching and learning. The coaching meetings aimed to (i) identify educational problems and possible solutions for resolution, (ii) design and implement solutions to the educational problems identified, and (iii) critical reflect on the solutions designed for those problems identified.

A negotiated schedule of 'low-participant' classroom observations of each teacher were undertaken by the research team. The observed situations were 'authentic' in keeping with the essence of a naturalistic approach (Cohen, Manion, & Morrison, 2007). All the written documents produced by the participants as a consequence of the research innovations introduced were collected for analysis. There were external sources of information introduced by the educational researchers as they worked and the university teachers, too, introduced relevant chapters into the discussions. These were logged and discussed, and commonly appear in some of the contributions to scholarship catalogued in the following sections, focused on academic growth.

Research Outcomes

Teacher A

Figure 15.4 shows some of the forms of teaching strategies used by Teacher A on his curricular units during two academic years (2012/2014).

Strategies	Description	Academic year	
		2012/2013	2013/2014
Microtalk	Conducting 4 lectures by researchers in Microbiology, and filmed by Educast system	Adaptation	Maintenance
Exploration of microbial world	Conducting a face-to-face session in Microbiology with the following aims: to stimulate students' oral questioning; to design questions according to ASI system (acquisitive, specialist and integrative questions) (authors, 2004, 2006).		Innovation
Scitable	Exploring an online tool with scientific contents in Genetics (Nature Publishing Group)	Maintenance	Maintenance

FIGURE 15.4   Teaching strategies used by Teacher A (2012/2014)

Teacher A first attempted the Microtalk strategy with the aim of stimulating students' knowledge about research in microbiology, in this case the topic of bacteria with antibiotic resistance. Each talk comprised a twelve-minute presentation by researchers from the Department of Biology, followed by five minutes for discussion with students. The Microtalks were filmed using EDUcast service, making it available on Moodle so that students could re-view them and submit further questions and/or queries either directly to Teacher A or to the researchers. In the early stages, Teacher A saw the implementation of this teaching strategy as an opportunity for students to understand several microbiology topics related to the curricular unit contents. Students found them interesting and asked for the Microtalks to happen more often.

During the academic year 2013/2014 a new session was implemented entitled 'Exploration of microbial world'. This development allowed him to focus on the scientific information captured through students' questions. It followed our previous project (Pedrosa-de-Jesus, Lopes, Moreira, & Watts, 2012) encouraging questioning as a strategy for developing students' learning [2nd interview].

Based on this, he also asked his Microbiology and Genetics students to answer questions using Moodle. This task aimed at selecting the top five most complex questions he had placed there and to see if they could find the answers either through the Internet and/books suggested for the discipline. Teacher A was aware that collegiate meetings were consonant with a broader drive for change within the university. The teacher also considered the very positive potential of using 'Scitable' in Genetics. He stressed the potential of this online learning tool by stating that it is a good base to have as a starting point of information. And then it also leaves an open door for those [students] that are more interested in certain topics and want to explore it more [1st interview].

Strategies	Description	Academic year	
		2012/2013	2013/2014
Online questionnaire	Designing an online questionnaire with a presentation of a practical problem in Microbiology. The aim was to stimulate students' questioning, submitting questions for its resolution	Adaptation	
Rubric assessment questionnaire	Drawing a rubric with assessment criteria for the students' responses of the online questionnaire in Microbiology	Adaptation	
Mini Questionnaires	Designing 5 short questionnaires in order to promote students' involvement in the preparation of laboratory classes of Microbiology and Genetics		Innovation

FIGURE 15.5   Teaching strategies used by Teacher B (2012/2014)

Teacher B

Figure 15.5 shows some of the teaching strategies used by Teacher B in curricular units "Microbiology" and "Genetics" during the two academic years (2012/2014).

Teacher B enjoyed the importance of questioning and stressed her own practice by trying to align teaching, learning and assessment [1st interview]. She, too, shared her view that their work should be valued not just in terms of developing teaching competencies, but also in terms of scientific production [2nd interview]. Her ideas and thoughts are better expressed and explained in Chapter 17.

Teacher C

Figure 15.6 shows some strategies of teaching, learning, assessment and feedback used by Teacher C in the curricular unit "Evolution" during the two academic years (2012/2014).

This teacher developed a task requiring student 'critical analyses' related to the topic of evolution. Students worked in groups and the Teacher provided written group-based formative feedback for the task. This particular task of critical analysis entailed a considerable amount of work both from the teacher and students. He took the opportunity to peer-observe classes of other university teachers. The teacher considered that the task allowed him to develop students' competences, such as 'selection and evaluation of scientific information', and 'group work collaboration' [1st interview].

Strategies	Description	Academic year	
		2012/2013	2013/2014
Critical analyses	Producing a critical analyses of a selected press note related to the topic of evolution (i.e., the advent of genetic diseases) – Group work	Innovation	Maintenance
Teacher's written feedback	Sending written formative feedback of critical analysis (through e-mail) to 21 groups of students	Innovation	Maintenance
Students' written feedback	Sending written formative feedback of critical analysis (through a excel document and e-mail) to 21 groups of students		Innovation

FIGURE 15.6   Teaching strategies used by Teacher C (2012/2014)

However, the following year he recognized that providing extensive written formative feedback to 21 groups involved a huge effort in terms of time commitment [2nd interview].

When asked about the effect of these innovations on his classroom practice, he recognized that it was very useful since it helped him to better align teaching with learning outcomes, therefore change the way he taught. Teacher C also noted the need for the university organisation as a whole to be more committed to the development of such interdepartmental collaboration projects [2nd interview].

Strategies	Description	Academic year	
		2012/2013	2013/2014
Questions online	Designing an online questionnaire, which requested students' questions about Microbiology	Adaptation	Maintenance
Teacher's oral feedback	Oral feedback (through Moodle) to Questions in Microbiology online	Maintenance	Maintenance
Teacher's written feedback	Written feedback (through Moodle) to Questions in Microbiology online		Adaptation
Mini Questionnaires	Designing 5 short questionnaires in order to promote students' involvement in the preparation of laboratory classes of Microbiology		Innovation

FIGURE 15.7   Teaching strategies used by Teacher D (2012/2014)

Teacher D

Figure 15.7 shows some teaching, learning, assessment and feedback strategies used by Teacher D in the curricular unit "Microbiology and Pharmacology" during 2012/2014.

When interviewed, Teacher D recognised that she had started using more time asking questions during classes [1st interview]. Being surprised by students' lack of preparation for lab sessions, she instigated a question-system at the beginning of a session in order to check that students had read the preparatory work before arriving at the session [1st interview]. When reflecting about the impact of this research collaboration on her academic development, Teacher D was also very positive as can be seen in the following transcript during the 2nd interview

> Yes, it had some good impact. Let me think … I reduced the contents in the discipline … I also have been asking more questions to the students, from year to year. I have also being trying not to respond in advance to questions. I think I have done that in the beginning [of the research project] … but now I try to give them [students] indirect clues, in order they could answer at least, they could figure out what was intended with that particular question, and try to articulate the contents or apply them in a practical way …. (2nd interview)

Discussion

The various forms of disciplinary and interdisciplinary 'instructional coaching meetings' entailed colleagues make explicit to each other some of their pedagogic content. They did this through face-to-face and email conversations, commenting and advising on each other's ideas and their implementation, organising peer observation – meanwhile 'nudging' the university to take this kind of activity seriously. As can be seen in this short interview extract, the list of 'innovations' include working with a 'questioning colleague', personal reflection, instigating, restructuring course content, developing classroom questioning strategies amongst many more that were discussed elsewhere and else when.

In reference to the MAI model, there were few examples of 'leadership' by anyone of the four university teachers. So, for example, Teacher A decided to apply for national funding (FCT), including Teachers B and D and the two of the educational researchers as team members, intended as follow-up research on teaching. The project submitted was entitled 'Microtemas – A strategy for promoting Microbiology students autonomous learning competencies'. The purpose of the project was to develop a 'virtual space' for learning in microbiology, linking formal with non-formal higher education (e.g. use of 'massive open online courses' (MOOCs). Although the project was not funded, we consider this is a SoTL indicator where the teacher was autonomous in seeking to transfer their academic knowledge to other educational contexts, knowledge developed principally throughout this collaboration.

While, as noted above, they occupied different departmental roles and status in relation to each other, they tended to work easily and collaboratively together, each one taking different initiatives at different times, moving the spotlight around within the group. In addition, while they contributed to university initiatives as discussed below, they were rather more pre-occupied in ensuring ideas were tested and embedded in their own practice than leading innovations at university level.

SoTL is focused on university teachers' academic development by: drawing on literature and research on teaching to inform practices; publishing and make presentations about teaching and applying for funding for research on teaching. In general, university teachers certainly grew in their understanding and appreciation of SoTL through these activities, engaging them in the complexities of teaching and learning at this level. Some indications of the 'SoTL products' have emerged from the project. They range from contributions to internal university teaching and learning events, to external international conference presentations (Guerra et al., 2015).

In our work, the four university teachers were not content just to innovate and reflectively evaluate the developments in their teaching; they used the collaborative research process in order to gain access to a world different from their own specialist fields. While they are all involved in academic scholarship within their own disciplines, they undertook to present and publish within SoTL.

SoTL 'Academic Growth Opportunities'

This chapter presents a study of collaboration between educationalists and four university biology teachers across the academic years 2012/2014, and weighs the impact on these teachers' academic development and growth. As indicated at the start, our main goals have been to: (i) work alongside university teaching colleagues in designing and adopting novel practices to meet new demands on their time and teaching; (ii) evaluate such innovative teaching and learning strategies in action, and (iii) promote university teachers' academic reflection on issues of teaching and learning at this level.

Making changes to university teachers' conceptions of teaching and learning in the context of higher education is difficult and challenging. From the beginning, our work has been focused on understanding just how to promote university teachers' academic development throughout the design of innovative teaching, learning, assessment and feedback strategies. Our collaborative study shows the extent to which experimentation with innovative strategies by this group is strongly influenced by their particular conceptions of teaching. Results from classroom observation, individual and group meetings and teachers' individual interviews indicate how they have interpreted their academic experiences concerning the design of innovative strategies.

We have generated data from the naturalistic settings of classrooms-in-action and face-to-face conversations and discussions, and have organised the data using an analytical framework for academic development (MAI model). This allows analysis of these university teachers' ability to enact upon their teaching and the changes in their critical thinking.

There are drawbacks and limitations to conducting naturalistic research, not least forging a balance between the number of participants possible given the depth, richness and complexity of the data generated over this kind of timescale. The sample in this chapter is small and, necessarily, drawn from a very specific locale and working context. We do not feel, however, that this detracts from the quality of the growth evidenced in the section above, and the time span involved – over a two-year period – has allowed us to chart the development of these teachers in considerable detail.

One key benefit has been the close collaboration between colleagues. This has occurred across different disciplines, departments and institutions, resulting in new ideas and shared understandings. As Barefoot and Russell (2014, p. 161) note, such collaborations can enhance discussion of 'how I can improve students' experiences' of learning and assessment within a discipline-specific context. The four teachers here introduced a number of innovations to their teaching such as MicroTalks, peer observation, using students' own questions on Scitable, tasks for critical thinking and analysis and the like.

SoTL happens in the classroom, in committee meetings, in engagement with students and colleagues (peers and educational researchers). In this instance, academic development has occurred when something discussed during the 'instructional coaching meetings' and/or 'individual interviews' have generated change in university teachers' self-academic reflection in their experimentation practices and the salient outcomes of their practices (academic growth and students' learning).

Their overall comments on the project are unequivocal and pleasing. They would not have undertaken and benefited from this kind or level of educational enquiry without the collaborative input and support from each other and from educational colleagues.

Their analysis and evaluation of the innovations is clear. While they weighed the benefits to students each teacher was also acutely aware of any new demands on their own time and teaching. Some innovations were patently attempts to be time- and labour-saving, others were undertaken in the understanding that they made considerable extra call on personal resources.

On the whole they, too, have been pleased with the outcomes, resolved in places to continue to refine their own approaches and, in others, to try ideas from their colleagues. Their reflections are measured and focused, exploring what exactly happened in certain circumstances, what sense to make of it, and what was significant. In Chapter 17 they present 'situated' and reflexive comments, where they discuss the role of the institution, how their own professional practices play sometimes with, sometimes against, organisational structures and contexts.

As Bolton (2014, p. 8) points out, being reflexive is a struggle against a sense of immutability, of 'it's just how things are', or 'it's just common sense'. These teachers were prepared on occasions to occupy uncomfortable spaces. Of particular note is the extent to which these colleagues have engaged in scholarship outside of their discipline areas. It is not just Weston and McAlpine (2001) who see this as a worthy direction, Cleaver, Lintern, and McLinden (2014) also argue that, equipped with high-level enquiry-based skills, 'academics can move beyond a synthesis of the latest thinking, research and scholarship within their subject area, to actively enter into and lead debates about appropriate modes of teaching and good practice in facilitating student learning' (p. 14).

We see some of this in our work where, as we illustrate above, while they may not yet be leading, these teachers have certainly entered and contributed to the debate at both a local, regional and international level. To this extent, we can see considerable growth both down and across the analytical framework model (MAI model), we propose in this chapter. Nevertheless, there is always room for further research.

References

Bardin, L. (2009). *Análise de conteúdo*. Lisboa: Edições 70.

Barefoot, H., & Russell, M. (2014). Enquiry into learning and teaching life sciences. In E. Cleaver, M. Lintern, & M. McLinden (Eds.), *Teaching and learning in higher education, disciplinary approaches to educational inquiry*. London: Sage Publications.

Barnett, R. (1997). *Higher education: A critical business*. Buckingham: Open University Press.

Bolton, G. (2014). *Reflective practice, writing and professional development* (4th ed.). London: Sage Publications.

Boyer, E. L. (1990). *Scholarship reconsidered: Priorities of the professoriate: Carnegie endowment for the advancement of teaching*. Princeton, NJ: Princeton-Hall.

Clarke, C., & Reid, J. (2013). Foundational academic development: Building collegiality across divides? *International Journal for Academic Development, 18*(4), 318–330. doi:10.1080/1360144X.2012.728529

Clarke, D. J., & Hollingsworth, H. (2002). Elaborating a model of teacher professional growth. *Teaching and Teacher Education, 18*(8), 947–967.

Cleaver, E., Lintern, M., & McLinden, M. (Eds.). (2014). *Teaching and learning in higher education, disciplinary approaches to educational inquiry*. London: Sage Publications.

D'Andrea, V., & Gosling, D. (2005). *Improving teaching and learning in higher education: A whole institution approach*. Berkshire: Open University Press.

Ennis, R. H. (1996). Critical thinking dispositions: Their nature and accessibility. *Informal Logic, 18*(2–3), 165–182.

Ennis, R. H. (1997). Incorporating critical thinking in the curriculum: An introduction to some basic issues. *Inquiry: Critical Thinking across disciplines, XVI*(3), 1–9.

Ennis, R. H. (1998). Is critically thinking culturally biased? *Teaching Philosophy, 21*(1), 15–33.

European Commission. (2013). *Report to the European commission on improving the quality of teaching and learning in Europe's higher education institutions*. Luxembourg: Publications Office of the European Union.

Gilmore, J., Maher, M. A., Feldon, D. F., & Timmerman, B. (2014). Exploration of factors related to the development of science, technology, engineering and mathematics graduate teaching assistants' teaching orientations. *Studies in Higher Education, 39*(10), 1910–1928.

Guerra, C., Pedrosa-de-Jesus, H., Correia, A., Cunha, A., Almeida, A., & Watts, D. M. (2015). Promoting academic development trough situated critical reflection. In L. Leite, M. A. Flores, L. Dourado, M. T. Vilaça, & S. Morgado (Eds.), *Proceedings of the ATEE annual conference transitions in teacher education and professional identities* (pp. 267–278). Braga: University of Minho. Retrieved from https://repositorium.sdum.uminho.pt/handle/1822/36281?locale=en

Higher Education Academy. (2011). *The UK professional standards framework for teaching and supporting learning in higher education*. Retrieved November 28, 2013, from http://www.heacademy.ac.uk/assets/documents/ukpsf/ukpsf.pdf

Hutchings, P., Huber, M., & Ciccone, A. (2011). *The scholarship of teaching and learning reconsidered: Institutional integration and impact.* San Francisco, CA: Jossey-Bass.

Hutchings, P., & Shulman, L. S. (1999). The scholarship of teaching: New elaborations, new developments, change. *The Magazine of Higher Learning, 31*(5), 10–15.

Kreber, C. (1999). A course-based approach to the development of teaching-scholarship: A case study. *Teaching in Higher Education, 4*(3), 309–325.

Kreber, C. (2002). Controversy and consensus on the scholarship of teaching. *Studies in Higher Education, 27*(2), 151–167.

Kreber, C. (2015). Furthering the "theory debate" in the scholarship of teaching: A proposal based on MacIntyre's account of practices. *Canadian Journal of Higher Education, 45*(2), 99–115.

Kreber, C., & Cranton, P. A. (2000). Exploring the scholarship of teaching. *Journal of Higher Education, 71*(4), 476–495.

Malthouse, R., Roffey-Barentsen, J., & Watts, D. M. (2014). Reflectivity, reflexivity and situated reflective practice. *Professional Development in Education, 40,* 597–609. doi:10.1080/19415257.2014.907195

McKinney, K. (2006). Attitudinal and structural factors contributing to challenges in the work of the scholarship of teaching and learning. *New Directions for Institutional Research, 129,* 37–50.

OECD. (2009). *TALIS technical report.* Paris: OECD Publishing.

Pedrosa-de-Jesus, M. H., Guerra, C., Moreira, A., & Watts, D. M. (2014, July 9–13). *The role of teacher's written formative feedback on students' critical thinking* (pp. 221–238). Proceedings of The European Conference on Education 2014 (IAFOR), Brighton. Retrieved from http://iafor.org/iafor/iafor-european-conference-series-2014-conference-proceedings-now-online/

Pedrosa-de-Jesus, M. H., Lopes, B., Moreira, A. C., & Watts, D. M. (2012). Contexts for questioning: Two zones of teaching and learning in undergraduate science. *Higher Education, 64*(4), 557–571.

Pedrosa-de-Jesus, M. H., Moreira, A., Lopes, B., & Watts, D. M. (2014). So much more than just a list: Exploring the nature of critical questioning in undergraduate sciences. *Research in Science & Technological Education, 32*(2), 115–134. doi:10.1080/02635143.2014.902811

Shulman, S. (1987). Knowledge and teaching: Foundations of the new reform. *Harvard Educational Review, 57*(1), 1–22.

van Schalkwyk, S., Cilliers, F., Adendorff, H., Cattell, K., & Herman, N. (2013). Journeys of growth towards the professional learning of academics: Understanding the role of educational development. *International Journal for Academic Development, 18*(2), 139–151.

Weston, C. B., & McAlpine, L. (2001). Making explicit the development toward the scholarship of teaching. *New Directions for Teaching & Learning, 86,* 89–97. Retrieved from http://onlinelibrary.wiley.com/doi/10.1002/tl.19/pdf

CHAPTER 16

Assessment and Feedback

Helena Pedrosa-de-Jesus, Aurora Coelho Moreira, Betina da Silva Lopes, Cecilia Guerra and Mike Watts

Introduction

There exists a substantial literature on the forms and function of assessment and feedback within systems of higher education. In this chapter we discuss our own work in this area throughout the 'Aveiro Project' and, in broad terms, this entails

1. Discussions on the nature of feedback, its applications and impact.
2. Our own approach to what we call 'active constructive feedback'.
3. Project interventions and examples of innovation in assessment and feedback, and the technological approaches we have adopted in order to support teachers in delivering feedback to students.

An important principle embedded in students' activity is their criticality: the capacity to receive and give suitable critique with and of others, as well as of self, while the teacher quite clearly has a series of responsibilities in relation to ensuring good quality, timely feedback and support, the student, too, has a key role to play. For example, there is need for students to engage with the process and understand the marking system, criteria and grade descriptors used for each assessment, helping them understand the requirements. They need to recognise the different types of feedback they can expect to receive and apply comments to subsequent pieces of work – continually referring to feedback as they review their work in progress. In the work we discuss here, we also encourage students to engage in collaborative learning by giving, discussing and comparing their feedback with peers to support their analysis.

Feedback

Feedback to learners is considered to be one of the most influential factors in the improvement of their learning achievements. Evans (2012) has noted the current strong degree of consensus as to what constitutes effective feedback practice, particularly where assessment is considered as an integral aspect of teaching. In summarising the increasing body of research, Yorke (2003) highlights formative assessment as critically important for student learning. Without informative feedback on what they do, students will have relatively little by which to chart their development (p. 48). Providing clear requirements for participation, and ensuring approaches to assessment and feedback are congruent with intended learning outcomes, are both important design goals (Orsmond & Merry, 2011). While Hattie and Timperley (2007, p. 102) consider that feedback typically occurs '… after instruction that seeks to provide knowledge and skills or to develop particular attitudes', formative and summative assessment are more often referred to as opposite methods for assessing students work. In reality they are simply ends of the same spectrum, both of which are commonly tutor-led and dominated (Fallows & Chandramohan, 2001; Kingston, 2009 p. 31) and, according to O'Neil, Huntley-Moore and Race, it would probably be wise to stop fussing about which assessment elements were intended to be formative or summative, and to concentrate on giving students useful feedback on all the elements of their work which are assessed (2007 p. 15).

Tunstall and Gipps (1996) have shown that evaluative feedback can actually have little impact on students' performance. Ideally, when receiving feedback on their work, students deal with their difficulties and improve the next element of their assessed work (Black & Wiliam, 1998; Hattie & Jaeger, 1998; Race, 2005). In addition, Nicol, Thomson and Breslin (2014) think that feedback has positive effects when it facilitates the development of students' reflection and self-assessment in learning. According to O'Neil, Huntley-Moore, and Race (2007) 'feed-forward' is also a critically useful part of feedback, where students know exactly how to go about improving their learning. In this vein, Race (2005) has already presented several aspects often referred to as 'feed-forward': details of what would have been necessary to achieve better marks or grades, expressed in ways where students can seek to improve their future assignments or answers; direct suggestions for students to try out in their next piece of work, to overcome problems or weaknesses arising in their last assignment; suggestions about sources to explore, illustrating chosen aspects of what they themselves are being encouraged to do in their own future work.

Being Constructive

A key problem with many types of feedback is that it commonly focuses on the past, on activities that have already occurred – seldom on the variety of opportunities that can happen in the future. As such, feedback can be limited and static, as opposed to expressive and dynamic and, as noted, not uncommonly producing discomfort on the part of the giver and defensiveness on the part of the receiver. Even constructively delivered feedback is often seen as negative because it necessarily involves a discussion of mistakes, shortfalls, and problems. The organisational model currently used for teaching and learning in HE in the UK (Fallows & Chandramohan, 2001) further compounds this potential problem because it attempts an impersonal, summative grading system, at the expense of learner-centred formative assessment. A main strength of self- and peer-assessment and feedback relates to the enhancement of student learning by means of reflection, analysis and diplomatic criticism, and the overwhelming view (Falchikov, 2006) seems to be that it is a useful, reliable and valid exercise. Some of the advantages are that it encourages student involvement and responsibility, and prompts reflection on their role and contribution to the process of the group work. The agreed marking schemes and criteria related to the assignment become visible and this reduces confusion about assignment outcomes and expectations. Important for us is that peer assessment and feedback focuses on the development of student's judgment skills as they become involved in the process and are encouraged to take part ownership of the process. Going further, Askew and Lodge (2000) describe co-constructive feedback as a type of feedback with the following characteristics: dialogic, democratic, bi-directional, of sharing responsibilities, reflective, situated, metacognitive, formative, problem solving, enhancing learning. Besides the relevance of the teacher's role in providing oral and/or written feedback, it is also important that students engage and use feedback.

A key issue here lies in students' 'judgement skills', their capacities to be analytic and offer real but tactful critique. Ennis (1987) presented one of the most well-known definitions for critical thinking competency, distinguishing between abilities and attitudes and so-called 'dispositions'. Abilities refer to the cognitive dimensions, while dispositions relate to more affective aspects. The abilities are organised into five areas: elementary clarification, basic support, inference, elaborated clarification, and strategies and tactics. In our case, we have been interested in developing critical analysis competency in order to mobilise students' critical thinking, broadly using Ennis' (1987) taxonomy, to:

1. Judge the credibility of a source, for example, through the selection of the press cutting
2. Identify where clarification was needed during the process of knowing the aims and the scope of the research
3. Enable inferential abilities during the evidence and research outputs evaluation, and scientific articles recommendations
4. Encourage strategically and tactical abilities, described by Ennis (op cit) as 'deciding on an action' and 'interacting with others'.

TABLE 16.1 Quality of co-constructive written formative feedback (Pedrosa-de-Jesus & Guerra, 2018)

		Category	Description
A. Evaluative feedback		A.1 Positive feedback	A.1.1 To approve students' work or engagement
		A.2 Negative feedback	A.2.1 To disapprove student's work or behaviour
B. Descriptive feedback (Dimension)		B.1 Achievement feedback	B.1.1 To identify aspects of successful attainment
			B.1.2 To diagnose work performance using assessing criteria
			B.1.3 To specify failures in work performance
			B.1.4 To correct errors in work performance
			B.1.5 To provide strategies to improve work performance
		B.2 Constructing feedback	B.2.1 To use students 'best work exemplars'
			B.2.2 To discuss strategies for work improvement
			B.2.3 To specify new criteria as they emerged in students' work
			B.2.4 To involve students in evaluating standards definitions and applications
			B.2.5 To compare work with previous students' performance
			B.2.6 To focus the relevance of future development

Table 16.1 presents our 'co-constructive written formative feedback' model, developed by Pedrosa-de-Jesus and Guerra (2018), on the basis of the adapted Tunstall and Gipps (1996) feedback typology, and the results achieved during 2012/2014 academic years' experience.

Evaluative feedback (A) includes a 'qualitative summative assessment approach' with criticism about the students' assignment (both positive and/or negative), while Descriptive feedback (B) is associated with a 'qualitative formative assessment approach'. 'Achievement feedback' (B.1) shows a 'mastery-oriented approach' to formative assessment, demonstrating specific guidelines for work performance improvement (critical analysis). 'Constructing feedback' (B.2) shows a 'social constructivist approach' (Vygotsky, 1978) to formative assessment, where the teacher (or peer) is more a 'facilitator' of students' self-regulation of their learning.

Innovative Assessment and Feedback Strategies in Large University Classes

In this section we present and discuss three different teaching strategies that include the promotion and delivery of feedback to (and from) undergraduates by one teacher in the context of one semester long curricular unit focused on the biological concept of 'Evolution' (Figure 16.1). The strategies were designed and implemented in a time span of seven academic years (2007/2008 to 2012/2013). Those three feedback strategies aimed at promoting students' autonomous learning, contributing for their critical thinking development. Each strategy was implemented on at least two separate occasions, benefitting from updates based on the field knowledge we acquired along the way, and which can be read elsewhere (Silva Lopes, Moreira, & Pedrosa-de-Jesus, 2012; Pedrosa-de-Jesus, Moreira, Silva Lopes, & Watts, 2014). Here we focus on the general design of each strategy and we focus on the final version in order to discuss our general aims, the decisions and actions made by the teacher provide efficient and fair feedback to his students. Descriptions of each strategy will be followed by a reflective balance provided by the teacher's 'voice', including the benefits and constraints he saw for the diverse forms of feedback he used.

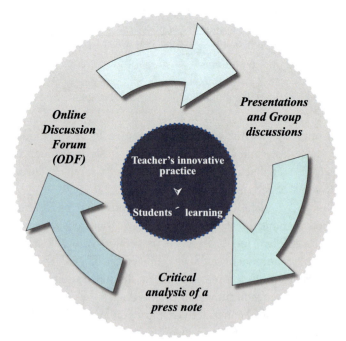

FIGURE 16.1   Feedback strategies developed in the teaching context of 'Evolution' (2006/2014)

Our discussion is based mainly on the data we generated by naturalistic non-participant classroom observations and through semi-structured interviews conducted with the teacher and some of his students, across those years. All written documents produced by the participants (teacher and students) were also analysed and we use some excerpts here in order to amplify the discussion. For further information considering methods and techniques of data gathering please see Chapter 12.

The Online Discussion Forum (Over)

The central goal of creating an Online Discussion Forum (ODF) was to allow students to interact with each other and to think about Evolution on a more regular basis than only once a week during the 2-hour lectures. This strategy was adopted during four academic years, from 2007/2008 to 2010/2011. The forum was allocated to the e-learning platform of the university (Moodle) and was opened during the entire semester, a period of nearly four months, being organised as a formative period (one month) and a summative period (three months). Both periods were deliberately initiated by a message posted by the teacher in order to 'trigger' discussion (Garrison & Cleveland-Innes, 2005). The quality of students' participation during the summative period was assessed and, and included in their final grade classification, with a weighting of 10% of their final grade (2 values out of 20).

At the beginning of the semester a written document that the assessment criteria for the quality and the frequency of the posts was given to the students and discussed with them. Concrete examples of 'desirable' types of posts were explored and the assessment criteria were negotiated with the students. At the end of the formative period, one lecture was used to explore with the students the most common errors being made so far and also their difficulties, highlighting the guidelines they should consider when making an intervention, namely:

1. Never forget to label your post by giving it a title. It will help others to identify the key-idea that is being discussed;
2. Your opinion has to be sustained with relevant argumentation (information sources);
3. Assure that you have read the previous posts when posting your idea. If you don't, there is a high risk of repeating an idea. In this case this will not have positive impact on your assessment mark and it will only contribute to an overload of information, demotivating you and your colleagues of reading further.

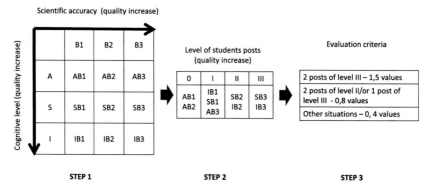

FIGURE 16.2 Translation of quality criteria of students' posts into a quantitative mark for assessment purpose

The criteria for assessing the students' posts included the cognitive level of the expressed reasoning, being based on Pedrosa-de-Jesus, Almeida, Teixeira-Dias & Watts's (2006) ASI categorization system, and also on the scientific accuracy revealed in each post. The combination of these two dimensions resulted in four different levels for assessing the general quality of the posts (Figure 16.2). New questions and topics for discussion were valued, as long as they were supported by argumentation. Each student was required to post at least two questions/comments during the semester to assure that their participation would be considered for final grades.

During the summative assessment period, the students posted a total of 218 messages, more than half of the class (n=53), indicating a high commitment to this strategy. The three most common themes discussed were: 'The evolution of the human being' 'Natural Selection' and 'Science and Religions'. Participation along the semester was not homogenous: students' had posted his participation in the forum. Indeed, content analysis of the forum interactions revealed that the teachers' messages were central to focusing, correcting or facilitating the flow of ideas.

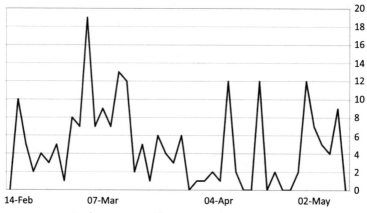

FIGURE 16.3 Students' posts on the ODF over three months

ASSESSMENT AND FEEDBACK

Day	15/02	03/03	06/03		17/03			26/04			Total Posts
Post	1	2	3	4	5	6	7	8	9	10	
Instructional design				X		X				X	3
Facilitation		X	X	X	X	X	X		X	X	8
Direct instruction	X	X		X		X	X	X		X	8

FIGURE 16.4 Categorization of the teachers' posts according to Garrison et al.'s (2001) model 'teaching presence'

> " (…) The theme of 'human evolution' is quite diverse and very interesting! (…) we have to approach this in parts.. If my mind is not tricking me "Nemo" and the anemone have an favourable ecological relationship (+,+), which is not obligatory Filipe* (posts on 10th march , 10:27), do you believe that this particular relationship emerged randomly?
> It would be interesting try to understand in an evolutionary perspective the appearance of human egocentrism, as well as environmental consciousness…Perhaps reading the following contributions of your colleagues could be a good starting point: Carla's contribution at 8th March 2:16 could be a good starting point (Carla, please remove the association to Lamarck, Catarina's contribution on 9th march, 9:53 and Claudia's question on 15th march … on what concerns to the exaggeration of human evolution, you already answered!

FIGURE 16.5 Example of one type of feedback posted by the teacher's to the students' on the OFD710

When reflecting on this particular pedagogical strategy the teacher valued its functionality as a complementary learning environment, one that created the possibility of knowing better the students' ability and their personal interests:

> After a few lectures I was even able to associate a specific face to the students name … some students indeed stood out at the ODF … I ended up bringing those posts to the lectures and discuss some ideas with the other students … this was positive … and was very useful when I was correcting the final exam.

But he also recognized the enormous investment in time that it implied, empathising that this would never be feasible without external support, suggesting the collaboration with other colleagues from his department:

> The most difficult was managing my communication at the forum … the feedback to students has to be on time and adequate … this is not an easy task! It requires a lot of time and mental disposition … managing this is very difficult … it takes a lot from us … and something has to be left out … but if I had more time I would have discussed more ideas … Even though

this is very exhausting ... in a next opportunity I would probably invite some colleagues to help me with this ...

Evaluating this high diversity of posts ... it is quite difficult to take the decision ... In some cases I had to read the same post several times ... but the criteria that we defined together was were very useful ... it made the task a little bit easier (...).

Presentations and Discussions

This strategy was implemented in two academic years (2008/2009 and 2009/2010) mainly as a response to one student's suggestions. He felt it was unfair that online and participation in the ODF contributed to the final assessment grade, but that oral participation during lectures did not. Acknowledging that there could be more students feeling the same way, the teacher proposed the implementation of two group discussions related to the contents discussed on the ODF, also valuing the importance of oral discussion and argumentation. The first group discussion took place during one class time, was a formative and was intended to introduce students to some basic rules, such as giving to identify themselves before intervening, and to talk in a calm and respectful way, making their questions and arguments clearly. Since this 'special' lecture would be considered for evaluative purposes (0,5 values out of 20) it was important that the students would not talk at the same time and participate in a concise and proficient way, but without losing direct interaction with each other.

The summative discussion lasted two hours and some 20 or so students participated. In 'normal' lectures the mean value of participating students was 4.5. While the teacher tended to formulate around 37 questions per lecture, in this discussion he made only 8 interventions, the discourse being definitely dominated by the students, as it was the intention. In fact, several student-student interactions emerged during the discussion, which is very rare in traditional lectures. It was also interesting to note that many students were taking notes of what was being said by their colleagues in order to prepare their own interventions. Some students also brought printed documents and books, marked on specific pages in order to sustain their discussion, revealing a previous preparation, for example, the books *'Climbing Mount Improbable'* and the *'The Blind Watchmaker'* by Richard Dawkins.

In this strategy, specific written documents to support feedback and assessment were also produced. One of our educational research team (AM) developed a specific observation grid in order to check for evidences of students' competences, such as critically and clarity, during their interventions. This educational researcher completed the observation grid for each student

> Student A: For example the case of the butterfly that is studied in relation with pollution, if there is some species that would be adapted to just one dry climate ... (noise)
> Teacher: (claps hands). This is important what your colleague is saying ...and I want comments at the end. Sorry that I interrupted you, please continue...
> Student A: If there is a species that is adapted to a dry climate ... all the things they have are ...
> Teacher: All things? Their characteristics?
> Student A: Yes, their characteristics, and then the environment where they are starts slightly to change, for instance rain, but on a large time span, slowly. Then they will along the time start to create different characteristics and they will start to adapt to the new environment. But if it is a drastic change...then in this case the species does not have opportunity to change, then this is a bad thing...
> Teacher: Does everybody agree? (one student raise his hand) Yes, please.

FIGURE 16.6   Transcripts of an excerpt from the student debates highlighting examples of oral feedback given by the teacher

who participated in the discussion in order to allow the teacher to concentrate fully and engage in the discussion (Figure 16.6). Afterwards, the annotations were discussed with the teacher, and the students oral participation was ranked on a scale from 0.1 (level 1) to 0.5 points (level 3) (see Figure 16.7). Again, this strategy allowed the teacher to know better the learning abilities of his students as well as their difficulties and constraints, even before the final module examination. As previously stated, some evidence of successful promotion of study methods was also observed. In order to participate with their own ideas and knowledge, several students started to seek reliable information beyond the specified course books. The teacher considered this to be very rewarding: "Some of the comments were quite objective and concise ... I noticed that ... this is also an important learning aspect".

In our view, the advantages and disadvantages of this strategy, are that:

1. In general, many more students' participated than was commonly the case in traditional lectures
2. There was less teacher intervention when compared to regular lectures; the teacher's primary role was mediating and conducting the discussion
3. Students were given qualitative feedback before the final examination, and before final grades were delivered, which was generally seen to have positive effects on their progression in learning – they were motivated to feel well-prepared for these discussions and so invested in autonomous and continuous study
4. These moments gave the students the opportunity to interact with each other in an organized manner, to express themselves, their knowledge and competences receiving qualitative feedback in appropriate time
5. Based on the outcomes revealed by students' interventions, the additional effort by the teacher in making this strategy part of summative assessment was overall very positive.

Level	1	2	3
Relevance	Superficial opinion without any relevant arguments/ non fitting arguments	The student answers partially to the topic under discussion	The student expresses a relevant opinion, using valid arguments
Criticality	The students doesn't show any criticality. They do not question the intervention of colleagues.	The students show some criticality. They sometimes question the intervention of colleagues on what concerns the relevance and accuracy.	The student evidences clearly a spirit of criticality, questioning colleagues' interventions on what concerns the relevance and accuracy.
Cognitive Level	The student participates in order to clarify, confirm ideas or information	The student participates in order to understand, compare and relate the topics under discussion	The student participates in order to explore and/or hypothesize arguments
Clarity	The student's interventions are unclear. Ideas are mixed up. There is no evident logical sequence.	The student's ideas are presented in a clear and understandable mode.	The students' ideas are presented in a clear, understandable mode. The students' interventions evidence a clear effort of organizing information
Scientific accuracy	The student's intervention are scientifically incorrect	Some of the student's interventions are scientifically incorrect, that is, have some scientific incorrectness	Student's interventions are scientifically correct.

FIGURE 16.7 Levels of student skills and competencies assessed during group discussion

First feedback		Intermediate feedback		5 May	Final feedback	
3 April	6 April	19 April	21 April		19 May	2 June
Definition of group composition and selection of the 'press notes' for analysis	1st teacher written feedback: (Evaluative positive/ approving feedback) (Descriptive/ achievement feedback)	1st Group feed-forward	2nd teacher written feedback: (Descriptive/ achievement feedback)	Group Delivery of the first version of critical analysis	3rd teacher written feedback: (Descriptive/ achievement feedback) (Descriptive/ improved feedback)	Group delivery of the final version of critical analysis, and 2nd Group feed forward

FIGURE 16.8   Example of the teacher's written feedback profile considering the critical analysis of one group of students

Critical Analysis of a Press Note over Academic

Within this strategy, implemented during two academic years (2012/13 and 2013/14), the students where challenged to write a critical analysis based on the selection of a press release from newspapers, books or Internet blogs related to the theme of 'Evolution'. This critical analysis required that students not only understand the science involved, but it also tested their capacity to judge whether the news content of the press release had either been 'managed' or 'mismanaged'. Additionally, each group had to undertake a blind review process of other groups' critical analysis. Undergraduates organised themselves in small groups from 2 to 4 students.

A supporting learning tool called 'Guidelines for a critical analysis of a topic about Evolution' was designed in an Excel form to help students during the process of doing the critical analysis. The document had a brief explanation and some guiding questions in each of the sections and formatting requirements. The teacher gave feedback on several structured occasions (Figure 16.8), those being mainly of a positive evaluative/judgmental as well as of constructive/descriptive nature, according to Tunstall and Gipps's (1996) quality feedback categorization system. Evaluative feedback includes the criticism about the assignment (both positive and/or negative), while Descriptive feedback presents questions for reflection, aspects that could be improved and suggestions that can lead to the improvement of the critical analysis.

The group work was supported by the teacher's written feedback, principally by e-mail. Teacher written comments included questions for reflec-

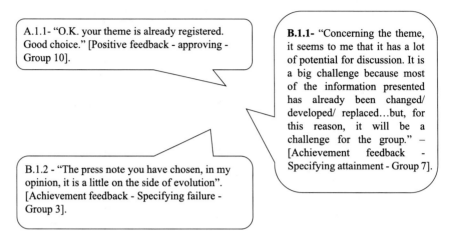

FIGURE 16.9 Example of the teacher's written feedback profile considering the critical analysis of one group of students

tion, suggestions for improvement (i.e. further reading) and also critical observations (Figure 16.9). Students had to submit the final assignment, having in mind the teacher's written feedback. After receiving the written formative feedback of the first version of critical analysis, which was focused on students' critical thinking performance, student's had to compare it to the assessment rubric criteria defined in order to assess critical analysis, and were: 'Clarity and relevance of the theme'; 'Suitability of the document development'; 'Degree of thoroughness treatment of the topic'; 'Transparency and writing correction'; 'Relevance of the findings'; 'Originality of the contribution'; 'Variety and relevance of sources', and 'Appropriate use of the Vancouver norms NP 405 AP (or other database)'. Each group submitted the final version of the critical analysis together with written feed-forward (which was optional).

The teacher considered that this strategy increased opportunities for students to search for further information, to negotiate and take decisions within their group and to reflect before sending their final critical analysis to the teacher. Group work also allowed the development of further higher-order competences, such as collaboration and argumentation. Students' common difficulties were related to group organisation issues, such as schedule, compatibility and commitment were also identified. The teacher stressed the enormous effort in carrying out written feedback for 20 groups, over a 10-week period. However, he faced this strategy as a personal challenge and recognised several benefits for students:

> My comments (teacher's written feedback) really, in my perspective, were made in order to improve the groups' critical analysis, sometimes aiming at a better 'speech articulation', at better prose. Other times, I simply

asked for a better scientific support of their statements. Frequently, I also advised them to add references supporting what they were saying in the critical analysis and, therefore, that gave me some work.

Furthermore, he considered that the self-assessment process could be integrated into students' summative assessment, making it a mandatory feature:

> Self-assessment is very important. Some students were extremely objective when doing their own critical analysis. Some even said that peers/colleagues only saw the text at the end. Anyway, here we have some critics and I think that this experience was extremely important for students at this stage. However, the fact of knowing how to work in a group, accepting opinions of others ... is not always easy. To develop/write text documents, to search ... I think it was worth it for all of this.

The teacher also stressed how important is to involve groups during the critical analysis feedback process. He considered that it helped to develop several students' competences, such as argumentation:

> In the end, to agree with my suggestions and opinions, they could disagree with me. However, it was required that they prove/justify their opinion and some groups were looking for extra readings in order to argue against what I was saying about their critical analysis.

Results shows that this 'critical analysis assignment' increased opportunities for students to search for further information, to negotiate and take decisions within their group, to reflect before sending their final critical analysis to the teacher. Group work also allowed the development of further higher-order competences, such as collaboration and argumentation. Students' common difficulties were related to group organisation issues, such as schedule, compatibility and commitment were also identified. Furthermore, the learning benefits highlighted during students' interviews, and the richness of written data, were seen of enormous relevance. Further results were presented and discussed in Pedrosa-de-Jesus, Guerra and Watts (2017) and Pedrosa-de-Jesus and Guerra (2018).

Discussion

All of the three strategies for feedback and assessment that we discuss above were adapted towards the particularities of the teaching-learning situations of the teacher involved, and were all designed in accordance with the main learning goals for the teaching module on Evolution. It was important, both for the teacher and ourselves, that we evaluated quite diversified strategies for giving student feedback. The use of these three main strategies by the same teacher revealed very positive effects on student motivation for learning, being recognised as a way of attending to individual differences, valuing different competences and capacities, resulting in what was seen to be a more fair and transparent assessment system. Our strong sense derived from this work is that there is no one feedback/assessment strategy that 'fits' all purposes equally well. Such a single all-purpose 'super' feedback/assessment system would not be desirable, not least because the exercise of constructing a custom-built approach is an excellent strategy for promoting academic reflection – and therefore of promoting academic growth. In our view, academic growth entails being willing and able to reinvent and construct a strategy whenever required, to be flexible, creative and sensitive to the needs and opinions of the students involved. While some teachers are able to do right from the beginning, support and guidance is needed for others.

A key conflict associated with giving student feedback is that 'summative' feedback associated to the final grade, s not particularly useful to the student. The work is done, the task complete (for better or for worse) and the feedback might be of interest but not of much practical value. On the other hand, giving – and organising – detailed feedback is resource-intensive, it requires investment in time and energy (Crisp, 2007). Because formative feedback occurs best during the process, and not at the end of a teaching programme, generates much more for. It is time intensive not least because dialogical feedback – dialogue both surrounding the assessment process and the actual implementation of the strategy itself – is not a quick process. Teacher and students need understand each other in the process, engaging in a two-way dialogue in which the student is an equal partner (Nicol, 2010). That said, there are currently useful and supportive strategies (for example, online tools), and the adoption of collaborative and co-researcher models have proved very fruitful in our case. Our intention here has been to illustrate the excellent opportunities for peer collaboration that can exist between teams.

References

Askew, S., & Lodge, C. (2000). Gifts, ping-pong and loops – Linking feedback and learning. In S. Askew (Ed.), *Feedback for learning* (pp. 1–18). London: RoutledgeFalmer.

Black, P., & Wiliam, D. (1998). Assessment and classroom learning. *Assessment in Education, 5*(1), 7–74.

Crisp, B. (2007). Is it worth the effort? How feedback influences students' subsequent submission of assessable work. *Assessment & Evaluation in Higher Education, 32*, 571–581.

Ennis, R. H. (1987). A taxonomy of critical thinking dispositions and abilities. In J. B. Baron & R. J. Sternberg (Eds.), *Teaching thinking skills: Theory and practice* (pp. 9–26). New York, NY: W. H. Freeman & Co.

Evans, C. (2012). Assessment and feedback: We can do better. *Reflecting Education, 8*(1), 1–9.

Falchikov, N. (2006). Peer feedback marking: Developing peer assessment. *Innovations in Education and Training International, 32*(2), 175–187.

Fallows, S., & Chandramohan, B. (2001). Multiple approaches to assessment: Reflections on use of tutor, peer and self-assessment. *Teaching in Higher Education, 6*(2), 229–246.

Garrison, D. R., & Cleveland-Innes, M. (2005). Facilitating cognitive presence in online learning: Interaction is not enough. *American Journal of Distance Education, 19*(3), 133–148.

Hattie, J., & Jaeger, R. (1998). Assessment and classroom learning: A deductive approach. *Assessment in Education: Principles, Policy & Practice, 5*(1), 111–122.

Hattie, J., & Timperley, H. (2007). The power of feedback. *Review of Educational Research, 77*(1), 81–112.

Ivanič, R., Clark, R., & Rimmershaw, R. (2000). What am I supposed to make of this? The messages conveyed to students by tutors' written comments. In M. R. Lea & B. Stierer's (Eds.), *Student writing in higher education: New contexts* (pp. 32–46). Buckingham: The Society for Research into Higher Education and Open University Press.

Kingston, E. (2009). *Self-theories of emotional intelligence in higher education: Assessment feedback and non-continuation* (Unpublished PhD thesis). Roehampton University and University of Surrey, Surrey.

Nicol, D. (2010). From monologue to dialogue: Improving written feedback processes in mass higher education. *Assessment & Evaluation in Higher Education, 35*(5), 501–517.

Nicol, D., Thomson, A., & Breslin, C. (2014). Rethinking feedback practices in higher education: A peer review perspective. *Assessment & Evaluation in Higher Education, 39*(1), 102–122. doi:10.1080/02602938.2013.795518

O'Neill, G., Huntley-Moore, S., & Race, P. (Eds.). (2007). *Case studies of good practices in assessment of student learning in higher education*. Dublin: AISHE.

Orsmond, P., & Merry, S. (2011). Feedback alignment: Effective and ineffective links between tutors and students understanding of coursework feedback. *Assessment & Evaluation in Higher Education, 36*(2), 125–136. doi:10.1080/02602930903201651

Pedrosa-de-Jesus, M. H., Almeida, P., Teixeira-Dias, J. J., & Watts, D. M. (2006). Students' questions – building a bridge between Kolb's learning styles and approaches to learning. *Education + Training, 48*(2–3), 97–111.

Pedrosa-de-Jesus, M. H., da Silva Lopes, B. Moreira, A. C., & Watts, D. M. (2012). Contexts for questioning: Two zones of teaching and learning in undergraduate science. *Higher Education, 64*(4), 557–571.

Pedrosa-de-Jesus, M. H., & Guerra, C. (2018). Teachers' written formative feedback on students' critical thinking: A case study. *MIE Journal of Education, 9*(1), 2–21.

Pedrosa-de-Jesus, M. H., Guerra, C., & Watts, D. M. (2017). University teachers' self-reflection on their academic growth. *Professional Development in Education, 43*(3), 454–473. doi:10.1080/19415257.2016.1194877 (Published online 24 June 2016)

Pedrosa-de-Jesus, M. H., Moreira, A. C., da Silva Lopes, B., & Watts, D. M. (2014). So much more than just a list: Exploring the nature of critical questioning in undergraduate sciences. *Research in Science and Technology Education, 32*(2), 115–134. doi:10.1080/02635143.2014.902811

Peelo, M. (2002). Struggling to learn. In M. Peelo & T. Wareham (Eds.), *Failing students in higher education*. Buckingham: SRHE/Open University Press.

Race, P. (2005). *Making learning happen*. London: Sage Publications.

Silva Lopes, B., Moreira, A. C., & Pedrosa-de-Jesus, M. H. (2012). "Questions in biology". Designing an online discussion forum for promoting active learning about Evolution. In F. Gonçalves, R. Pereira, W. Leal Filho, & U. M. Azeiteiro (Eds.), *Contributions to the UN decade of education for sustainable development* (pp. 235–254). Frankfurt am Main: Peter Lang.

Tunstall, P., & Gipps, C. V. (1996). Teacher feedback to young children in formative assessment: A typology. *British Educational Research Journal, 22*(4), 389–404.

Vygotsky, L. S. (1978). *Mind in society: The development of higher psychological processes*. Cambridge, MA: Harvard University Press.

Yorke, M. (2003). Formative assessment in higher education: Moves towards theory and the enhancement of pedagogic practice. *Higher Education, 45*, 477–501.

CHAPTER 17

Teachers' Reflections

Helena Pedrosa-de-Jesus and Mike Watts

Introduction

In the poem The Dry Salvages, T.S. Eliot (1943) wrote, 'We had the experience but missed the meaning'. We might argue that one purpose of teaching and research is actually to foster connections between experience and meaning – potentially so that together teacher and learner gain from both. Throughout the many years of the Aveiro Project we have worked very closely with a number of university teachers. This penultimate chapter provides space and time to give air to some of their reflections on the processes and products that have emerged from the project as they worked. We have already discussed some of their various comments along the way, for example about the introduction of a 'Micro-talk strategy' in Chapter 13, and to the introduction of a question sheet, in Chapter 14. In this chapter we look not just at some of the positive comments and feedback we received as we worked on the project, but also some of the perceived frustrations and drawbacks.

Reflection itself represents the human capacity for higher-order thinking, specifically, our ability to make connections between thoughts, ideas and practice. Critical reflection can support professional development through the evaluation of both decision-making and actions, and it can lead to improvements in teaching and the experiences of learners. We ask it of students and here we ask it of ourselves. It offers a way for practitioners to gain insight into their own professionalism. In the world of education, critical reflection features strongly in professional development and, in adult education literature (for example, Brookfield, 1987; Mezirow, 1981), the broad approach is to encourage individuals to take a critical attitude to their own work and to position themselves in relation to the ideas and practices they encounter (Leach et al., 2000). Schön (1996) describes critical reflection as an 'act of professional artistry' (p. 12) that can involve reflection-on-action (after the event) and reflection-in-action (at the time of the event). In Chapter 11, Richard Malthouse and Jodi Roffey-Barentsen even make the case for PReflective activities (before the event) – although, this being the penultimate chapter of the book – we have resisted Richard and Jodi's invitation to do that. Elsewhere, we have referred to university teachers' academic reflections as their 'situated critical reflection' (Malthouse, Roffey-Barentsen & Watts, 2014), building on ideas from Kolb (1984), Schön (1987) and Gibbs (1988). Our sense has been that 'situated critical reflection' seeks to '... add to the body of knowledge in a way that enables people to make sense of their world by observing the prevailing extended or external influences' (p. 4). These perspectives correspond with the notions that critical reflection can support professional competency and professional development, where self- and peer-forms of critical reflection can be used to gain insights and assess thoughts and actions.

In talking about the teachers' overt reflections in the way we do, we have ignored the very substantial field of informal unconscious unintentional learning, a field that has been well summarised in the recent work of Rogers (2014), called 'The Base of the Iceberg: informal learning and its impact on formal and non-formal learning'. Each one of those university teachers brings to his or her intentional self-directed learning a vast amount of *unconscious* learning, of both knowledge and skills that they have accumulated over many years from daily experience – but which they do always not know that they have. This field of informal learning has been the focus of extensive studies of adult learning over the last twenty years, and is directly relevant to self-directed intentional learning (c.f. Vygotsky, making the unconscious conscious; Michael Polanyi's tacit dimension). What these teachers bring to their teaching and research, to their discussions and evaluations of innovative interventions, are considerable funds of knowledge (and banks of skills) from their 'workplace' learning (Eraut, 1994). They bring pre-understanding and meaning frames (Mezirow, 1995) and social imaginaries (Taylor, 2003) they bring their ideals, values, constructed both intentionally and unintentionally and unconsciously from their everyday experiences, background and social interactions with students and colleagues.

The teachers here are all busy professional academics, with a full load of teaching, assessment, administration, external commitments, their own specialist areas of research (as well as personal and home lives) and yet they still found time to work with us on ways to improve their teaching and students' learning. In the context of the project, 'working closely' has entailed regular project meetings, observation of their classes, discussions of their teaching plans, resources, materials, semi-structured interviews, phone calls, emails, 'coffee chats', 'corridor conversations', involvement in writing and presenting results in national and international contexts using both formal and informal interaction. In this chapter we engage in a form of 're-storying' (Clark & Rossiter, 2008, p. 61). Our writing here is based on a view of the narrative quality of human life (Bruner 1987), people discussing and giving accounts of – in this case – their work experiences. Stories are based on events and occurrences and illustrate the cultural working habits and practices that teachers observe in their daily life and work. These Portuguese teachers' reflected on their experimentation with new teaching practices and, by re-storying their comments, offering evidence from interviews, conversations, discussions, we interpret their commitments to reform, their concerns and challenges as they work in new ways. This form of writing has rapidly gained legitimacy in educational research (Clandinin & Connelly, 2000; Ollerenshaw & Creswell, 2000): it is an engaging way through which lived experience can be shared and reflected upon. Our process of re-storying highlights the teachers' narratives – they are our interpretations, a bricolage, of our gist of all the very varied data that we have collected, and have available, over time.

As we noted at the start of the book, our own roles have been that of supportive co-researchers, facilitating and enhancing discussion and scholarship on strategies for teaching and learning, learning outcomes, and modes of assessment. The university teachers in turn had considerable support in enacting, reflecting upon, analysing and evaluating new approaches to teaching and learning. The need to encourage and support the academic development of university teachers is recognised internationally (for example, Higher Education Academy, 2011; Clarke & Reid, 2013). In Portugal, Pinto (2008) and Huet, Costa, Tavares, and Baptista (2009) have also highlighted the importance of promoting programmes in order to stimulate teachers' academic development. Our research preference has been for a transitional 'instructional coaching approach' (Burkins & Ritchie, 2007; Kennedy, 2005; Knight, 2004; Schrum, English, & Galizio, 2012). Such an approach entails co-researcher investigations (Macaro & Mutton, 2002), which allow each participant to benefit from the enterprise. In our case, this has taken place within a positive change environment that has enabled academic growth to take place. As already mentioned, research data were collected through informal contacts with the teacher (before or after classes) and 'low-participant classroom observation' of various classes in naturalistic contexts. Participant observation took place during the regular meetings with the research group, and semi-structured interviews were conducted with both teachers and students (24) at different points in the project. The observed situations were 'authentic' in keeping with the essence of a naturalistic approach (Cohen, Manion, & Morrison, 2007). All the written documents produced by the participants as a consequence of the research innovations introduced were also collected for analysis and discussion. There were external sources of information introduced by the educational researchers as they worked and the subject specialist teachers themselves drew up some of these. Several innovative teaching, learning, assessment and feedback strategies were designed, implemented and evaluated within four curricular units: "Microbiology" (1st semester) and "Genetics", "Microbiology & Pharmacology" and "Evolution" (2nd semester).

When teachers describe episodes, write comments or tell stories about their work to others, they reveal something about their thoughts, intentions, emotions and 'teaching ethos' – as Betina discusses in Chapter 14. They relate their experiences in the form of narratives and choose, from among the many possibilities, a discourse that they can use to discuss even those experiments that did not always work well. When we, as researchers, analyse and re-tell the teachers' stories, we do so within the frame of our own stories. Central to our approach is our aim to research with these teachers: we do not wish to speak for them, as we are conscious of how we might unwittingly distort their experience. That said, we could never reproduce the teachers' voices purely as they are, but only as a kind of ventriloquism through our own researcher's voice.

Wrestling with Teaching Problems

The three 'teaching problems' we discuss here belonged to no one teacher alone, they are hybrids. It is certainly the case that they were broadly the province of one of the teachers involved, but the general sentiments that lie behind the problems were articulated and shared by others within the project – teachers and researchers both. The problems – though not quite as tidily summarised as they are here – generated considerable discussion and debate round the table – not just about 'the way students are these days' but also about university practices, demands and requirement, within departments, across the university and across the sector as a whole. These are not the only problems that were articulated (by far!), but serve as illustrations here:

> *Problem A*: There are several teaching approaches within modules in the sciences, some being in standard lecture format, small group tutorials and often the essential lab-work. In the latter, the students are often asked to undertake tasks, usually experiments that have been designed to develop laboratory skills as well as to further theoretical ideas. One of the key issues for the teachers here was that students commonly arrived at the lab unprepared so that, although pre-reading and orientation materials were provided (and required), these were seldom used and a good deal of time at the start of the session was 'lost' in 'catching the students up' in what they needed to do. Teacher A found herself increasingly irritated and frustrated by this, time was limited for all the teaching sessions and having to spend time rehearsing what should already have been done was exasperating – to say the least.

Problem B: Teacher B was unhappy with the quality of feedback he was providing to students. The seat of this unhappiness took several forms: the size of the class limited him in what he could meaningfully achieve in feedback terms; students did not seem to be responding to his comments on their work and were continuing to make the same kinds of mistakes in consecutive assignments – he found himself repeating the same feedback comments time and again. He also felt that the students needed to take greater ownership of 'quality matters' in their work. He wanted to develop students' competences in such areas as the selection and evaluation of scientific information, and in group-work collaboration

Problem C: students in the course seemed relatively passive and unresponsive. They might attend sessions well, be their 'in body', but interaction between themselves and the lecturer was not high. In this case, the teacher was interested in promoting greater degrees of critical thinking, requiring the students to engage with the materials more fully, challenge, respond, debate, and be critical of issues, have opinions and to air these. Teacher C was of the opinion that this passivity was largely the result of the strong examination ethos within the programme, "I realised of course that, in the nature of the final exam, some students are simply unable to demonstrate their critical opinions".

Our 'round table' discussions centred on ideas that teaching, learning and assessment design must take into account strategies to help learners develop such critical competencies. The intervention strategies we discussed provided an overall working framework for organising successful student development of, for example, critical questioning, showing how students' capacity to be critical can be brought into being, developed and honed. As researchers, it was part of our role to foster ideas and then generate the empirical data to help evaluate and illustrate some aspects of these innovative intervention strategies, giving evidence on how it may be possible to develop criticality, as well as 'critical environments' where such competencies could be promoted. So, while each of the teachers, in general, owned one of the particular problems, the others – teachers and researchers round the table – all contributed to the broad discussion, the possible solutions, and means of evaluating these. As already suggested, these discussions took place over time and in varying contexts, none of the approaches that were eventually adopted, trialled and assessed were drawn up or implemented on the spur of the moment, they were the product of considerable discussion and conversation. As one teacher said:

> For me as a teacher, these strategies are extremely pleasant since I'm going to the lectures always taking something new. I'm not going just to transmit knowledge for students to memorise and then they go to the exam ... no ... this is a deliberate strategy having a specific purpose, where all the intermediate steps are planned in order to maximise the final result [the students learning outcomes]. Therefore, this is what I most value in these strategies being develop during this curricular unit as a result of this collaboration.

The 'Up-Side' of Innovation

The teachers we worked with were very positive, enjoyed participation in the project. Results from classroom observation, individual and group meetings and teachers' individual interviews indicate their enjoyment and the benefits they drew from the discussions, the interventions and the analysis and evaluation of the outcomes. The project clearly had a strong impact, they said, not least in terms of prompting creative ideas, real suggestions, shared endeavours. For example, in terms of Problem A above, as we have suggested, one of the teachers was considerably exercised by students' lack of preparation for lab sessions,

> ... [the module guidelines] require them to read the practical protocols [lab session materials] because, when they read the protocol, they should then know what to do in the lab lessons ... and get much more advantage from the lab sessions than if they don't prepare in advance. But they *don't* read the lab protocols, and so then they don't know what they should be doing.

One of the project group's suggestions was simply to instigate a quiz-system at the start of a lab session in order to check that students had read the preparatory work before arriving at the laboratory. For instance, the instructions on the worksheet were jumbled and, as a brief group task, they had to be sensibly re-ordered (and agreed) before commencing any practical activities. This served to challenge the students without creating an overly hostile or authoritarian atmosphere within the class. Later, in the second year of the project, the teacher reflected back on this:

> ... from my point of view ... It was absolutely the best strategy in order to take more advantages of the practical classes, and motivate students to

read the practical protocols. Of course, I then had to integrate this kind of quiz activity in students' assessment, because otherwise it would not be fair and not result in being a formal requirement ...

Teacher B had always 'tinkered' with his approaches to lectures and to teaching, but – he freely admitted – this was the first time (within the project) that he had undertaken such an elaborate and extensive innovation. He initiated an elaborate process of peer assessment in groups, so that the students were developing criticality as well as learning through collaborative activities. Overall, he was pleased with this experience; he thought that the activity he devised with students had promoted their individual critical reflection. In addition, it had also developed collaborative group work. And for these two reasons alone, he thought, it had been well worth the effort,

> The self-assessment is so very important. Some students were extremely objective when doing their own critical analysis. Anyway, here we have generated some criticality and I think that this experience was extremely important for students at this stage. Moreover, the fact of knowing how to work in a group, accepting the others' opinions ... is not always easy. To develop, write text documents, to search ... I think it was worth it for all of this.

When asked about the impact of this type of teaching and learning strategy on his future academic practice, he said that

> it was very useful since it helped me to better align teaching with learning outcomes, therefore changing the way I will taught evolution.

In terms of Problem C, all of the teachers and researchers were interested in generating a greater degree of interaction and responsiveness in classes. As we have noted elsewhere in other chapters, this was achieved through a range of strategies – some in-class, some after and beyond-class strategies. So, there was a greater emphasis on in-class questioning, a much more 'dialogic' approach, a variety of stimuli, class activities, formats that challenged students to respond, be creative and air opinions. Depending on the nature of the class and the topic, sometimes the classwork was successful, sometimes the greater results were achieved through the online forums or 'chat' facilities that students accesses after hours. Overall, the teachers considered that, in their different forms, these interventions helped to develop several students' competences – such as argumentation. The important point was to create an atmosphere so that students could respond, a 'critical climate' within the teaching session. One of the teachers was delighted by the extra effort some of the students put in:

> In the end, it was really not necessary for student to agree with my suggestions or opinions at all, they could very easily disagree with me. However, I did require that they prove or justify their opinions. Some groups spent considerable time looking for extra bibliographic sources in order to argue against what I was saying about their critical analysis.

There is evidence, too, from their many comments, for the 'transference' of the change process, as academic development and confidence grows. A teacher's small change in approach one year leads to a larger change the following year; a change in one part of her work might lead to a similar change in another, with a different group or different teaching topic. These teachers clearly learned from each other – what worked for one teacher one year might be adopted and adapted in some form by another teacher in the next. That said, the same strategy suggested for different teaching groups commonly had different outputs, and these differences were a constant source of amusement and debate. The conversations, the ideas, the 'pros and cons' of different ways of working were discussed and shared and – as already noted – while some teachers took greater ownership of the problems and solutions, the collaboration was such that sharing took place quite naturally. When asked about new developments for the following academic year, the teachers all stated the importance of continuing to implement these kinds of learning activity, providing the same sort of guidelines and suggesting ideas aimed at promoting students critical thinking. Regarding the teacher's role during this process, one mused on the possibilities of being a non-participant observer during group work so that he could collect additional information about their learning process:

> If I had the opportunity, I'd be a non participant observer when groups were developing their critical analysis. I think it would be extremely interesting for me to understand some of group the dynamics taking place.

During the ensuing discussions, however, he clearly understood some of the practical difficulties in doing this,

> Obviously, they would probably feel very uncomfortable with me looking over their shoulders at their work and listening in to them!

and reflected, anyway, that much of the group work probably took place away from the session via social media or discussion facilities, away from the possibilities of his gaze:

> I have the idea that most of the work is developed during the evening interacting through distance web tools, email, etc. I also think that the groups do this because they had few opportunities to meet. Mind you, I also consider it important to know how they use all these new web tools, too.

Some 'Down-Sides' of Innovation

There is little doubt that introducing innovation within a busy teaching load requires additional work. Some of the smaller interventions were not, of themselves, enormously demanding so that, devising a quiz for the start of lab-sessions, for example, was not of itself a major undertaking. However, added to all of the other demands on time and energy within a hardworking department, might have required extra motivation, extra effort, extra commitment to see it through for all of the sessions of the module. In terms of Problem C, for example, the teacher involved made the clear point that sending detailed formative feedback to 21 groups of students in the exercise he had developed involved him in a huge effort, not only from the point of view of the time spent, but also in the identification of student mistakes, and the design of their questions and his suggestions for improvement:

> This feedback exercise involved a lot of work. Because ... the feedback was given as follows: I made an overall assessment ... therefore, I had an Excel sheet for each group where I registered a general review of their critical analysis. Then I reviewed, in detail, the entire critical analysis. Each document handed in has x text lines and each of my comments were reported to line y or z. Those comments really, from my perspective, were made in order to improve the groups' critical analysis, sometimes aiming at a better 'speech articulation', or better written prose. Other times, I simply asked for better scientific support of their statements. Frequently, I also advised them to add references supporting what they were saying in the critical analysis and, therefore, this gives me some work.

As with Teacher A above in terms of the 'lab quiz', this teacher too felt the need to institutionalise this kind of self- and peer-assessment process, to integrate this somehow into students' summative assessment, making it mandatory, so that student effort was 'properly recognised and rewarded'.

The teachers were all aware, too, of the size of the task they were attempting. As one said,

> After all, we are working with 18 year-olds who just arrived at the university ... and this is just one curricular unit for them. I actually think that the effort these students have made to accomplish this learning activity is very high. It was necessary to read texts, to analyse the texts, and not all of them are prepared to do that. It is actually a fact we [the teachers] have no time to do this kind of work!

And 'developmental impetus' did not always come from their work with students. The teachers were aware that our collegiate teacher-researcher project meetings were consonant with a broader drive for change within the university:

> The fact is that there exists an external push ... a kind of top-down audit. Well I don't think it is exactly an audit, but there is a push to change every year, with reflection on what is being done and, therefore, these [the meetings] have been very important.

That university 'push', though, often came without perceived recognition of the time required for planning and development, leading to the criticism that:

> There is no 'upstream' work to prepare the ground, for example, in terms of distribution of the teaching time. I think these (inter departmental) projects are extremely useful if we teachers want to participate ... and collaborate. The university should be aware of this type of collaboration and should arrange conditions in order to enable the different outcomes that the project wants to achieve ... and that, for example, could be in terms of teaching duties [i.e. number of teachers attached to each curricular unit] and so on.

Summary

We are enormously indebted to these teachers not least because without them, of course, there would have been no project, no longitudinal study, no stories of change, development and academic growth. John Dewey (1997) defines reflection as 'active, persistent, and careful consideration of any belief or supposed form of knowledge in the light of the grounds that support it, and the further conclusions to which it tends' (p. 6). Simply put, reflection involves spending significant time on one topic in order to explore it thoroughly, and this is exactly what the Aveiro Project allowed. Our teachers certainly displayed 'active and persistent' reflection through their time with the project. Dewey went on to state that reflection involves a conscious and voluntary effort to establish belief upon a 'firm basis of reasons' (p. 6). We cannot do justice to the wealth of knowledge and understanding they brought to the discussion table. But we did have the advantage of not only listening to what they said, but also of watching what they did and how they acted. Our naturalistic ethnographic-type observations allowed us to note and discuss their actual behaviour, their engagement in their classrooms. This, in turn, brought to the surface some considerable food for thought, issues for consideration, areas for debate and – to their enormous credit – these teachers did not flinch from the 'critical gaze' of we researchers, but welcomed us in, and allowed us full 'researcher reign' while they worked. Through long conversations and discussions, they have critically reflected upon their own learning experiences in ways that have allowed us to 're-story' aspects of their professional lives. Our premise has been that the act of reframing and re-storying their past learning experiences provides a means of sense-making that engages multiple means of learning and creates a learning context in which transformational learning can occur.

We opened the chapter with TS Elliot, we close with Fernando Pessoa's (1998) poetic reminder that our accounts are just that: our accounts of one aspect of each person,

> Countless lives inhabit us.
> I don't know, when I think or feel,
> Who it is that thinks or feels.
> I am merely the place
> Where things are thought or felt.

References

Burkins, J., & Ritchie, S. (2007). Coaches coaching coaches. *Journal of Language and Literacy Education (Online), 3*(1), 32–47.

Clandinin, D. J., & Connelly, F. M. (2000). *Narrative inquiry: Experience in story in qualitative research.* San Francisco, CA: Jossey-Bass.

Clarke, C., & Reid, J. (2013). Foundational academic development: Building collegiality across divides? *International Journal for Academic Development, 18*(4), 318–330. doi:10.1080/1360144X.2012.728529

Cohen, L., Manion, L., & Morrison, K. (2007). *Research methods in education* (6th ed.). London: Routledge.

Dewey, J. (1997). *How we think.* New York, NY: Dover.

Eliot, T. S. (1943). *Four quartets.* New York, NY: Harcourt, Brace &World.

Eraut, M. (1994). *Developing professional knowledge and competence.* London: Routledge.

Gibbs, G. (1988). *Learning by doing: A guide to teaching and learning methods* (Further Education Unit). Oxford: Oxford Polytechnic.

Higher Education Academy. (2011). *The UK professional standards framework for teaching and supporting learning in higher education.* Retrieved November 28, 2013, from http://www.heacademy.ac.uk/assets/documents/ukpsf/ukpsf.pdf

Huet, I., Costa N., Tavares, J., & Baptista, A. V. (Eds.). (2009). *Docência no Ensino Superior: Partilha de Boas Práticas.* Aveiro: Editorial da Universidade de Aveiro.

Kennedy, A. (2005). Models of continuing professional development: A framework for analysis. *Journal of In-Service Education, 31*(2), 235–250. doi:10.1080/13674580500200277

Knight, J. (2004). Instructional coaches make progress through partnership. *Journal of Staff Development, 25*(2), 32–37.

Kolb, D. A. (1984). *Experiential learning: Experience as the source of learning and development.* Upper Saddle River, NJ: Prentice-Hall.

Macaro, E., & Mutton, T. (2002). Developing language teachers through a co-researcher model. *Language Learning Journal, 25*(1), 27–39.

Mezirow, J. (1995). Transformative theory of adult learning. In M.Welton (Ed.), *In defense of the lifeworld.* Albany, NY: State University of New York Press.

Malthouse, R., Roffey-Barentsen, J., & Watts, D. M. (2014). Reflectivity, reflexivity and situated reflective practice. *Professional Development in Education, 40*(4), 597–609. doi:10.1080/19415257.2014.907195

Ollerenshaw, J., & Creswell, J. W. (2000). *Data analysis in narrative research: A comparison of two "restorying" approaches.* Paper presented at the American Educational Research Association Annual Meeting, New Orleans, LA.

Pessoa, F. (1998). *Countless lives inhabit us – Selected poems* (R. Zenith, & F. Pessoa, Trans.). New York, NY: Grove Press.

Pinto, P. R. (2008). Formação pedagógica no ensino superior. O caso dos professores médicos. Sísifo. *Revista de Ciências da Educação, 7*, 111–124. Consultado em agosto de 2013 em http://sisifo.fpce.ul.pt

Rogers, A. (2014). *The base of the iceberg: Informal learning and its impact on formal and non-formal learning.* Opladen: Barbara Badruch.

Schön, D. (1987). *Educating the reflective practitioner.* San Francisco, CA: Jossey-Bass.

Schrum, L., English, M. C., & Galizio, L. M. (2012). Project DAVES: An exploratory study of social presence, e-mentoring, and vocational counselling support in community college courses. *The Internet and Higher Education, 15*(2), 96–101.

Taylor, C. (2003). *Modern social imigaries.* Durham, NC: Duke University Press.

CHAPTER 18

Summary

Helena Pedrosa-de-Jesus and Mike Watts

Here, we add our own reflections to those of the teachers' reflections in Chapter 17. We have subtitled the book 'questions and answers'. An old Chinese proverb says that 'one foolish man can ask more questions than ten wise men can answer'. In this respect we poor fools have probably raised hugely more questions than our many contributors here can possibly answer. Our purpose has not been to answer all questions related to universities. In 2012, Holmes, Mayhew and Keep asked 'Ten big questions' of higher education, questions such as: *Does going to university make students more productive in the labour market? What should a degree programme look like? Does increasing graduate numbers lead to faster economic growth? Does having more graduates make society function better?* Significant as they are, these are not questions we can address here. Their tenth, and final question in that article was: *Given that HE institutions have many roles and finite resources, what balance is to be struck*?

There will be very few answers in the book to the first set of questions but, in amongst all of the discussion, the reader may well find some suggestions in relation to that final one. There clearly *is* a balance to be struck. One of the key questions in the UK is, in the light of the Research Excellence Framework (REF), the Teaching Excellence Framework (TEF), the university league tables, the National Student Survey (NSS), shrinking funding – and many other demands – *What is the balance to be struck with all the competing demands being made on university teachers?* There is no doubt from the reflections of the contributors engaged in the Aveiro Project that this is an important question in many other countries too – not least, as Júlio Pedrosa points out in Chapter 2 – the challenge of changing demographics in Portugal. We do hope that throughout the book, readers will find discussions that resonate with their own situations, be they teachers of physics as is Nilza Costa, a head of a development unit like Fiona Denney, education specialists like Richard Malthouse, Jodi Barentsen-Roffey and Sarmin Hossain, or researchers such as Betina Lopes and Cecília Guerra. And, in the midst of that resonance, that they find ideas, suggestions, routes, solutions to some of their own questions and predicaments.

Our own questions arise in the form of the future work and future research needed in this field of academic and professional development. Historian

David Pace (2004) acknowledges the increasing calls for this combination of teaching and research:

> A consensus has formed within growing circles in academia that there is scholarly research to be done on teaching and learning, that the systematic creation of rigorous knowledge about teaching and learning is a crucial prerequisite to responding to major challenges facing academia, that this knowledge must be shared publicly and should build cumulatively over time, and that the explorations of this area should be conducted by academics from all disciplines, not just those with appointments in schools of education. (p. 1174)

So, following on from the chapters of the book, what are our 'top research questions' that relate to teaching, learning, and conducting researching on these? Safe in the knowledge that there are a myriad more questions than just these, we propose the following six:

First, is student-centred learning really an achievable goal? Part of the underlying philosophy of this kind of learning is that no university context can have just one style that remains applicable throughout time. The teachers, students and institutions need to continuously reflect on their teaching, learning and infrastructural systems in such a way that would continuously improve the learning experience of students and ensure that the intended learning outcomes of a given course or programme component are achieved in a way that stimulates learners' critical thinking and transferable skills. While we have explored a number of ways of working to achieve this, none are perfect. Given the pressures on university teachers, is consistent student-centred learning 'do-able'?

Second, we have made little or no mention within these pages of diversity, inclusivity, equity or social mobility. Do all of our students have equal opportunities to take advantage of the teaching that takes place within our classrooms? This is a growing question for universities in Portugal and the UK – not only access to universities, but – following entry – access to first class teaching and learning and, of course, to first class degrees. Universities have the potential to be a force for social progress but also a means of reinforcing inequalities. They are small parts of a very large social machine and so cannot be expected to find solutions for all of society. In Chapter 2, Júlio Pedrosa points, for example, to the increase in mature students to the system, and the particular needs that they bring with them. However, these sensitive issues deserve our greater attention in how we organise and manage our teaching.

Third, while we have made tangential reference in several chapters to the advent of technology, as Aisha Alkaabi and Sarmin Hossain do in theirs, there is no doubt that major changes are just around the corner. There are no mentions here of 'flipped classrooms', of 'learner analytics' or 'the quantised learner', of 'adaptive learning' or 'mobile collaborative learning theory', and so there is considerable work to be done to adopt, adapt and assess each and every shift in the technological firmament. And there are many of those – let alone the vast number of educational theories that accompany them! But, at a very basic level, in a digital on-line world, it becomes increasing difficult, for example, to monitor academic dishonesty, especially plagiarism. How and when do we create appropriate environments to teach our students about academic honesty and integrity?

Fourth, as universities 'shape-shift' with the times, there is now an array of employment contracts, careers and short-, medium- and long-term 'academic lives'. The traditional life of an academic, the 'ivory tower existence' (if that were ever a reality), is long gone to be replaced by a spectrum of 'opportunities' within departments and research units, in the way that Fionna Denny describes in her chapter. There is clear need to explore how these changes impact on academic development and growth.

Fifth, there is growing pressure for undergraduate and postgraduate programmes to be inter- and cross-disciplinary in their focus and working. Certainly, programmes are, and should be, flexible and constantly evolving. As Carlinda Leite discusses in Chapter 3, the impetus for research-led teaching first entails a commitment to academic research in its own right. And academic research – by its very nature – is highly specialised, seldom inter- or cross- disciplinary. So, if it is important that research in higher education should look beyond the discipline alone, to include input from other disciplines, how do teachers manage to teach new programmes through their personal research activities?

Sixth, internationalisation and globalisation: at one level, internationalisation is seen as a 'good thing', particularly focused on science, technology, engineering and mathematics (STEM), since STEM skills are considered critical for innovation, technological progress, industrial performance, economic growth and thus national development. The number of international students is very much on the rise, and this changes the composition of the student body in university classrooms. How might we cater best for their diverse needs? Moreover, local stakeholders are challenging many universities regarding the imbalance between global endeavour and prestige, and local commitment. So, what is the ideal balance a teacher might strike in this respect?

Ideally, answers to these questions, and the evaluative research behind those answers, will be the topic of a new book. We leave the last word to Lee Shulman, president emeritus of the Carnegie Foundation for the Advancement of Teaching, who says:

Scholarly teaching is what every one of us should be engaged in every day that we are in a classroom, in our office with students, tutoring, lecturing, conducting discussions, all the roles we play pedagogically. Our work as teachers should meet the highest scholarly standards of groundedness, of openness, of clarity and complexity. But it is only when we step back and reflect systematically on the teaching we have done, in a form that can be publicly reviewed and built upon by our peers, that we have moved from scholarly teaching to the scholarship of teaching. (2004, p. 166)

References

Holmes, C., Mayhew, K., & Keep, E. (2012). *Ten big questions for higher education* (SKOPE Issues 31). Oxford: University of Oxford.

Pace, D. (2004). The amateur in the operating room: History and the scholarship of teaching and learning. *American Historical Review, 109*(2), 1171–1192.

Shulman, L. S. (2004). *Lamarck's revenge: Teaching among the scholarships. Teaching as community property: Essays on higher education* (pp. 164–172). San Francisco, CA: Jossey-Bass.

Index

Academic careers
   contracts   50, 58
   development   xii, xv, 7, 15, 46, 52, 57, 145, 148, 172, 187, 189, 194–197, 219, 224, 231
   progression   45, 51, 52, 55

Bologna process   15–16, 19, 24, 26, 27
Brunel University London   xii, xiv, 53

CARE question processes   111

E-learning   81, 100
Educational development units   8 43, 44
European higher education   13

Feedback
   feedforward   130, 133, 137–140, 189, 201, 212
   formative   193, 203, 212, 214, 225
   oral feedback   202, 209
   summative   189, 214
   written feedback   202, 211, 212

Group work   212, 213

Higher Education Academy (HEA)   xiii, xv, 38, 48, 51, 58, 219
Higher education policy, xii

Journals   xiii, xiv, xv, xvii, 1, 27, 33, 36, 37, 39, 77

Learning
   active learning   60, 65, 70, 82, 102, 167
   blended learning   81
   collaborative learning   78, 88–94, 96–100, 200, 231
   inquiry-based learning   xv, 2, 5, 9, 20, 102–114, 118, 126, 161, 163, 167
   inquiry-led learning   xi, xvi, 160–168
   problem based learning   15, 23, 117, 119
   self-directed learning   130, 161, 163, 218
   self-regulated learning   130, 161, 163, 218
Learning styles
   cognitive style   xiii, 8, 74–83, 92, 93
   learner differentiation   4
   learning habits   139, 140
   learning preferences   167
   questioning styles   xv, 102–114, 160–163, 177, 188, 195, 221, 223
Kolb's Learning Styles Inventory (LSI)   9

Peer assisted learning
   peer instruction   60
   peer assessment   202, 223, 225
Portugal's higher education   8, 12–15, 24–26, 60, 65

Question-based learning (QBL)   17
Questioning skills   xv, 102–104
Questions
   acquisition questions   161, 162
   factual questions   106–109
   integrative questions   162
   investigable questions   162
   question matrix   109, 110
   specialisation questions   161
   thought provoking questions   104, 106–110, 114
   wonderment questions   123

Reflection
   in practice   21, 23, 64, 154,
   on practice   2
   Preflection   9, 134–136, 138, 140, 141
   Situated critical reflection   189, 218
Research
   and teaching   xii, xiii, xiv, 19–27
   naturalistic research   10, 147, 156, 196
   qualitative research   2, 153
   validation of   6
Research data gathering
   case studies   151–152
   interviews   154–155
   observations   153–154
   questionnaires   154–155
   surveys   136–138
Research Excellence Framework (REF)   50, 229

Scholarship of Teaching and Learning (SoTL)   xii, 1, 8–10, 31–39, 60, 66, 70, 186–197
Self-questioning   102, 130, 134, 135

Student centred learning 3, 4, 10, 160, 166–168, 230
Student fees 51
Subject disciplines
  cross-disciplinary 231
  interdisciplinary
    biology xii, 146–149, 192, 196
    chemistry 146, 148, 149, 152, 155, 156, 161, 165, 167, 173
    engineering xiv, 8, 15, 32, 51, 59–62, 64–66, 69–71
    evolution 193, 223
    genetics 147, 148, 192, 193, 219
    microbiology 147, 148, 163, 164, 176, 178, 179, 192–195, 219
    neuroscience 74, 75, 92
    physics xi, xvi, 8, 59–71, 117, 167, 173, 229
    psychology xi, xii, xiii, xiv, xv, 74, 75, 92, 104, 105, 109, 111,

Teaching and learning qualifications xiii, 3, 45
Teaching approaches
  approaches to Teaching Inventory (ATI) 154, 175

research-led teaching 20, 32, 231
transmission teaching 167, 179, 180
laboratory classes 151, 165
lectures 153–154
microtalks 163, 164, 192, 196, 217
seminars 1, 165, 190, 191
tutorials 1, 5, 10, 149, 161, 162, 165, 220
Teaching Excellence Framework (TEF) 46–48, 229
Teaching modes
Thinking skills
  critical thinking xiv, 5, 6, 10, 24, 99, 118, 141, 167, 188, 196, 202, 204, 212, 221, 224, 230
  higher-order 217
  metacognitive processes 79, 88

UK's higher education xii, xiii, 8, 14, 32, 34, 38, 43, 49, 51, 53, 56, 202
University of Aveiro xi, xii, xiii, xv, xvi, 1, 9, 15, 16, 60, 65, 145–148, 156
Unknowns
  extrinsic 121, 122
  intrinsic 121, 122

Voice 2, 16, 77, 82, 204, 220

Printed in the United States
By Bookmasters